Library of Congress Cataloging in Publication Data
Main entry under title:

Savings and capital formation.

   Papers presented at the first annual conference of the Savings Forum Federal Reserve
Bank of Philadelphia, May 1985 sponsored by Beneficial Corporation.
   Includes index.
   1. Saving and investment—United States—Congresses.
   2. United States—Economic policy—1981–   —Congresses.
   I. Adams, F. Gerard (Francis Gerard), 1929–   .
   II. Wachter, Susan M.   III. Savings Forum (U.S.).
   Conference (1st : 1985 : Federal Reserve Bank of
   Philadelphia)   IV. Beneficial Corporation.

   HC110.S3S24   1986   339.4'3   85–40328
   ISBN 0–669–11017–5 (alk. paper)

Copyright © 1986 by D.C. Heath and Company

Published simultaneously in Canada
Printed in the United States of America
International Standard Book Number: 0–669–11017–5
Library of Congress Catalog Card Number: 85–40328

The paper used in this publication meets the minimum requirements of American
National Standard for Information Sciences—Permanence of Paper for Printed Library
Materials, ANSI Z39.48–1984.

The last numbers on the right below indicate the number and date of printing.

10   9   8   7   6   5   4   3   2   1

95   94   93   92   91   90   89   88   87   86

Savings and Capital Formation

The Policy Options

Edited by
F. Gerard Adams
University of Pennsylvania

Susan M. Wachter
University of Pennsylvania

Lexington Books
D.C. Heath and Company/Lexington, Massachusetts/Toronto

Contents

Preface and Acknowledgments

The chapters in this book are papers presented at the Federal Reserve Bank of Philadelphia in May 1985 at a conference, "Towards a National Savings Policy," sponsored by Beneficial Corporation. This was the first national conference of the newly formed Savings Forum, a nonprofit center to encourage research on savings. The conference was attended by approximately 100 invited government, academic, and business leaders. Funding for the conference and this book was provided by a grant from Beneficial Corporation and facilities for the conference were provided by the Federal Reserve Bank of Philadelphia.

The conference and this book represent the work of many individuals. We wish to express gratitude to Edward G. Boehne, Richard Lang, John Bell, and Lawrence Murdoch of the Federal Reserve Bank of Philadelphia; Finn M.W. Caspersen and Ann Stephenson of Beneficial Corporation; and William Alrich, David Melnicoff, Donald Mullineaux, Yung-Ping Chen, and Sherry Elliot of the Savings Forum. Finally, many thanks are owed to the participants and to those, too many to name, without whose help the conference and the book would not have become realities.

The opinions expressed in this volume are those of the respective authors and do not necessarily reflect the views of the Federal Reserve Bank of Philadelphia, of the Federal Reserve System, or of Beneficial Corporation.

1
Introduction and Overview

F. Gerard Adams
Susan M. Wachter

John Adams once said that "confusion, and distress in America arise, not from constitutional defects, or from want of honour, but from downright ignorance of the nature of coin, credit, and circulation." Today he might have added, "and from deficits, taxation, and insufficient saving." A national savings policy cannot be formulated without an understanding of the determinants of savings (including the impact of government policy) nor without an understanding of the economic effects of the national savings rate. We do know that our net national savings rate is lower than our major trading partners'. We also know that private and business savings in the United States do not balance our government's dissaving. Hence, we rely on foreign capital. We are fast becoming a net debtor nation. We also know that our relatively low savings rate has made the U.S. economy vulnerable to three major sets of problems.

The first set of problems derives from the U.S. economy's increased dependence on foreign capital inflows. Our present and growing reliance on foreign capital could at worst lead to a "crash-landing" scenario: some unforeseen, adverse events precipitate a flow of funds out of the United States, giving rise to devaluation, resurgent inflation, high interest rates, monetary restraint, and a severe recession. Even in the absence of this catastrophe, at best, we are no longer in a zero-sum game. High interest rates and the resulting strong dollar reduce our international competitiveness. In addition, we do not owe the debt entirely to ourselves, as we once did. The result is a reduction of future American consumption to fund that portion of the debt which is foreign owned.

The second set of problems brought about by the low U.S. net savings rate derives from high real interest rates and the crowding out of plant, equipment, and R&D investment. High real interest rates may already have aborted a potential long-run boom. "The paradox of thrift" notwithstanding, our long-run growth depends on savings to fund capital formation. Private investment must compete with government demand for funds in the capital market. It is investment which fuels growth.

A third set of problem derives from the juxtaposition of a low savings rate with a heavy reliance on Social Security and Medicare for retirement income and health benefits, respectively. If we are to reduce these benefits to avoid large tax increases, we must increase our reliance on private savings.

Today, the nation is debating government tax and expenditure policy. It is crucial to consider the impact on savings of any changes in these areas. That is why we must consider savings not only in a conceptual context (what is saving and how is it determined?) but also in a policy context (how can government policy affect saving and what is an appropriate national savings policy?).

Such a consideration of savings from these two perspectives is the objective of this book. It contains the papers presented at the first annual national conference of the Savings Forum held May 2–3, 1985 at the Federal Reserve Bank of Philadelphia under sponsorship of Beneficial Corporation.

The Savings Forum is an organization founded, fittingly, in Benjamin Franklin's adopted town of Philadelphia to study the determinants of saving. The Savings Forum sponsors conferences, research, communication, and scholarship on savings. It is a nonprofit academic organization which promotes knowledge on savings and related topics. It does not seek to advance any particular point of view.

The conference on which this book is based was intended to take a broad-base view of savings, presenting the fundamentals of definition, measurement, and theory as well as the more controversial aspects encountered in policy discussions. Since the book is the product of a lively, indeed often controversial conference, it is not always possible to keep the content of each participant's presentation within narrow bounds. Our efforts to reorganize the material into narrow categories have been stymied in many cases. The same issues will appear in different contexts and in different viewpoints throughout several of the chapters. But there is some logic in the organization of the book nevertheless.

Part I deals with conceptual and empirical issues. The first chapter in this section is by Michael Boskin and focuses on the concept and definition of saving. Alternative definitions and data sources are evaluated. While the different concepts and measures give very different results, the author concludes that by almost any definition of saving, the savings rate in the United States is low and has been falling, in large part because of government dissaving in recent years. But the question of whether or not the savings rate is low can be evaluated not only in historical terms or relative to savings rates in other countries, but also relative to conceptual and empirical analyses of optimal savings rates. Boskin carries out such analyses. The conceptual and empirical issues facing such studies are not trivial—they include time preference, technical change, accumulation of human capital, and treatment of government capital expenditures, for example. But allowing for these factors as well as possible, he concludes that the net savings rate is "well below its optimum."

Boskin next considers two major current savings controversies of relevance to public policy making. He argues, first, that the pure life cycle hypothesis can be rejected, although this does not mean that the propensity to consume is independent of age. He also maintains that tests cast doubt on the alternative intergenerational altruism model which would contend that government debt policy does not affect the consumption savings choice. Another important controversy, one which raised its head at numerous points during the conference, was over the extent to which changes in the after-tax rate of return affect private savings. Referring to his own extensive empirical studies of the question, Boskin concludes "there is at least a modest positive interest elasticity of private savings in the United States." However, recent tendencies towards tax-exempt savings such as IRA and Keogh plans, as well as lower marginal tax rates have tended to mitigate the adverse impacts of the tax structure on savings. Boskin suggests in conclusion that unfunded Social Security and Medicare obligations and public debt do crowd out some private saving, a factor which explains a significant portion of the decline of net savings in the United States.

The second conceptual chapter is by Irwin Friend. It is concerned particularly with the issues of the impact of taxation and other government policies on private saving decisions. Friend's appraisal of the empirical relationships is not greatly different from Boskin's on the issue of the importance of the deficit's contribution to our too low savings rate, but he doubts any positive result through raising the after-tax rate of return. Nonetheless, he points out that there are other aspects of the tax structure which also matter to some degree. "An obvious way to cut down any depressive effects on both capital and labor of a given total of taxation would be to minimize the marginal rates, keeping them consistent with a desired rate of progressivity in the average tax-income ratios." In general, Friend sees only limited scope for public policy to influence saving. Comparing savings rates in different countries, he says: "The apparent paucity of noncoercive economic measures which could be taken by the government to increase household or private saving may seem strange in view of the extremely large observed differences in the underlying saving-income ratios for different countries. Although these differences have not been satisfactorily explained in the literature . . . they (may) represent cultural differences. . . . As a consequence, it may be possible to increase private saving more effectively through noneconomic means than through economic policies." This represents a preview of the next section of the conference which was concerned specifically with the contrast between U.S. and Japanese saving.

Written by Lawrence Summers, the third conceptual chapter reviews a number of issues relating to the policy goal of increasing national savings. The first section considers the measurement and definition of national savings. As other conference participants noted, current U.S. savings rates are low compared with those of other countries and with the past U.S. experience, a comparison which Summers refers to as "disquieting, especially given the disappointing performance of the U.S. economy over the past decade and a half." The second section considers possible avenues through which public policy can increase national savings. Summers concludes that changes in public savings or dissavings through budget surpluses or deficits are the most potent and reliable policy tool for altering the savings rate. However, Summers would not neglect tax reform since he argues that it "would be likely to have a significant effect on the private savings rate."

Summers is concerned about the allocation of savings. He presents empirical estimates and econometric model simulations which suggest that a surprisingly small share of induced extra savings will find their way into increased plant and equipment investment while much savings will find their way into residential construction and consumer durables. He finds that the major effect of increased savings would be to reduce international capital inflows and to improve American competitiveness.

The second part of the book focuses on the contrast between saving behavior in Japan and in the United States. What financial, institutional, and cultural factors lead the Japanese to save at a much higher rate than Americans?

A chapter by John Makin contrasts Japan and the United States. Makin compares their savings rates over a twenty-eight-year period and concludes that "Japan's net saving rate is strikingly above that for the United States, standing at two and one-half to three times the U.S. rate." The question is more fundamental than it first appears. The high savings rate is an important ingredient in the competitive race between the U.S. and Japan. The need to explain the contrast is vital. Striking differences come to mind at first glance at the United States with its relatively high capital stock, large percentage of elderly in the population, greater availability of pension plans, and opportunities for capital-intensive leisure-time activities. Undoubtedly, these factors help to explain the large difference between savings rates in the U.S. and Japan. Other reasons include the typical early retirement age (at 55) in many Japanese firms, which leaves a period not covered by retirement plans, and the difficulty of raising funds to finance home purchases due to the fact that in Japan a large share of the price of a home is paid in cash and that interest is not tax-deductible.

The second part of Makin's chapter deals with tax policy and saving behavior. Lower tax burdens on interest income and nondeductibility of interest expenses are strong incentives for Japanese households to save. His savings equations for both countries suggest a low interest elasticity of saving, an elasticity lower than other recent studies have indicated. Nonetheless, the high savings rate in Japan has provided a channel of savings flow (directed from oversaving or, as Makin prefers to call it, "underconsumption") to the United States.

As the U.S. increasingly relies on imported savings on which it will ultimately have to pay a return, there is a serious problem if those savings have not been invested productively. "A fuller understanding of reasons for different savings rates is important if policy errors related to trade flows in commodities and savings are to be avoided."

Elliehausen and his associates take a new empirical look at saving in the United States on the basis of the 1983 Survey of Consumer Finances. The central idea here, as in the previous chapter on Japan, is the impact of pensions and social security on the levels of savings and household portfolios. Theoretical results about saving are ambiguous, which places a premium on empirical evaluation. Emergencies were listed as a predominant reason for saving, one mentioned more frequently in 1983 than in previous surveys. In contrast, saving for retirement was mentioned less frequently, perhaps as a result of the greater prevalence of retirement plans in recent years. While on the surface the data appear to support findings of earlier studies that pensions stimulate savings, that phenomenon may well reflect interactions of saving with income, age, and occupation. This is because the relatively strong retirement saving motive among higher income professionals and managers may have offset any negative effects of pension coverage on retirement saving. In most but not all cases, the authors find support for the life-cycle savings model that persons covered by pensions will have lower nonpension wealth to finance retirement than uncovered families will, thus indicating that there may be a negative relationship between pensions and nonpension saving after all.

Part III presents views on the impact of policy on saving. Not surprisingly, these chapters are colored by the perspective from which the authors observe the economic scene. Robert Ortner challenges the dicta that (1) government deficits are depressing the economy by crowding out other borrowers and (2) the inflow of foreign capital is financing and stimulating a large part of the economy's expansion. He argues that "deficits are stimulating, while foreign capital inflows . . . and the trade deficits which accompany them—act as a drag on the economy." A focus on net saving understates the availability of resources to finance investment activity and the foreign capital inflow provides additional funding, though admittedly the trade deficit which it finances reduces demand for domestic manufacturing products. Notwithstanding, Ortner sees these halcyon days coming to an end. "We have been living beyond our means. . . . Bringing the current account into balance will mean that for a time we will have to produce more than we consume—working harder and enjoying it less."

The paradox in the case of deficits and savings is that looking at the world from the same perspective does not always lead to the same conclusion. Barry Bosworth echoes Ortner's views of the domestic and foreign deficits. He registers skepticism that much will be done by the Congress and the administration in the near future since the damage of current overspending will only appear in a long-run perspective. He also notes the difficulty of disentangling theoretically and empirically the impact of taxation on savings. Bosworth sees merit in tax reform and recognizes the potential of tax changes to affect the efficiency of saving, but in the light of the massive needs for adjustment to cope with our low savings rate, he sees little hope that much can be accomplished by tax system changes alone. "Their consequences for long-term investment and wealth accumulation pale in magnitude when compared to the effects of basic budget policy—the balancing of revenues and expenditures."

Paul Craig Roberts, one of the architects of the supply-side approach, takes the position that "a defense of saving is not only a defense of a higher real GNP growth and better productivity performance, but also a defense of the western alliance." He focuses on the adverse effect of taxation on savings and investment, arguing that the effect of taxation on the cost of capital can easily swamp the effect of interest rates.

Lawrence Klein looks at the question from an international perspective. Klein's concern is with the low rate of national saving in the United States as compared to other countries and the resulting sensitivity of the U.S. economy to the willingness of foreigners to direct capital flows to the United States. Given the large domestic and foreign deficits, the Federal Reserve has two policy options in response to a change in international capital flows. The readjustment could take the form of a "crash scenario" of rapidly diminishing capital inflows, rising prices and interest rates, and a sharp drop in real GNP if the Federal Reserve maintained restraint. Or we could see a "soft-landing" scenario where the Federal Reserve's efforts to bring down interest rates could lead to a slow adjustment in the current account without significant recessions.

F. Gerard Adams and Susan M. Wachter's brief summing up reviews the conclusions of the conference—insofar as unfinished business can have conclusions—and presents an agenda for additional research. Despite a large measure of agreement among the participants about fact, if not always about policy, there remain striking differences in the evidence which the conference participants bring to bear and in their evaluations of its implications. Savings is clearly important, no matter what the perspective, but how to explain saving and how to influence it remain uncertain. Yes, taxes make a difference, but which ones and how much? Yes, pension plans and social security make a difference, but again the discussions at the conference, especially in the summary panel moderated by Marshall E. Blume, brought out the disagreements among panel participants more sharply than do the chapters themselves.

If only one thing is clear and agreed upon by all or almost all participants, it is that further research is required. The issues debated here can only be resolved with increased data availability and more empirical resources. The final chapter of this book considers the broad outlines of an agenda for research which could serve as an input into the formulation of a consensus on savings and savings policy.

Part I
The Conceptual and Empirical Issues

2
Theoretical and Empirical Issues in the Measurement, Evaluation, and Interpretation of Postwar U.S. Saving

Michael J. Boskin

Introduction

A large number of conceptual and empirical issues cloud analyses and interpretations of postwar U.S. consumption and saving, and, therefore, the implications of alternative economic policies. The purpose of this chapter is to raise an important subset of such issues. The hope is that by bringing up these issues and giving the most tentative preliminary answers to them, we will provide additional impetus for further research on these important questions.

The chapter is organized in five sections. First, we analyze alternative concepts of net national saving and alternative data sources from which to estimate them. We see that these data sources provide very different answers, in part because of their conceptual differences (for example, inclusion of capital gains and losses, and treatment of consumer durables and government assets). Despite these differences, all of the measures suggest that the net national saving rate is low and falling. We also discuss various issues in concepts and measures of saving. For example, what specific adjustments to budget deficit or surplus figures should be made to come close to an economist's concept of government saving or dissaving? How should one treat human investment? Are business and household or private and government saving perfect substitutes?

Second, we address the issue of how much should an economy such as the United States save? This question has numerous subissues, but we

I would like to thank John Roberts, David Starrett, Larry Summers, and participants at the conference for their valuable comments and advice. I also thank John Roberts for his excellent research assistance.

suppress all short-run macroeconomic-fluctuation issues and analyze the factors that should be considered in determining an optimal long-run saving policy for the United States. We demonstrate that the optimal saving policy depends on a number of empirically estimable parameters, although some of them are conceptually difficult to estimate from available data. Further, a variety of potential relationships between saving and the rate of economic growth, as opposed just to a transition to a different growth path, must be evaluated. In any event, my evaluation is that the optimal rate of net saving, based on very preliminary analyses of the relevant parameters, is likely to be much larger than the rate of net national saving in the United States.

Third, we discuss some recent analyses of simple models analyzing private saving behavior, such as the pure (no-bequest) life-cycle model and the infinite-horizon altruism model. We conclude that the empirical data refute both extremes. We also discuss several recent econometric studies and their results concerning the propensity to save by age and vintage, and also concerning the interest elasticity of saving. We conclude that there are substantial differences in the marginal propensity to consume by age, that there has probably been a substantial shift in the propensity to consume by household vintage (particularly in terms of people born prior to the Great Depression as opposed to those born afterwards), and that saving is likely to be at least somewhat responsive to real after-tax rates of return.

Fourth, we derive the implications of the theoretical and empirical results for analyzing various fiscal policies, such as structural changes in tax policy, unfunded Social Security obligations, and the public debt on private saving decisions. A brief conclusion summarizes the results and discusses several major outstanding research issues.

How Much Do We Save in the United States?

The saving behavior of an economy reveals much about the nature of a society, since it reflects various values, institutions, and incentives. It is a fundamental reflection of the relative values placed on the future and the present by its citizens and, perhaps, its political institutions. There used to be a presumption that saving and thrift were beneficial, at least to the individual or household concerned, and perhaps to society as a whole. Throughout economic history, however, there has also been a concern about insufficient total spending, an idea most prominently developed by Keynes. Keynes and the postwar stagnationists were deeply concerned that insufficient spending would lead to chronic and massive unemployment, so they argued for policies designed to soak up excess saving. It is not my purpose here to present my own views or a summary of others' concerning this Keynesian proposition. Suffice it to say that the force of that argument has been mitigated considerably by recent analytical and empirical research in economics, and that at best it is probably a weak temporary proposition.

However, it is clear that in the long run we could save too much. In order to save more, we must forego current consumption. We must somehow balance the benefits of increased consumption in the future against the cost of foregone consumption opportunities today. In fact, we could save so much that we reach capital saturation and drive the marginal product of capital to zero! Obviously, this conceptual difficulty is not one that is about to plague any modern economy.

Saving can be defined as foregoing consumption and providing funds either directly or indirectly to capital markets to channel into productive investments, whether in tangible, financial, or human capital. It is a neat concept, but there are an inordinate number of difficulties in measuring it. We begin with a discussion of recent postwar saving behavior by focusing on the most commonly used measure, total net national saving as a fraction of GNP, as measured in the national income and product accounts (NIPA). These results are presented as decade averages for 1951–1980, and annually since then, in table 2–1. Total net national saving is the sum of net private saving, the state and local government surplus (or deficit), and the federal government surplus (or deficit). Private saving, in turn, is the sum of personal saving and corporate saving. Further, gross private saving is the sum of net private saving and the capital consumption allowance. These data are also presented as memoranda in the table.

Even a cursory examination of the table suggests that the total net saving rate has fallen substantially from the 1950s and 1960s. While net private saving rebounded somewhat in 1984, approaching its historic norms, net government dissaving (the federal government deficit minus the state and local surplus) more than offset this rebound in net private saving.

Numerous conjectures have been made concerning whether the appropriate rate to study is net or gross, private or total, or disaggregated personal and corporate private saving. For example, David and Scadding (1974) find that the gross private saving rate at full employment is remarkably constant, reinforcing the finding of Denison (1958). They infer from this that households see through the corporate veil and that movements between personal and corporate saving reflect various factors such as changes in the relative tax advantages of the two forms of saving. However, they strongly reject the "ultra rationality" argument that households see through the government veil, an argument associated with

Table 2–1
U.S. Net National Saving, 1951–1984

	1951–60	1961–70	1971–80	1981	1982	1983	1984
Total Net Saving	6.9%	7.5%	6.1%	5.2%	1.6%	1.8%	4.0%
Net Private Saving	7.2	8.0	7.1	6.1	5.4	5.9	7.4
Personal Saving	4.7	4.7	4.9	4.6	4.4	3.6	4.3
Corporate Saving	2.5	3.3	2.2	1.4	1.0	2.3	3.2
State and Local Government Surplus	−0.2	0.1	0.9	1.3	1.1	1.3	1.4
Federal Government Surplus	−0.2	−0.5	−1.9	−2.2	−4.8	−5.4	−4.8
Memoranda: Capital Consumption	8.9	8.5	9.9	11.2	11.7	11.4	11.0
Gross Private Saving	16.1	16.4	17.0	17.2	17.1	17.3	18.4

Source: U.S. Department of Commerce, National Income and Product Accounts.

Notes: Data are averages (except for 1981–1984) of annual flow, as percentages of gross national product. Total net saving and total net investment differ by statistical discrepancy. Detail may not add to totals because of rounding.

Martin Baily (1962) and Robert Barro (1974). However, focusing on gross saving and its apparent stability seems odd, since virtually all of our theories are in terms of how households, firms, and even governments wish to form their *net* wealth position. In brief, any rationality hypothesis seems somewhat out of balance if it ignores the fact that depreciation is estimable. There has been much less stability in the net private saving rate and in the net national saving rate than in the corresponding gross figures, as can be seen by examining the annual data rather than the decade-average data. We shall return later to conjectures concerning why the saving rate may have fallen.

Before turning to a discussion of other potential data sources and concepts, it is worth noting some problems with traditional figures. First, household saving in the national income accounts is estimated as a residual, after subtracting consumer expenditures, taxes, and interest payments to business from estimated personal income. The measurement errors in these components, each of which is potentially large relative to net saving, will show up dollar for dollar in the numerator of the net saving rate. This could lead to nontrivial mismeasurement. Second, the NIPA's measure of saving excludes net capital gains or losses in its measures of saving, as in its measures of income. Third, the NIPA treats expenditures on consumer durable goods as consumption rather than as saving (although the recent classification of home computers as investments may be the first step toward an improved classification system). It would be preferable to treat expenditures on consumer durables as saving, and the imputed rental flow of the durables as consumption. Fourth, the treatment of government saving or dissaving in the national income and product accounts is a mechanical reporting of the budgetary position, with no attempt to develop a separate capital account on the expenditure side for government units in reporting a surplus or deficit on current operating account. Of course, the federal government's own budget suffers from this difficulty, but the Department of Commerce does attempt to estimate government capital stock, investment, and depreciation (although these estimates are not devoid of their own problems). However, these estimates are not implemented in the reported figures for the government surplus or deficit, but perhaps this is sensible given the vagaries of classification and reporting. Still, during periods of rapid increases or decreases in the rate of federal or state and local investment-type expenditures relative to the depreciation of the existing government stock, these numbers can be quite misleading (see Boskin 1982, 1985; Eisner and Pieper 1984). Worse yet, no adjustment is made for (unfunded) accruing pension and Social Security liabilities, which could swamp the asset-accumulation side of the balance sheet.

Table 2–2 reports several alternative methods of estimating net na-

Table 2–2
U.S. Net National Saving, 1951–1984, Alternative Concepts

	NIPA Net Saving	Flow of Funds	Adjusted Net Saving, S_a out of NNP*	Adjusted Net Saving, S_a out of Private NNP*
1951–60	6.9	9.3	12.4	16.6
1961–70	7.5	9.2	13.6	17.8
1971–80	6.1	16.6	12.2	15.7
1981	5.2	3.5	10.8	13.8
1982	1.6	−10.2	6.8	8.7
1983	1.8	3.7	8.0	10.1
1984	4.0	NA	10.1	12.7

Source: Author's calculations.

NNP* = NIPA NNP + the rental flow from consumer durables net of depreciation + the rental flow from government tangible capital net of depreciation.

$$S_a = \frac{NNP^* - C^* - G^*}{NNP^*}$$

C* = NIPA consumption + the rental flow from consumer durables net of depreciation less durables expenditures.

G* = NIPA government expenditures plus the rental flow from government capital net of depreciation less government investment expenditures.

See text for further discussion of measurement.

tional saving incorporating some of these adjustments. The first column merely reproduces the data from table 2–1, the NIPA net saving rates. The second column, however, provides data from the Federal Reserves' flow-of-funds balance sheets for the U.S. economy. In principle, they reflect current cost estimates for the assets and liabilities of each sector of the economy (households, businesses, and government). An inflation adjustment allows us to define saving as the difference in the real net worth from the end of one year to the end of the next, which is much closer to the economist's definition of saving. Unfortunately, bonds are valued at par, and therefore capital gains and losses due to inflation will not be reported to the extent that there are net external bond holdings. However, this should not be terribly important since the overwhelming bulk of corporate and government bonds are held internally, and the capital gains and losses merely cancel among sectors.

The flow-of-funds figures generally estimate higher net saving rates than do the NIPA net-saving figures. This probably primarily reflects real net capital gains and also wealth accumulated from the underground economy. For 1981, however, the flow-of-funds estimates reveal smaller net saving than do the national income and product accounts and actually show a substantial decline in real net worth in 1982, negative saving, and a rebound to a net saving rate of about twice the NIPA level in the early stages of the recovery in 1983. It should be noted that these data are based on the November 1984 revisions of the national balance sheets provided by the Federal Reserve Board of Governors, while the negative saving for 1980 and 1981, previously noted by Auerbach (1983) and Shoven (1984), were based on earlier versions of the data. Another difference between these estimates and those presented by Auerbach and Shoven is that we use the GNP deflator, which is almost identical to the personal consumption expenditure deflator, whereas they use the consumer price index (CPI). The widely documented overstatement of inflation by the CPI, in part because of its peculiar treatment of housing in this period, may have contributed to their estimates of negative saving rates.

Thus, a comprehensive measure of net national saving would adjust the national income and product account definition to include purchases of consumer durables and government tangible capital as saving, subtracting out these purchases from consumption, while adding to the NIPA consumption figures the imputed rental flow of services from consumer durables and government capital. More formally,

$$NNSR = \frac{NNP^* - C^* - G^*}{NNP^*}, \qquad (2.1)$$

where *NNSR* is the net *national* saving rate and equals adjusted *NNP* minus both private consumption and government consumption, with the remainder divided by adjusted *NNP*. Adjusted *NNP* is NIPA *NNP* plus the rental flow from consumer durables and from government tangible capital, each net of depreciation. C^* is NIPA consumption plus the rental flow from consumer durables net of depreciation less expenditures on consumer durables; G^* is NIPA government expenditures plus the rental flow from government capital net of depreciation, less government investment expenditures. Since the rental flow is imputed for both durables and government capital as the product of a net capital stock and a real opportunity cost plus depreciation, errors in measurement of the real opportunity cost or depreciation will carry over dollar for dollar into errors in the measurement of private and government consumption and net national product. Therefore, improved measures of the stock of consumer durables and the stock of government tangible capital, and the depreciation and the real opportunity cost of using each, are urgent research priorities. We now present several alternative estimates of these numbers, which vary substantially and therefore cause the net national saving rate to vary substantially as well.

Column 3 of table 2–2 reports net saving, adjusting the NIPA data for a consistent treatment of durables. We add durables expenditures, both government and private, net of depreciation to saving, and treat the imputed rent from the stock of consumer and government durables as consumption. These adjusted net national saving figures are roughly double the traditional national income account figures. The denominator in the third column is net national product, not gross national product, and is adjusted for the imputed rent to government capital and household durables, less depreciation thereof. These adjustments are conceptually simple, but subject to large potential measurement error in practice. Since errors in consumption carry over dollar for dollar to errors in saving, this should be borne in mind. A discussion and alternative estimates are presented in an appendix. The data on which tables 2–2 and 2–3 are based are from Boskin and Kotlikoff (1985).

Finally, table 2–2, column 4 reports the same net national saving figure out of private net national product, as adjusted for the treatment of durables. Private net national product is defined to be adjusted net national product less government consumption.

Again, columns 2, 3, and 4 suggest a substantial decline in the net national saving rate in the 1980s relative to the previous three decades. While we shall later discuss in more detail some conjectures concerning the reasons for this decline, particularly as they relate to government economic policy, it is worth noting here that the most interesting and important demographic features of the economy (declining fertility rates, dramatic increase in life expectancy of the elderly, and the accelerating trend to earlier retirement) all seem more likely to lead to an increase in saving rather than to its decrease, other factors being equal.

An interesting alternative perspective is presented in table 2–3, where we see different measures of consumption as a percent of net national

Table 2–3
Consumption as a Percent of Adjusted NNP

	C^*/NNP^*	G^*/NNP^*	$(C^* + G^*)/NNP^*$	$C^*/(NNP^* - G^*)$
1951–60	62.6	25.0	87.6	83.4
1961–70	63.0	23.4	86.4	82.2
1971–80	65.8	22.0	87.8	84.3
1981	67.7	21.4	89.2	86.2
1982	70.9	22.3	93.3	91.3
1983	70.7	21.3	92.0	89.9
1984	69.3	20.6	89.9	87.3

Source: Author's calculations.

NNP^* = NIPA NNP + the rental flow from consumer durables net of depreciation + the rental flow from government tangible capital net of depreciation less durables expenditures.

C^* = NIPA consumption expenditures plus the rental flow from consumer durables net of depreciation less durables expenditures.

G^* = NIPA government expenditures plus the rental flow from government capital net of depreciation less government investment expenditures.

See text for further discussion of measurement.

product. First, we examine the ratios of private and government consumption (including adjustment for durables as saving) to NNP. We then see the sum of the two as fractions of adjusted NNP, with the adjustments being for the imputed rent to government capital and consumer durable stocks less depreciation thereof. Finally, we have the ratio of private consumption to adjusted net national product minus government consumption, a measure of disposable income net of government expenditures. The data reveal that since the 1950s the private consumption rate has increased substantially, as has the total consumption rate out of adjusted NNP.

It is vital to reiterate the potential importance of a conceptually proper separation of capital and current account (including revaluation of their assets) for government units in the United States. As discussed in Boskin (1982, 1986) and Eisner and Pieper (1984), government assets are large and have been growing. These include substantial financial assets, tangible capital such as buildings, inventories, equipment, and, as discussed in Boskin, Robinson, O'Reilly, and Kumar (1985), a significant value of land and mineral rights. Indeed, until the big increase in the national debt associated with the recent deficits, the value of oil and natural gas rights for the federal government alone exceeded the value of privately held national debt. There are a number of intrinsic difficulties in trying to get replacement or market valuations for government assets. The overwhelming bulk of such values can be estimated, as suggested in methodologies in the papers cited. Just saying that it is difficult to value the Grand Canyon misses the point that the bulk of government assets do have a value which can be reasonably estimated. However, many such assets are much harder to value than private assets. They also depreciate and obsolesce in a different manner (military equipment being a prime example) and in a way that is difficult to estimate from market data. Furthermore, they may be subject to systematic changes in prices relative to the prices of private investment goods and commodities in general. As noted, plausible differences in depreciation of government capital can cause large differences in measures of net national saving.

Thus a priority area of research is improved government capital budgeting. This is important not only to improve data on net government capital formation and, therefore, net national saving and wealth accounts. Probably it could be an important input to improved budgetary outcomes as well. A few cautious attempts in this direction have been recommended recently, but we still remain the only major advanced economy in the world without a separate capital account.

It is clear that a separate capital account for the government is not only harder than capital accounts for the private sector but also more likely to be politically manipulated. But even a cursory examination of the data suggest that the numbers are very important. With respect to the data just described, we note that the big increase in tangible investment by the federal government occurred in the 1960s with the buildup of the interstate highway system and public infrastructure. Subsequent declines in military spending on investment-type goods reduced the rate of investment substantially until recently, when the increased rate of government investment in military equipment has more than offset the decrease in other types of federal government investment outlays. Further, some of the investment expenditures of the government were driven by demographics, such as the buildup in expenditures on school buildings following the baby boom.

Once again, the issue of the extent of substitution among different types of saving is important. By no means has the issue been exhausted analytically or empirically. Better theoretical and empirical understanding of the interrelationship among capital formation (net saving) of households, businesses, and federal, state, and local governments are other high priority items. Indeed, the data reported in table 2–3 reflect this important distinction. Private consumption is reported both with respect to NNP and NNP minus government consumption. If government consumption is a perfect substitute for private consumption, the private sector's ultimate disposable income is simply NNP, and the private saving rate coincides with the net national saving rate. On the other hand, if government consumption does not enter private decision making at all, or enters it separably, in choosing its consumption level, the private sector would view NNP minus government consumption as its ultimate disposable income, since current government consumption must be ultimately financed by the private sector. Thus, in choosing the measure we wish to use to analyze saving, we implicitly assume a theory of the relationship of government and private saving.

Finally, while we have noted some difficulties with the national income and product accounts measurement of saving, and have therefore presented alternative estimates, we should mention one primary advantage of the NIPA measures relative to flow-of-funds figures: NIPA measurements are reconciled with independently obtained estimates of investment, usually with only a minute statistical discrepancy.

Regardless of which set of figures one uses, U.S. net national saving in the 1980s plummeted from already low levels. Is this a problem? Should we be concerned about it? Were we saving enough prior to this plunge? To these issues we now turn.

How Much Should We Save?

We begin with the assumption that *long-run* capital formation in an advanced economy such as the United States must ultimately be financed by domestic saving rather than imported capital. Certainly the short-run supply of foreign capital to the United States is quite elastic. It is my view that for the types of long-run issues to be discussed here, we can take investment as constrained by the supply of domestic saving.[1]

There have been three approaches taken to analyze the question of the optimal rate of saving or investment for an economy and, hence, to decide whether a particular economy is over- or undersaving/investing. The most direct approach is that usually followed in deadweight loss or cost-benefit analyses: compare the demand price as a measure of marginal social benefit with the supply price as a measure of opportunity cost;[2] in the case of investment and saving the relevant prices are the gross marginal product of capital and the net return to savers. If these are equal, in the absence of externalities, the individual's consumption time profiles will be socially optimal; if the demand price differs from the supply price, we can both measure the deadweight loss and estimate the optimal saving/investment rate once we have knowledge of the interest elasticities of saving and investment.

With perfect capital markets, in the absence of taxes, consumers will save to the point where their subjective time discount rate, ρ, equals the rate of interest, i, which in turn equals the marginal product of capital. As is well known, capital income taxes reduce the net return to savers well below the marginal product of capital. Given this distinction, both the deadweight loss and the shortfall below the optimal saving rate are increasing functions of the interest elasticities of saving and investment.

For the United States economy, the marginal product of private capital has been estimated in a variety of ways: Feldstein and Summers (1979) examine the ratio of pretax capital income to the value of the capital stock for the nonfinancial corporate sector, obtaining estimates of about 0.12.[3] Boskin (1978) estimates a CES production function with Harrod neutral technical change for the entire private nonfarm economy, and his estimates imply a marginal product of about 0.08. Because of the separate corporate tax, we would expect this difference in estimates. Recent studies by Corcoran and Sahling (1982), and Brainard, Shoven, and Weiss (1980) attempt to use financial market data to estimate the real net cost of capital—which without taxes will equal the marginal product of capital in competitive equilibrium. Corcoran and Sahling present recent estimates in the 8% range; Brainard, Shoven, and Weiss's estimates are on average both higher and considerably more variable. Thus our 8% estimate probably is conservative.

The real net-of-tax return to savers averaged over the postwar period through 1984 was less than 0.03. Thus, a substantial wedge was driven between the marginal product of capital and the net return to savers (an approximation in an economy with no technical progress in the steady-state to the pure rate of time discount; in an economy with technical progress, this will overstate the pure time discount rate as discussed below). Thus, the return to investment exceeds the pure time discount rate by a factor of three or four in the U.S. economy. Were investment demand extremely elastic, even a modest interest elasticity of private saving of 0.3 or 0.4 would imply that our saving rate is only half its optimal level! Empirical evidence on the interest elasticity of saving will be discussed below.

A second alternative relates to the so-called "golden rule" of economic growth, or dynamic efficiency.[4] Basically, this approach asks whether some balanced growth paths are more desirable than others. In a simple neoclassical growth model, each saving rate leads to a particular steady growth path, so that the most desired growth path implies a most desired saving propensity. Usually, the analysis focuses on which steady growth path (over all those that are sustainable) maximizes per capita consumption. Along such a growth path, per capita consumption is given by

$$c = (1 - s) f(k^*(s)) = f(k^*) - gk^*, \qquad (2.2)$$

where s is the saving rate, g the growth rate, and $f(k)$ output per capita written as a function of the capital/labor ratio, k.

To obtain the maximum steady growth path in per capita consumption, differentiate with respect to s and obtain

$$dc/ds = (f'(k^*) - g) \, dk^*/ds = 0, \qquad (2.3)$$

or

$$f'(k^*) = g. \qquad (2.4)$$

Thus, along the steady growth path that maximizes per capita consumption, the marginal product of capital should equal the growth rate, which is approximately the sum of the rates of population growth and technical change. The real growth rate in an economy such as the United States over long periods of time averages perhaps 3 to 3.5%, whereas the marginal product of capital appears to be more than twice as large. Thus, society is underinvesting, and expansion of our capital stock is in order until the marginal product of capital is driven down to our growth rate.

Sometimes, this analysis is faulted because it occurs in a simple one-sector certainty environment. This is a legitimate criticism, but the interpretation that we should be comparing the real growth of the economy to the real rate of return on a "safe asset" I believe to be incorrect. In the world of the capital asset pricing model, suppose the risky asset is the market portfolio, and there is another safe asset. The real return to the safe asset (say, Treasury bonds) is below *g* (as it usually has been historically, except for the last few years), but the expected real return on the market portfolio exceeds the growth rate. Are we under- or oversaving and -investing? To my knowledge, this issue has not been addressed rigorously, and I am in the process of doing so. Intuitively, it seems that the answer almost certainly will be that we ought to be equating the expected return on the market portfolio to the growth rate via our national saving policy, and thus, we are grossly undersaving in the United States.

A third and more rigorous approach to optimal saving has been taken in utilitarian optimal-growth models, such as those of Mirrlees (1967).[5] While authors such as Arrow (1977) have assumed the identity of utility function and discount rates between the government planner and the representative consumer, some analyses have allowed these to differ (Arrow and Kurz 1970) and examined whether the government instruments being considered could achieve the fully optimal, or the second-best policy.

This approach adopts a general social-welfare criterion, rather than the maximization of per capita consumption. It pays particular attention to the decline in the marginal utility of income (consumption) as each generation becomes wealthier due to technical progress enhancing labor productivity. It therefore provides a more explicit criterion for welfare comparisons across generations than does the golden rule.

For convenience, most authors have assumed that utilities are additive in successive time periods and that governments therefore attempt to maximize a sum of discounted utilities. Intragenerational equity issues are suppressed, and intergenerational equity is implicit in the choice of a discount rate. In a world where private intergenerational transfers operated to make individuals maximize the sum of discounted utilities, or the government adopted this policy criterion, we would

$$maxU = \int_0^\infty e^{-(\rho + \sigma\mu - \mu)t} u(C_t) dt \qquad (2.5)$$

where ρ is the pure time preference rate, σ is the elasticity of marginal utility, μ is the labor augmenting rate of technological progress, and C is consumption per effective worker. The worker's income at any point in time is net interest income on accumulated wealth $(r - \mu)a$, plus earnings, w. Labor is taken to be inelastically supplied. Capital accumulation per effective worker is

$$\dot{a} = (r - \mu)a + w - c. \tag{2.6}$$

The current value Hamiltonian is, therefore,

$$H = U(c) + q((r - \mu)a + w - c) \tag{2.7}$$

where q is the shadow price of wealth per efficiency unit of labor. The consumer chooses C to maximize H; q evolves according to the differential equation

$$\begin{aligned} \dot{q} &= \left((\rho + \sigma\mu - \mu)q - \frac{\partial H}{\partial a} \right) \\ &= (\rho + \sigma\mu - \mu)q - (r - \mu)q \\ &= (\rho + \sigma\mu - r)q. \end{aligned} \tag{2.8}$$

In the steady state, therefore, consumer equilibrium implies

$$r = \rho + \sigma\mu. \tag{2.9}$$

The rate of interest, net of tax, is a constant equal to the pure rate of time discount plus the elasticity of marginal utility times the Harrod neutral rate of labor augmenting technical change. Since these are presumed constant in what follows, the net rate of interest converges to a constant: in the steady state the supply of capital is perfectly elastic.

Let us now take a specific example to analyze the optimal saving rate at any point in time. Suppose population growth is constant at rate n and utility is isoelastic in per capita consumption

$$U(C) = \frac{c^{1-\sigma}}{1 - \sigma}, \tag{2.10}$$

where σ is the elasticity of marginal utility, $-c(U_{cc}/U_c)$. Let production be parameterized by a CES function, $f(k) = A(1 - b - bk^{-h})^{-1/h}$ where the elasticity of substitution, $\epsilon = 1/(1 + h)$. It can be shown that the optimal saving rate at time t, s_t, is

$$s_t = (\mu + n)\left(\frac{K}{y}\right)_t \left[\frac{f'(k_t)}{\rho + \sigma\mu}\right]^{\epsilon} \tag{2.11}$$

and depends, as the original analysis suggests, on the difference between the current gross return to capital and the optimal net rate in the steady state.[6] While we have rough empirical estimates of ϵ, μ, n, K/y, and $f'(k)$, we need to know ρ and σ to estimate s. Roughly speaking $f'(k_t)$ is about .08 to .12; K/y about 3; ϵ about 1/2 to 1; μ about 0.01 to 0.02; and n about 0.01. This yields

$$.06\left(\frac{.08}{\rho + \sigma\mu}\right)^{1/2} \le s_t \le .09 \left(\frac{.12}{\rho + \sigma\mu}\right). \tag{2.12}$$

While many writers, most notably Frisch, have attempted to estimate σ from demand behavior, we note that it is not invariant to monotonic transformations of the assumed additively separable utility function. A logically consistent method of estimating σ is from behavior toward risk under certain strict assumptions. In any event, numbers such as 1/2, 1, or 2 are usually suggested (see Feldstein 1978). A σ of 2 implies, for example, that a 10% increase in income from say $30,000 to $33,000 is associated with a 20% fall in the marginal utility of income, that is, the household values dollar number $33,000 at only 80% of dollar number $30,000.

In the long-run certainty analysis considered here, however, it is important to be careful in generalizing from estimates of σ based on shorter-run behavior toward risk in stylized portfolio allocation models. In the latter, σ may well be larger than 2, as individuals are reluctant to risk a sharp change in their living standard. In the model discussed here, what is at stake is the rate of decrease of the marginal utility of income as a certain income rises over decades. Credit market imperfections would make it heroic to translate behavior in the former situation to the latter one.

Likewise, opinions on ρ differ markedly. Without borrowing constraints, we would expect ρ to equal the net rate of interest in an economy without technical progress, while equalling somewhat less than the net rate of interest with technical progress as derived above. Perhaps then, ρ is between 0 and 0.03.[7] In a study described in more detail later, Boskin and Kotlikoff (1985) derive a finite approximation to the infinite horizon optimization problem with isoelastic utility and conclude that among such functions, in the sense that predicted consumption best approximates actual U.S. time-series aggregate consumption, the maximum likelihood estimates of σ and $(\rho + \mu\sigma - \mu)$ are 1.5 to 2.0 and 0.03 to 0.04 for the various specifications. Taking these as central values and presenting a modest sensitivity analysis produces the estimates of the optimal net saving rate presented in table 2–4.

The optimal net saving rates increase as the pure rate of time pref-

Table 2–4
Optimal Net Saving Rates (Various Parameter Values) Pure Rate of Time Preference (ρ)

Risk Aversion (σ)	Substitution (ϵ)	Technical Progress (μ)	0.0	0.01	0.02	0.03
1.5	1.0	.01	32.%	19.2%	13.7%	10.7
1.5	1.0	.02	24.%	18.0	14.4	12.0
1.5	0.5	.01	13.8	10.7	9.1	8.0
1.5	0.5	.02	14.7	12.7	11.4	10.4
2.0	1.0	.01	24.0	16.0	12.0	9.6
2.0	1.0	.02	18.0	14.4	12.0	10.3
2.0	0.5	.01	12.0	9.8	8.5	7.6
2.0	0.5	.02	12.7	11.4	10.4	9.6

Source: Author's calculations.
N.B. Assumes $n = 0.001$ and $f'(k) = 0.08$. With $\epsilon = 1$, optimal saving rates are proportional to $f'(k)$. Proportionally higher or lower estimates would produce proportional changes in the corresponding entries in the table. For example $f'(k) = .10$ implies the entries with $\epsilon = 1$ would each be one-quarter larger.

erence and the elasticity of marginal utility fall and the elasticity of substitution in production rises. The effect of (presumed) exogenous technical change is ambiguous: more rapid productivity growth means extra saving, while investment raises the productivity of workers whose productivity is rising more rapidly and hence, other factors being equal, leads to greater future output from the extra capital. But by making us wealthier faster, it decreases the marginal utility of the higher future output.

Even with conservative assumptions, optimal *s* in general is quite a bit larger than recent net national saving in the United States. The optimal saving rates most compatible with the estimated discounting in Boskin and Kotlikoff (1985) with $\mu = .02$ are $\rho = 0$, $\sigma = 2.0$ and $\rho = .01$, $\sigma = 1.5$, or $\rho = .01$, $\sigma = 2$ and $\rho = .02$ and $\sigma = 1.5$. These imply a range of optimal net saving rates of 11.4% to 18.0%, clustering in the 11% to 14% range. This range approximates quite closely the adjusted saving rates reported in table 2–2 for 1950–1980, but exceeds the net national saving rate for the decade of the 1980s to date substantially. Let me repeat, we are quite some distance from precise estimates or implied values of parameters such as ρ and σ. But I believe the estimates of optimal net saving rates use reasonable ranges of the relevant parameters and conservative estimates of the marginal product of capital.

Thus far we have adopted the usual convenient assumption of constant exogenous technical progress. If, however, in the process of investment and production, new techniques of production or new products (so-called learning-by-doing) are apt to be developed, increasing output produces an external benefit raising the growth rate, and optimal saving rates may be still higher than estimated above.[8] This will be reinforced still further if the learning-by-doing is more important in the production of investment than of consumption. In short, it will rise (at least over some range) with *s*, thus either raising or lowering optimal *s* depending on whether the extra output effect offsets the declining marginal utility of income effect.[9]

While the analysis is heuristic, it is instructive to examine the cases where greater μ leads to higher or lower *s*, to examine the likely effect of a greater μ from higher *s* due to learning. An examination of table 2–4 indicates that the only cases where higher μ leads to *lower* optimal saving rates are those few combinations of parameters which produce very large saving rates. For virtually all of the cases, raising μ raises optimal *s*. In brief, learning-by-doing is likely to lead to still higher optimal *s* except in those cases where *s* is enormous already.

The issue of embodied technical change is somewhat more subtle. If advances in technology are embodied only—or disproportionately—in new capital, higher saving and investment rates may raise the rate of technical progress or at least temporarily diffuse the new technology more rapidly.[10]

Finally, some saving and investment takes the form of human capital. While it is difficult to separate the investment from the consumption component in, for example, direct education expenditures, and even more difficult to impute the value of foregone earnings in education and job training, such investment is likely to be important. However, those who argue for inclusion of human capital expenditures in saving figures ignore the depreciation of the stock of human capital (Schultz 1960). Conceptually proper treatment would deduct depreciation and include only net saving embodied in labor force knowledge and skills. As Auerbach (1985) notes, "Because all workers eventually die, their human capital must fully depreciate." Thus, comparisons of savings rates across countries such as the U.S. and Japan which seek to explain large differences by offsetting human capital expenditures almost certainly overstate that case.

Further net human investment in our model is perfectly equivalent to labor augmenting (Harrod-neutral) technical progress. Thus, our discussion establishing the relationship between higher rates of technical progress (brought about through higher rates of *net* human investment) and optimal saving in "regular" capital applies. While further refinements of measures of human investment expenditures *and* depreciation of the stock of human capital are desirable, they are not likely to raise the *net* saving rate more than a small amount (perhaps 1% or so) and are unlikely to cause us to alter the conclusion that currently the net national saving rate in the U.S. is low, falling, and well below its optimum.

Some Recent Studies Testing Theories of Private Saving Behavior

The two leading theories of private saving behavior are the pure life-cycle theory set forth by Modigliani and Brumberg (1954) and Ando and Modigliani (1963) and intergenerational altruism model of Barro (1974). In the Barro model it is unclear whether the government can affect national saving, since the private sector will seek to undo any change in government saving or borrowing. While problems exist with the Barro model, were it correct, the long-run saving rate would approximate estimated optimal rates if current savers had accurate information about the parameters, and there were no capital market restrictions (for example, nonnegative net worth), and so forth. The life-cycle model provides no automatic mechanism for individual households to account for the fact that future generations will be richer except by issuing greater public debt. There is no bequest motive and the average propensity to consume over the lifetime is one. Various studies have attempted to demonstrate that life-cycle behavior can explain several important phenomena concerning aggregate wealth accumulation in the United States (see Tobin 1967). More recently, a variety of authors have attacked the pure life-cycle model for its concept of no bequest and its lifetime average propensity to consume of one. For example, Kotlikoff and Summers (1981) conclude that life-cycle saving can account for only about 20% of the aggregate wealth in the United States. Unfortunately, a mathematical error in their derivation of the formulae is part of the explanation for their result, and corrected, the number would be about 50%. This is still a telling indictment of the extreme version of the life-cycle hypothesis.

There have also been a number of studies attempting to examine the extent of dissaving after retirement. For example, Michael Darby (1979) demonstrated, using longitudinal household data, that there was surprisingly little dissaving postretirement, and concluded these results were incompatible with the pure life-cycle hypothesis. Mirer (1979), David and Menchik (1980), Blinder, Gordon, and Wise (1980), and Bernheim (1980) also find either no dissaving or too little dissaving after retirement to be consistent with the pure life-cycle model.

In recent work, Bernheim has established that in the presence of explicit annuities (or implicit ones, provided by family insurance as described by Kotlikoff and Spivak 1980) estimates of dissaving should be adjusted by including the simple discounted value of pension benefits (for example, Social Security payments) in total wealth, rather than the actuarial discounted value. He further concludes that the response to saving and dissaving rates to apparently involuntary annuitization is inconsistent with the pure life-cycle model.

Rejection of the pure form of the life-cycle model should not be taken to mean that there is no consumption smoothing over the life cycle, or that the propensity to consume is independent of age. It is the rejection of the assumption that the average propensity to consume over the lifetime is one, and that there is no bequest motive (even accounting for the fact that an uncertain date of death may require very slow dissaving in the absence of actuarially fair annuities).

A variety of studies presume the pure form of the life-cycle theory in analyses of public policy. We shall comment on several, but it is important to point out that one of the major conclusions from the pure life-cycle model is that public debt—explicit or implicit—crowds out private saving and, by our assumptions, capital formation. In an alternative model proposed by Barro (1974), extending work of Bailey (1962), and dating all the way back to Ricardo, a Say's law of public finance is developed in which increases in the supply of public debt call forth an increased demand for it. The argument is simply that in a world where there are intergenerational altruism and operative bequest motives—as well as many other assumptions such as lump-sum finance—the private sector can undo the government's attempt to redistribute resources across generations.

Many studies have tried to analyze the effect of some measure of deficits or public debt on consumption (for example, Feldstein 1982 and Barth et al. 1984 and the numerous studies cited in these works) or of unfunded Social Security liabilities on the consumption/saving choice (see Feldstein 1974, Barro 1978, and Feldstein and Pellechio 1979, among many). The conclusions are somewhat mixed. I believe that an accurate summary of the econometric literature is that Feldstein's original dollar-for-dollar estimate of the substitution of unfunded Social Security liabilities or public debt for private saving has been revised to 25 to 50 cents on the dollar.

Since concepts such as deficits, public debt, and unfunded Social Security liabilities are subject to vagaries of accounting procedures, more direct tests of the intergenerational altruism model are possible. To see this, note that in the intergenerational altruism model *aggregate* consumption depends only on *aggregate* resources, not on their age distribution. This forms the basis for the test developed by Boskin and Kotlikoff (1985). We develop a finite approximation to the intergenerational optimization problem for Barro-type behavior under earnings- and rate-of-return-uncertainty, as well as under demographic change, for the U.S. economy, and test whether, given the level of consumption predicted by this model, variables measuring the age distribution of resources influence actual consumption. Data on the age distribution of resources is obtained from the annual *Current Population Surveys*. Presented in a variety of forms using various measures of the age distribution of resources, the results reject the hypothesis that aggregate consumption is independent of the age distribution of resources. They therefore cast considerable doubt on the pure intergenerational altruism model and on the contention that government debt policy—explicit or implicit—does not affect the consumption/saving choice.

Thus, neither the pure life-cycle model nor the pure intergenerational altruism model seems sufficient to explain aggregate saving behavior or the effects of policy on saving. Undoubtedly, different people in the economy could be described in their saving behavior by different models, including a Keynesian liquidity constraint consumption/saving model, and the convex combination that results in aggregate saving is some complicated combination of these models.

I do believe that it is important to realize, however, that there are substantial differences in the propensity to consume by age, some lifetime smoothing, and substantial bequests in aggregate capital formation. Thus, elements of both the bequest model and the original pure life-cycle model are important in explaining saving behavior, despite the fact that each of the models in its most pure form is rejected in the data.

Another important controversy has arisen over the extent to which changes in the real after-tax rate of return affect private saving. As noted in the second section of this chapter, "Denison's law"—the apparent constancy of the gross private saving rate at times of full employment through the mid-1970s—was often taken to suggest that tax policy did not affect aggregate private saving, but only its composition between the household and corporate sectors. Since there has been substantial controversy about structural tax policy and its effects on effective tax rates on capital income, renewed interest has focused on this issue. The article by Boskin (1978) sparked a substantial amount of controversy. In that work, I consistently found estimates of the real net rate of return elasticity of private saving of about 0.4.

While hardly enormous, such a modest interest elasticity has important implications for public policy. For example, the social opportunity cost of public funds to be used in cost-benefit analyses of government programs is substantially lower than the private marginal product of capital since some of the funds freed from the private sector by either taxation or borrowing and made available to the government come at the expense of additional private saving, rather than just foregone private investment.

Were saving unresponsive to rates of return, all of the funds raised, for example, by government borrowing, would come from private investment, whose social opportunity cost is the before-tax marginal product of capital. Also, the intertemporal efficiency losses in our tax system are large and swamp the atemporal inefficiencies due to misallocation of the capital stock among assets and industries. (See Fullerton, Shoven, and Whalley 1983, who use my estimates.)

There are substantial difficulties in defining, estimating, and interpreting an interest elasticity of saving.[11] For a start, one must be careful in defining the conceptual experiment to decide whether one is holding a stream of income or wealth constant when one changes the real after-tax rate of return, for example, by tax policy. Are we causing a change in the future after-tax stream of capital income which is exactly matched by a reduction in the rate at which it is discounted, thereby leaving financial wealth unchanged, but perhaps affecting the valuation of future expected earnings, and through this change in human wealth affecting consumption and saving?

While studies of the interest elasticity of saving abound, greater clarity on the exact questions being posed and the conceptual experiment being analyzed is highly desirable. I confess to having been all too brief in my 1978 paper on this issue. Recent work has tended on the one hand either to confirm my earlier results or suggest that the rate-of-return elasticities are still larger (see Summers 1981, 1984) or on the other hand to cast doubt on these results (see, for example, Friend and Hasbrouk 1982, or Howrey and Hymans 1980).

A stylized finance model with labor earnings in period 1 and consumption out of interest income and assets in future periods yields the result that as risk-aversion rises, the response of saving to the rate of return eventually becomes negative. While adding uncertainty to the model is a step forward, we should be careful in reading too much into this result. First, with many periods, including subsequent periods of earnings, the result is unclear; second, as noted above, in aggregating households to determine the response of total saving to rates of return, surely much of saving is done for longer-term reasons, and examining behavior toward risk in portfolio allocation among the wealthy may be misleading.

While I do not think the issue is at all settled, I would like to share with you the preliminary results of a major study of postwar U.S. consumption that I have been conducting for the last three years with my colleague, Lawrence Lau. The major innovations in our study are the use of annual *Current Population Survey* information on cross-tabulations of income and household characteristics (especially age of head of household) plus the building of age cohort-specific wealth accounts with which to analyze the share of wealth consumed in goods and as leisure.

We build the simplest possible model that is a legitimate candidate for exact aggregation from individual behavior. The individual household's current-period consumption and leisure are functions of the spot prices of current-period consumption and leisure and forward prices of future-period consumption and leisure, wealth of the individual households, and the household's attributes. Under assumptions that expectations are stationary, we define the forward prices at each point in time. Since time-series data on individual households are not available, we use aggregate data on current consumption and leisure expenditures which satisfy necessary conditions for exact aggregation. They are consistent with "no-money illusion" and thereby impose various restrictions on the parameters. The estimated equations for the U.S. postwar period perform remarkably well, predicting the share of wealth consumed with but small deviations.

We then decompose the growth in consumption in the postwar period into its components. The approximate 3% average annual percentage change in consumption is decomposed into the total change due to changes in wealth, wage rates, rates of return, population growth, the age composition of households, wealth by age of the household, changes in female participation in the labor force, and the vintage of the household defined as whether or not the household head was born after or prior to 1939 and thus experienced the Great Depression first hand.

Several intriguing results emerge from that study. For the purpose at hand, suffice it to say that the estimated interest elasticities of saving are larger than from my previous studies, and are estimated relatively precisely. Thus, if anything, I would argue that my earlier results of positive elasticities tend not only to be confirmed, but that the interest elasticity is probably in the range 0.5 to 2.0 for persons age 45 to 54. These elasticities expressly include the revaluation of wealth due to the changes in the rates of return. The elasticity of consumption expenditures with respect to wealth is about 1.0. Finally, we note not only that the propensity to consume varies with age, but that there is an intriguing difference both in the elasticity of consumption with respect to wealth, and in the shares of wealth consumed.

There is also the shift in interest elasticity of saving between the vintages of households with heads born pre-1939 and post-1939. We find that *at the same age,* household heads born post-1939 have a higher propensity to consume out of their wealth than those born prior to 1939, but on the other hand, they are somewhat more responsive to changes in rates of return. I mention this study only to indicate that substantial refinements are possible in analyzing saving behavior and integrating various types of data despite the absence of full-blown panel studies providing accurate balance sheets on individual households.

I do not mean to suggest that the real net rate of return elasticity of saving is a closed theoretical or empirical issue, but my own judgment— as devoid of personal bias as possible for someone who has spent much time working on the problem—is that despite the numerous difficulties in such estimation, my work and the work of Summers, even adjusted for the criticisms noted, still lead me to believe that there is at least a modest positive interest elasticity of private saving in the United States.[12]

Implications of Analyses and Recent Empirical Results for Long-run Fiscal Policy

Recent empirical results just described combined with the analysis presented in the second and third sections of this chapter generate several implications for the analysis of fiscal policy, such as structural changes in tax policy, unfunded Social Security obligations, and the public debt. They suggest that a good working hypothesis is that unfunded Social

Security obligations and public debt do crowd out some private saving, but this is likely to be substantially less than dollar-for-dollar. The age distribution of resources does matter for aggregate consumption in the economy. Moreover, changes in the age distribution brought about by age-specific fiscal policy—such as increases in public debt or changes in the age structure of Social Security benefits and taxes—are likely to change saving behavior.

The size of these variables—a true measure of real public debt plus unfunded Social Security obligations including those projected in Medicare—is quite large (Boskin 1986). The unfunded liabilities in OASDI in present-value terms were as large as the privately held national debt prior to the 1983 Social Security Amendments. Various tax increases, the projected 1990–2015 building of a very large surplus of approximately one-third to one-half of GNP, and gradual increases in the age of eligibility for retirement benefits reduce this estimated present value of the unfunded liabilities in OASDI to approximately zero.

However, it would be naive to assume that the exempt amount in the income taxation of Social Security benefits will remain unindexed once the middle class has half of its benefits become taxable, and/or that we will passively accrue a surplus many times that of what Social Security has been able to accrue in the past. It is more likely that the surplus will be dissipated to pay part of the even larger deficit that is projected in the Hospital Insurance part of Medicare.[13] Thus, even a partial offset of Social Security's unfunded liabilities, and/or the growing public debt, on private saving is likely to be the most compelling problem for those concerned about raising the saving rate.

It is my belief that these effects have been mitigated substantially, even though we still have major structural tax problems, unproductively allocate the existing capital stock, and (while inefficiently subsidizing some types of investment) on balance curtail saving and investment via our system of income taxation. Reasons include the growth of employer-provided pension benefits and IRA and Keogh accounts as well as the recent reduction in effective marginal tax rates for corporations. Also, there is a controversy over whether effective marginal tax rates on capital income really rose as much in the 1970s as has been suggested by Feldstein and Summers (1979) and others, with King and Fullerton 1983 presenting the contrary view. Thus, we have been moving in a haphazard way toward a consumption tax system as opposed to an income tax system.

Much more could be done in this regard, but I do not believe that the structural nature of the tax system is sufficient to be the culprit by itself in the decline of our saving rate. I believe that the efficiency losses are large and that a substantial fraction of saving is done at the after-tax, not the before-tax, rate of return. (For example, approximately half of IRAs are at the limit allowed.) Thus, the study of the interest elasticity of saving remains relevant for these efficiency issues, but I do not believe that the increases in capital income tax rates in the 1970s plausibly can be estimated to have been large enough in combination with reasonable interest elasticities of saving to suggest that they are the *primary* reason for the decline in net saving. They probably contributed something, and may well have combined with our intergenerational transfer policies to reduce our net national saving rate.

Recent proposals to reduce tax rates and broaden the tax base have sometimes carried with them the notion that they would stimulate saving and investment. Of paramount importance is how the base is broadened. If depreciation allowances are slowed down, with tax-free savings vehicles limited, for example, it is likely that the inclusion of more investment income in the tax base will more than offset any lowering of the rates in the net effect on tax rates on saving and investment. Among the reform proposals, only broad-based consumption- or consumed-income-type taxes are likely to have a positive impact on U.S. saving. The reforms moving us closer to pure income taxation will likely do the reverse as they substantially extend the double taxation of saving, albeit at somewhat lower rates.

I might add that analyses of recent saving behavior have tended to suggest casually that the "supply-side" tax incentives did not work. While the investment boomlet we experienced in 1984 may well be in part a reaction to the tax incentives in ERTA/TEFRA, private saving has only rebounded slightly, and net private saving is still quite low. While there has been a substantial flow into IRAs, much of this comes from already existing assets, and only part is from accumulation of new wealth. Thus, some people see the sharp increase in real interest rates and the apparent modest response of saving as suggesting that there is not a very large interest elasticity of saving.

I would rather suggest that an important institutional factor has been overlooked in these data. As pointed out by Bernheim and Shoven (1985), there is virtually an automatic negative interest elasticity in the personal saving rate because defined-benefit pension plans will reduce their contributions substantially with increases in the interest rates assumed by actuaries which reflect historic experience in the economy. Thus, in 1984 there was a decrease of almost $30 billion in contributions to private defined-benefit pension plans. It is rather remarkable that net private saving actually increased as much as it did in 1984 in spite of this mechanical short-run automatic negative response of the defined-benefit contribution of private saving to these rates of return.

I conclude therefore that public policies can and do affect private and national saving, and that by virtue of their magnitude and likely response, intergenerational redistribution policies—explicit and implicit public debt—are probably quantitatively more important than capital income taxation, but that the latter certainly play some role. In any event, federal government dissaving is currently swamping any likely increase in private sector saving that could be produced by structural changes in tax policy in the near future. In order to increase our net national saving rate, we will have to decrease government dissaving.[14]

Appendix 2A

While an adjustment for including the expenditures on consumer durables and government capital, net of depreciation, is conceptually straightforward, as is the inclusion of the imputed rental flow in the corresponding consumption and income figures, a variety of assumptions and technical adjustments must be made to measure the rental flows and the depreciation. The numbers reported in table 2–2 define private and government consumption as their corresponding NIPA figures less private durables expenditures and government capital expenditures, respectively, plus the rental flows from the stock of private durables and the government's tangible capital stock, respectively. The rental flow is defined as the product of the sum of the real rate of interest plus depreciation and the capital stock. Thus, the adjusted consumption figures depend upon the choice of a real rate of interest and the measurement of depreciation. While the BEA provides estimates of depreciation, they are subject to substantial criticism, reflecting physical wear and tear much more closely than economic depreciation, for example, and not appropriately adjusting for obsolescence due to technical change or relative price changes.

The "real" rate of interest is the subject of a major controversy in economics. There are some who claim it is constant, others who attempt to estimate expected inflation in various ways to subtract from a nominal rate of interest, and still others who subtract ex post observed inflation from nominal interest rates to get a real rate. We then must choose the appropriate nominal rate of interest, as it can differ substantially by type of asset—for example, Treasury bill rates have been several percentage points lower than corporate bond rates in recent years.

The figures reported in table 2–2 use the BEA depreciation figures and a .02 real opportunity cost of the asset. As noted in the discussion of the multiplier effect of mismeasurement of consumption translating into a larger proportionate mismeasurement of saving because the latter is only a fraction of the former, we present in table 2A–1 a comparison of our adjusted consumption figures with the BEA depreciation and a 2% constant real rate of interest, with corresponding figures using the 2% real rate of interest and our depreciation, and our depreciation and ex post actual real interest defined as the T-bill rate less a four-quarter change in the PCE deflator.

Table 2A–1
Comparison of Consumption Concepts in 1972 Dollars

	Observed Real Rate(R)	C*, Using Observed R, Boskin–Kotlikoff Depreciation	C*, Using R = .02 and Boskin–Kotlikoff Depreciation	C*, Using R = .02, and BEA Deprec.
1951–1960	1.6	386.5	388.7	386.1
1961–1970	2.8	552.4	550.2	549.9
1971–1980	0.8	789.9	791.7	792.9
1981	7.8	974.1	939.7	938.9
1982	7.9	992.4	956.7	955.1
1983	6.5	1,015.7	987.7	986.9
1984	9.5	1,077.0	1,028.0	1,026.9

Source: Author's calculations.

(R) is T-bill rate, less four-quarter change in PCE durables deflator. Averages are geometric means for decade.

Our depreciation series uses a geometric rate of 20% for consumer durables and government equipment and 3% for government structures. Adjusted consumption for the private sector varies only modestly from 1951 to 1980. But because of the sharp rise in real interest rates from 1981 to 1984, our series using the observed real rate rather than a constant 2% rate produced larger estimates of adjusted consumption as indicated in table 2A–1. Consumption using either BEA or our depreciation with a 2% real rate was about 4% lower on average in the 1981–1984 period.

A similar comparison would reveal that government consumption would be 10% lower in 1981–1984 if we use .02 rather than the ex post real rate (with either depreciation series). Figure 2A–1 presents the baseline adjusted saving rate (BEA depreciation and .02 real interest rate) and figure 2A–2 presents a comparison of the actual ex post real rates to the baseline. All this serves to underscore the tremendous importance of obtaining improved measures of depreciation as an input into our understanding of net capital formation. It is not even clear that the BEA and our depreciation form reasonable bounds on what true depreciation might really be.

Notes

1. For conflicting views on this subject, see Harberger (1980) and Feldstein and Horioka (1980).

2. This approach is most fully developed by Harberger (1971).

3. Of course, average and marginal returns may differ and there are some pure profits included in capital income.

4. See Phelps (1962).

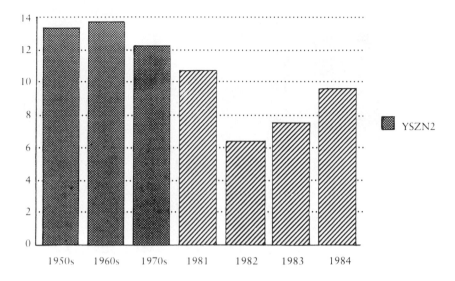

BEA depreciation; .02 real rate.

Figure 2A–1. Savings Rate

5. The discussion that follows is based on Mirrlees (1967) and Arrow (1977).

6. I discuss the implications of a similar analysis in Boskin (1981).

7. However, survey information among groups which may well be constrained in borrowing suggest ρ is much higher. (See Kurz et al. 1977 and the discussion in Friedman 1957.)

8. This concept is developed by Arrow (1962).

9. Were the social welfare function defined to maximize the sum of discounted consumption per capita, rather than the utility of that consumption, the optimal s would be larger than those reported in table 2A–4 as the declining marginal utility effect would be ignored. (See Sheshinski 1967.)

10. In the Cobb–Douglas case Phelps (1965) demonstrates that the long-run age structure of the capital stock is independent of the saving rate, but a higher saving rate still will move us to a higher growth path more rapidly and these output gains may be large for a long time. With more general technology, the embodiment of new technology can lead to a higher growth rate. The Phelps result above is only an approximation for small changes. (See Sheshinski and Levhari 1967.)

11. This has led some people to search for "deep structural parameters" using the Euler equation approach to estimating parameters of intertemporal consumption, and has often led to a comingling of time-preference and risk-aversion parameters. While I am sympathetic to the Lucas critique that changes in the macro environment might alter not only the stability of consumption or saving functions but their interpretations as well, the Euler equation work has

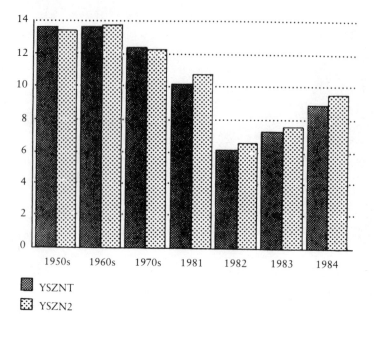

BEA depreciation; dark—actual ex post real rate; light—.02 real rate.

Figure 2A–2. Comparison of Fixed and Ex Post Real Rates

been done in a restrictive single-equation framework, usually assuming additively separable utility of a representative consumer. Such assumptions are extremely restrictive, and it is unclear that this approach introduces fewer problems than it solves. Hopefully, further research along these lines will improve our understanding of intertemporal consumption behavior.

12. The U.S. is an open economy in the short run at least. Thus in the short run, the supply of savings from the rest of the world is quite elastic.

13. See M. Boskin, *A Social Security Solution,* forthcoming 1986.

14. Two other avenues for fiscal policy to affect saving are increases in government consumption and redistribution from the rich to the poor if the latter are liquidity-constrained or have a higher propensity to consume. Neither of these factors appears to be large enough to cause much of a change in saving. (See Boskin and Kotlikoff 1985).

References

Ando, A. and F. Modigliani, "The Life Cycle Hypothesis of Saving: Aggregate Implications and Tests." *American Economic Review* 53 (March 1963):55–84.

Arrow, K., "The Economic Implications of Learning by Doing." *Review of Economic Studies*, 1962.

———. "The Social Rate of Discount with Imperfect Capital Markets." Discussion paper. Cambridge, Mass.: Harvard University, 1977.

——— and M. Kurz, *Public Investment, the Rate of Return and Optimal Fiscal Policy*. Baltimore: The Johns Hopkins University Press, 1970.

Atkinson, A.B., "The Distribution of Wealth and the Individual Life-Cycle." *Oxford Economic Papers* Vol. 23 (July 1971).

Auerbach, A.J., "Saving in the U.S. Some Conceptual Issues" in *The Level and Composition of Household Saving*, ed. P. Hendershott. Cambridge, Mass.: Ballinger, 1985.

Auderbach, A.J. and L.J. Kotlikoff, "An Examination of Empirical Tests of Social Security and Savings." National Bureau of Economic Research Working Paper no. 730, August 1981, Cambridge, Mass.

Bailey, M.J., *National Income and the Price Level*. New York: McGraw-Hill, 1962.

Barro, R.J., "Are Government Bonds Net Wealth?" *Journal of Political Economy*, November–December 1974:1095–1117.

———, *The Impact of Social Security on Private Savings*. Washington, D.C.: American Enterprise Institute, 1978.

Barth, J.R., G. Iden, and F.S. Russek, "Do Federal Deficits Really Matter?," *Contemporary Policy Issues*, 3 (fall 1984–85):79–85.

Bernheim, B.D. "Dissaving after Retirement: Testing the Pure Life Cycle Hypothesis," National Bureau of Economic Research Working Paper No. 1409, Cambridge, Mass., July 1984.

Bernheim, B.D., and J.B. Shoven, "Pension Funding & Saving," National Bureau of Economic Research Working Paper No. 1622, Cambridge, Mass., May 1985.

Blinder, S.A., R.H. Gordon, and D.E. Wise, "Social Security, Bequests and the Life Cycle Theory of Savings: Cross-Sectional Tests." National Bureau of Economic Research Working Paper no. 619, 1980, Cambridge, Mass.

Boskin, M., "Federal Government Deficits: Some Myths and Realities." *American Economic Review*, May 1982.

———, "Notes on the Tax Treatment of Human Capital," U.S. Treasury, *Conference on Tax Research*, 1976.

———, *The Real Federal Budget*. Cambridge, Mass.: Harvard University Press, forthcoming 1986.

———, "Some Issues in Supply-Side Economics" in *Carnegie-Rochester Conference Series on Public Policy*, vol. 14. North-Holland Publishing Company. Amsterdam, The Netherlands. (1981)201–20.

———, "Taxation, Saving and the Rate of Interest." *Journal of Political Economy*, 86(1978):S3–S27.

——— and L. Kotlikoff, "Public Debt and U.S. Saving: A New Test of the Neutrality Hypothesis." *Carnegie–Rochester Conference Series*, Summer 1985.

——— and L. Lau, *An Analysis of Post-war U.S. Consumption*. National Bureau of Economic Research, Cambridge, Mass., forthcoming 1985.

———, M. Robinson, T. O'Reilly, and P. Kumar, "New Estimates of the Value of Federal Mineral Rights and Land." *American Economic Review,* forthcoming December 1985.

Brainard, W., J. Shoven, and L. Weiss, "The Financial Valuation of the Return to Capital" in *Brookings Papers on Economic Activity,* Washington, D.C., 1980.

Corcoran, P. and L. Sahling, "The Cost of Capital: How High Is It?" *Federal Reserve Bank of New York Quarterly Reviews,* Summer 1982.

Darby, M.R., *The Effects of Social Security on Income and the Capital Stock.* Washington, D.C.: American Enterprise Institute, 1979.

David, M. and P. Menchik, "The Effect of Income Distribution and Redistribution on Lifetime Saving and Bequests." Discussion Paper no. 582. Madison, University of Wisconsin Institute for Research on Poverty 1980.

David, P.A. and J.L. Scadding, "Private Savings: Ultrarationality, Aggregation, and 'Denison's Law.' " *Journal of Political Economy* 82 (March–April 1974).

Denison, E.F., "A Note on Private Saving," *Review of Economic Statistics* 40 (August 1958).

Eisner, Robert and Paul J. Pieper, "A New View of the Federal Debt and Budget Deficits." *American Economic Review* 74 (March 1984):11–20.

Federal Reserve System, Board of Governors, Flow of Funds Section, Division of Research and Statistics, "Balance Sheets for the U.S. Economy, 1945–83." Unpublished data document. Washington, D.C.: November 1984.

Feldstein, M., "Social Security, Induced Retirement, and Aggregate Capital Accumulation." *Journal of Political Economy,* 1974:905–26.

———, "Does the U.S. Save Too Little?", *American Economic Review,* 67, no. 1 (February 1977):116–21.

———, "Do Private Pensions Increase National Savings?", *Journal of Public Economics,* 10, no. 3 (December 1978):277–93.

———, "Government Deficits and Aggregate Demand," *Journal of Monetary Economics,* 9, no. 1 (January 1982):144–49.

Feldstein, M. and C. Horioka, "Domestic Savings and International Capital Flows." *The Economic Journal,* 1980.

Feldstein, M.S. and A. Pellechio, "Social Security and Household Wealth Accumulation: New Microeconomic Evidence." *Review of Economics and Statistics* 61 (1979):361–68.

Feldstein, M.S. and L. Summers, "Inflation and the Taxation of Capital Income in the Corporate Sector." *National Tax Journal* 32 (December 1979):445–70.

Friend, I. and J. Hasbrouk, "Saving and After-Tax Rates of Return." *Review of Economics and Statistics,* November 1983.

Fullerton, D., J.B. Shoven, and J. Whalley, "Replacing the U.S. Income Tax with a Progressive Consumption Tax: A Sequenced General Equilibrium Approach." *Journal of Public Economics* 20 (February 1983):3–24.

Hall, R. and F. Mishkin, "The Sensitivity of Consumption to Transitory Income: Estimates from Panel Data on Households." *Econometrica,* 1982.

Harberger, A., "Three Basic Postulates for Applied Welfare Economics." *Journal of Economic Literature* 9 (1971):785–97.

———, "Vignettes on the World Capital Markets." *American Economic Review,* 1980.

Howrey, E.P. and S.H. Hymans, "The Measurement and Determination of Loanable-Fund Saving" in *Brookings Papers on Economic Activity* 3 (1978). Also in *What Should Be Taxed: Income or Expenditure?*, ed. J.A. Pechman Washington D.C.: The Brookings Institution, 1980.

King, M.A. and D. Fullerton, *The Taxation of Income from Capital: A Comparative Study of the U.S., U.K., Sweden and West Germany.* National Bureau of Economic Research, Chicago: University of Chicago Press 1983.

Kotlikoff, L.J. and L. Summers, "The Role of Intergenerational Transfers in Aggregate Capital Accumulation." *Journal of Political Economy* 89 (August 1981):706–32.

Kotlikoff, L.J. and A. Spivak, "The Family as an Incomplete Annuities Market," *Journal of Political Economy,* 89, no. 2 (April 1981):372–91.

Kurz, M. et al., "Experimental Determination of Discount Rates" SRI International Memorandum, Palo Alto, California, 1977.

Mirer, T.W., "The Wealth-Age Relation Among the Aged." *American Economoic Review* 69 (June 1979).

Mirrlees, J., "Optimum Growth When Technology is Changing." *Review of Economic Studies* 34 (1967):95–124.

Modigliani, F. and R. Brumberg, "Utility Analysis and the Consumption Function: An Interpretation of Cross-Section Data" in *Post-Keynesian Economics* ed. K.E. Kurihara. New Brunswick, N.J.: Rutgers University Press, 1954.

Phelps, E., "The New View of Investment: A Neoclassical Analysis." *Quarterly Journal of Economics,* November 1962.

Phelps, E., "Second Essay on the Golden Rule of Accumulation," *American Economic Review,* September 1965.

Schultz, T., "Presidential Address to the American Economic Association." *American Economic Review,* 1960.

Sheshinski, E., "Optimal Accumulation with Learning by Doing" in *Essays on the Theory of Optimal Economic Growth,* K. Shell, ed. Cambridge, Mass.: MIT Press, 1967.

Sheshinski, E. and P. Levhari, "On the Sensitivity of the Level of Output to Savings: Embodiment and Disembodiment." *Quarterly Journal of Economics,* August 1967.

Shoven, J.B., "Saving in the U.S. Economy" in *Removing Obstacles to Economic Growth,* ed. M.L. Wachter and S.M. Wachter. Philadelphia: University of Pennsylvania Press, 1984.

Summers, L.H., "Capital Taxation and Accumulation in a Life Cycle Growth Model." *American Economic Review* 71 (September 1981).

———, "Tax Policy, the Rate of Return, and Saving." National Bureau of Economic Research Working Paper no. 995 (September 1982). Cambridge, Mass.

———, "The After Tax Rate of Return Affects Private Savings," *American Economic Review,* 74, no. 2 (May 1984):249–53.

Tobin, J., "Life Cycle Saving and Balanced Growth" in *Ten Essays in Honor of Irving Fisher* ed. by W. Fellner. New York: John Wiley and Sons, 1967.

3
The Policy Options for Stimulating National Saving

Irwin Friend

In discussing the policy options for stimulating national saving, there is an implicit assumption that the current overall rate of saving and prospective trends in that rate are unsatisfactory. The overall rate of national saving for the United States, as measured by the national income accounts, has averaged an extremely low 2% of the national income in the past three years (1982–1984) as compared to the 10% of the late 1970s. The 1970 figure was not too different from the historical norm. Only a small part of this decline in overall saving from the 1970s was attributable to a decrease in the rate of private (or personal and corporate) saving. Rather, practically all of the decline stems from the massive increase in the federal government deficit. As a result, private domestic saving may be regarded as largely financing the government's deficit, with domestic investment largely financed by net foreign investment in this country, much of it by short-term funds. This relatively recent development has received substantial attention and obviously raises many potentially serious problems.

The concern about an inadequate rate of national saving, however, predated these government deficits and reflected a feeling that the U.S. rate of private as well as government saving and the associated rate of realized saving or capital formation was responsible at least in large part for lagging increases in national productivity as compared with earlier years or with major foreign competitors, especially Japan and West Germany, where the private saving rates were several times as large. The disparity between the total saving rate of Japan and West Germany and that of the United States was even greater.

It should be noted that while many noneconomists and economists alike take for granted a close causal connection between economic growth and capital formation (especially in plant and equipment), there is no consensus among economic specialists in the productivity area about the closeness of the relationship.[1] My own appraisal, and I think that of most economists, is that capital formation is only one of a number of the ingredients in economic growth, but it is still an important one. Even economists who agree with this appraisal do not necessarily agree with the desirability of government policy measures designed to increase the rates of saving and capital formation over those rates implied by the free play of competitive markets. Again, my own reaction is that if the rates of saving and capital formation can be increased without excessive costs (for example, by measures which do not place a much greater burden of taxation on low-income groups and do not substantially reduce allocational efficiency), it would be desirable to do so. Of course, where saving and investment can be increased by government measures which eliminate artificial tax or other constraints that encourage consumption at the expense of saving and investment and which do not result in a regressive tax structure, virtually all economists would agree with the desirability of such a change in policy.

The most important step to take to increase the national saving at this time would be to substantially reduce and, if feasible, eliminate the current federal government deficit. Substantial deficits cannot easily be justified in a relatively prosperous peacetime period. To the extent that the deficit can be reduced by decreasing government outlays, the national saving will clearly increase. It would be necessary to ensure that reduced government spending does not adversely impact the truly needy, but major cuts in the budget can still be carried out within this constraint. Such reductions in government expenditures might well encompass cuts across the board in defense and nondefense outlays, including a less costly indexing of government and Social Security pension payments and a moderate increase in the Social Security retirement age.

There is not the same degree of agreement on the effect of higher taxes on the national saving, even in periods of relative prosperity like the present time. However, it is my judgment, and I believe that of most economists, that an increase in taxes at this time would not only reduce government dissaving but would also increase the national saving. On the other hand, it should be pointed out that this conclusion is based on the assumption that the increased government revenue is not dissipated in increased outlays. There are economists who argue that even under this assumption, the reduction in government dissaving as a result of higher taxes would be offset in its effect on total saving by a reduction in private saving. This argument has little scientific support. It obviously assumes a high—and in my opinion implausible—degree of substitutability between government and private (household and corporate) saving.

Substitutability between Government and Private Saving

There is a wide difference of opinion among economists on the substitutability between household and corporate saving and between household and government saving. While the rationality and ultrarationality theories which imply that an additional dollar of corporate or government saving would be offset by a dollar decrease in household saving make considerable theoretical sense for corporate saving—at least in the long run—they seem to me to make much less sense for government saving where among other things they assume a strange type of intergenerational tax calculation. My evaluation of the empirical evidence, based on the available literature—which includes papers by Feldstein, Feldstein and Fane, David and Scadding, Howrey and Hymans, Tanner, and Blume and Siegel[2]—is that there is a moderate degree of substitutability between household and corporate saving but at most only a modest degree of substitutability between household and government saving.

The published tests which are based on time-series analysis seem to me quite deficient, especially as they apply to the relationship between household and government saving where I am not convinced there is any appreciable substitutability. Time-series analysis of the relationship between household and corporate saving is subject to the usual deficiency of the inadequacy of the number of independent observations for distinguishing among the effects of a large number of relevant serially correlated variables, while once government saving in addition to household and corporate saving is introduced into the usual time-series analysis, substantial problems of specification arise. Under these circumstances it seems to me essential to carry out cross-section tests both across countries and, more importantly, across households where possible.[3] Both Japan and West Germany have for many years had much higher household and private saving-income ratios and a much higher government saving-income ratio than the United States.[4] The drastic growth in the U.S. government deficit in recent years has not been offset even in part by a growth in private saving.[5]

Before leaving this subject of the substitutability between nonhousehold and household saving, special attention should be paid to the effect of the social security system on household saving. It should be pointed out that it is net payments into this system, rather than a net increase in assets, which are reflected in government saving as measured in the U.S. national accounts. As stressed by Feldstein in a number of papers,[6] this system which is essentially on a pay-as-you-go basis can be considered a government-imposed scheme of intergenerational transfers which he maintains has had a major effect in reducing household saving. Barro and, more importantly from an empirical viewpoint, Leimer and Lesnoy have demonstrated the great overstatement in Feldstein's estimated effects.[7] A large number of other studies—some of them time-series, others cross-sectional based on household surveys and still others cross-sectional with countries as the unit of observation—have obtained conflicting results on whether social security retirement programs have had any effect in reducing household saving.[8]

Based on all this evidence, especially that supplied by Leimer and Lesnoy, there is no clear evidence that a future claim on social security has *any* effect in reducing household saving. It is my judgment, but not one based on strong evidence, that there is such an effect but that it is likely to be moderate and nowhere near complete. As a result, a completely funded social security system and one which does not affect other government revenues and outlays (so that a surplus or deficit in the social security fund is associated with a corresponding surplus or deficit in the unified budget) should enhance the national saving. In this connection, reference should be made to Albert Ando's careful study of the relationship between household saving in Japan and the present value of net benefits for its social security program plus the present value of retirement benefits provided by private employers.[9] No significant relationship was found in Ando's study, which the author points out probably reflects in part substantial random measurement error so that there may well be some negative association between social security and household saving. However, there is no support for the hypothesis of a complete offset.

Effects of Taxation on Saving

The importance of aggregate government expenditures and tax revenues on the determination of total saving has been referred to above. However, we have not yet discussed one of the most controversial areas in appropriate government policy for stimulating total saving via the private sector, especially the household sector. The question here is how to structure the tax system so as to encourage private saving for a given level of taxes and federal government expenditures. Because our basic interest is in realized saving and investment, we must give some consideration to the effects of the tax structure on the propensity to invest as well as on the propensity to save.

For a given level of federal government revenues and expenditures, the primary tax mechanisms for affecting the propensity to save are the allocation of total taxes between taxes on capital income (levied directly on individuals or indirectly through corporations) and taxes on labor income.[9] While this chapter mainly concerns the after-tax interest sensitivity of saving and investment propensities, and ultimately realized saving, we cannot completely ignore the effects of shifting taxes from capital income to labor income (or vice versa) on the incentive to work or on the burden of taxation on different socioeconomic groups. Thus, if lower taxes on capital income do increase realized saving, as frequently perceived, they might still be undesirable if they depressed work incentives or if they made the tax structure regressive, since the upper income groups receive a very much larger share of capital than of labor income. Some supply-side economists might question the implicit assumption that a decrease in tax rates is not likely to increase the demand for and income of both capital and labor sufficiently to offset the adverse effect of lower tax rates on the government deficit, but I know of no evidence, including the recent federal government experiment in supply-side economics, which would support their position.

Before examining the relevant theory and empirical evidence on the effect of capital income taxation on aggregate saving, it should be noted that recent estimates by Joseph Pechman indicate that, as a result of changes in the tax structure over the past decade, capital income is no longer taxed more heavily than labor income.[11] In fact, Pechman's estimates of the current tax burden imply that for most economic groups labor income is somewhat more heavily taxed than capital income—a finding characterizing marginal as well as average tax rates. These estimates also indicate that combining all forms of taxation, the present tax structure is only moderately progressive and in fact is less progressive than it was a decade earlier.

While there is no consensus among economists about the after-tax return elasticities of private or aggregate saving, my own assessment is that neither the relevant theory nor the empirical evidence provides much support for the belief that higher after-tax rates of return on assets stimulate the private sector's propensity to save. This assessment is documented by Irwin Friend and Joel Hasbrouck in "Saving and After-Tax Rates of Return" in *Review of Economics and Statistics,* November 1983. The article spells out the deficiencies in other papers which have arrived at a substantially different conclusion.[12] From a theoretical viewpoint, perhaps the main deficiency is the usual modeling of the relation between the after-tax return and saving is the neglect of the crucial role played by uncertainty of resources (human and nonhuman wealth) and needs in the determination of saving behavior. Uncertainty may well play a more important role in influencing the saving-income ratio than any other economic factor.

There is evidence that a redistribution of after-tax income from the lower- to the upper-income groups, regardless of the form it took, would increase the private sector's saving-income ratio at least in the short or intermediate run though not necessarily in the long run. (Some proponents of the permanent income and life-cycle consumption theories might even question the shorter-term effects.) Thus, it might be possible to stimulate the aggregate propensity to save by shifting the overall burden of taxation on both labor and capital incomes from the upper- to the lower-income groups, but there is no strong evidence that the effect on saving of this regressive shift would be either large or sustained.

A shift in taxation from corporations to individuals would probably increase the aggregate propensity to save, at least in the short and intermediate run, in view of the substantially higher propensity to save by corporations than by individuals. A rise in the aggregate saving-income ratio associated with a shift in after-tax income from individuals to corporations would probably be partly offset by a decline in the household saving-income ratio, reflecting lower direct saving by stockholders but, except perhaps in the very long run as higher corporate saving is associated with higher household wealth, it is unlikely that the offset will be anywhere near complete. Yet, it should be noted that the fairly pronounced shift in U.S. taxes over the past decade from capital to labor income, and from corporations to individuals, together with the general decline in the progressiveness of the tax structure, especially for the top income group, was associated with a decline in the ratios to income of personal, private, and total saving to some of their lowest levels since the post-World War II adjustment in the late 1940s. This was true in spite of the specific additional saving incentives provided by IRA, Keogh, and similar plans.

While the impact of capital income taxes on saving behavior via an after-tax return effect is not entirely clear, even in direction, both theory and empirical evidence seem to indicate a negative impact of the cost of capital on investment. However, for risky investment, the cost of capital is not necessarily positively related, as might be expected, to the level of income taxes. Theoretical considerations do suggest a positive effect of higher corporate income taxes on the cost of capital and hence a negative effect on stock prices and investment.[13] However, this is not necessarily true of higher personal income taxes, at least in the short run, since under certain plausible assumptions (including personal tax credits for investment losses), investor risk is decreased more than expected return so that the required rate of return on risky assets may be reduced by higher personal tax rates.[14]

On the other hand, both theory and empirical evidence point to a positive relation between the cost of capital and the level of corporate income taxation, and hence a negative relation between the cost of capital and the magnitude of investment tax credits and depreciation deductions. Even here, however, the effectiveness of changes in corporation income taxation on investment would be limited in the long run by the apparent long-run ineffectiveness of such changes on saving incentives.

In connection with this discussion of the effects of taxation on capital and labor incomes, it may be useful to point out that there does not appear to be a solid basis to the common assertion that the "unsatisfactory" rate of capital formation and economic growth in the United States as compared to other western countries can be mostly attributed to our high taxes on income from capital. The most careful comparative study I have seen in this area concludes, on the basis of an admittedly limited sample of four countries: "Germany has the highest overall effective tax on income from capital *and* the highest growth rate. The United States is second in both categories and Sweden is third. The U.K. has the lowest overall effective tax on income from capital *and* the lowest growth rate. If we look at growth of nonfinancial corporate capital, results are substantially the same. The United States and Sweden are reversed, but Germany is still the highest and Britain is the lowest."[15] Lower marginal rates of taxation on capital and labor incomes probably do contribute to investment and work incentives, but their effectiveness should not be exaggerated.

Combining these different strands of theoretical and empirical evidence relating to the separate effects of corporate and personal capital income taxation on saving and investment behavior, my judgment is that a reduction of capital income taxes, especially at the corporate level, would initially stimulate investment over the cycle, but the long-run effect on capital formation is likely to be moderate if our assessment of the apparently low after-tax interest elasticity of saving is correct. Maximizing the effect on investment would require strongly regressive changes in the tax structure such as might be effected by the combination of eliminating corporate income taxes and either raising taxes on labor income or substituting flat consumption taxes for progressive income taxes. Such changes would probably raise corporations' propensity to invest both in the short and long run, and stimulate aggregate saving at least in the short and intermediate run, in veiw of the higher saving propensity of the upper-income groups. Thus, it is possible but by no means certain that a significant increase in capital formation could be effected, at least for a number of years, by a substantial increase in the regressiveness of the tax structure.

In the long run, however, the apparently low after-tax interest elasticity of saving would limit any increase in capital formation and hence realized saving which might be associated with a more regressive tax structure or with the substitution of taxes on labor income for taxes on capital income. Moreover, any beneficial effect of such changes in the tax structure on economic growth as a result of the stimulation of investment might be offset at least in part by weakened labor incentives as the lower taxes on capital income are financed by higher taxes on labor income. More important for purposes of this chapter, changes in the overall structure of taxes are not likely to greatly affect the aggregate level of realized saving.

It was noted that the substitution of flat consumption taxes for progressive income taxes might raise saving appreciably, but only at the price of strongly regressive changes in the tax structure. However, the use of progressive consumption taxes supplemented by substantially increased estate taxes could at least in theory take care of the problem of regressivity and might still result in increased saving as compared to the rate under a correspondingly progressive income tax structure. The reason is that there is substantial variation in the propensity to save by households of equivalent means, and consumption taxes channel more of the burden of taxes to households with a relatively low propensity to save. Unfortunately, progressive consumption taxes pose very serious transitional, enforcement, and other problems.[16]

The fact that there is no convincing evidence pointing to a significant positive after-tax interest elasticity of household or private saving does not mean that policy makers interested in stimulated saving should be indifferent to the structure of taxes. To the extent that taxes do depress saving and labor incentives, it is clearly the marginal rather than the average tax rates which are relevant.

An obvious approach to diminishing the depressive effects on both capital accumulation and labor input of a given total of taxation would be to minimize the marginal rates of taxation paid on income, keeping them consistent with a desired rate of progressivity in the average tax-income ratios. So long as the desired rate of progressivity in average tax rates is not too high, it is quite feasible to have an increase in average tax rates with increasing income levels without imposing extremely high marginal rates at any income level. Current approaches to this objective are exemplified by the Bradley–Gephardt and Kemp–Kasten tax proposals and, more recently, by the Department of the Treasury and administration proposals in 1984 and 1985.

Another approach to the use of tax policy to stimulate national saving might be to provide tax incentives for private pension and retirement funds since such savings, like social security, seem to result in a significant net addition to total saving.[17] Thus, in their 1984 paper Diamond and Hausman find that a 1% increase in the expected private-pension to permanent-income ratio does decrease the personal-saving to permanent-income ratio, but only by 0.14% on the average. These same authors find a somewhat higher offset (but still well under half) for social security. More limited and less satisfactory evidence suggests that contributions to IRAs and Keogh plans also increase total household saving rather than simply representing a diversion of saving from one form to another.[18]

A final approach to the use of tax policy to stimulate national saving would be to eliminate the income tax deduction available for interest paid on credit purchases of consumer goods. (Consumer credit might also be made less freely available through appropriate actions of the monetary authorities.) Since greater availability of consumer debt stimulates consumer spending, especially on consumer durables, and increased expenditures on consumer durables seem largely to be associated with decreased saving in financial assets rather than decreased consumption of nondurables, a decline in the availability of consumer debt would also be expected to enhance saving, especially if saving is defined to exclude net investment in consumer durables.[19]

The United States seems to be one of the few major countries which permits such favorable tax treatment of the interest paid on consumer debt. Comparable tax deductibility is not permitted (or is permitted only to a trivial extent) in Japan, Italy, West Germany, France, Britain, and Belgium.[20] All of these countries have saving ratios significantly higher than those in the U.S., and I suspect the more favorable terms for consumer credit in the U.S. played some role in this result.

Yet the problem is broader than consumer debt. As pointed out by Galper and Steuerle:

> If a taxpayer can borrow and deduct the costs of interest while at the same time acquiring an asset yielding income that is partially or fully tax-exempt—a process that is known as tax arbitrage—the taxpayer may achieve a tax reduction with no increase in net saving whatsoever. . . . Tax arbitrage reduces incentives to save—and incentives to work—in two ways. First, it permits taxpayers to increase their disposable income without doing any additional saving or productive labor—and may, therefore, encourage them to devote more time and resources . . . to non-productive efforts. . . . Second, the loss of tax revenues due to arbitrage by some taxpayers necessitates increases in revenue collections from other taxpayers. Those in the latter group face higher tax rates on their labor income and on their income from capital—and, as a result, [may] have somewhat diminished incentives to work and to save.[21]

What Accounts for Major Country Differences in Savings-Income Ratios?

In spite of the absence of much strong support for most noncoercive economic measures which might be taken by the government to substantially increase household or private saving, there are major variations in the saving–income ratios for different countries. It would be useful to know the reasons for these differences which have not been satisfactorily explained in the literature. One explanation sometimes given for the higher savings-income ratios in other countries, especially Japan, is the allegedly higher tax on capital income in the United States, leading to lower after-tax rates of return. This attribution of a much higher household-saving rate in Japan than in the U.S. to the differences in their tax burden seems difficult to justify even on the basis of casual empiricism, since the only noteworthy difference in the comparative taxes on individuals in these two countries seems to be their different treatment of capital gains.[22] While the absence of a capital gains tax in Japan might help to explain a relatively greater demand for common stocks, it would not be expected to have a substantial impact on total household saving, and even the effect on net stock accumulation should be limited in view of the relatively moderate effective (as distinguished from nominal) capital gains tax in the United States, estimated in recent years to be about 5%.[23] Moreover, since institutional stock ownership in Japan is said to account for the great bulk of outstanding stock and for a substantially higher proportion of all stocks outstanding than in the United States (where it approximates 50%), it is not clear why the somewhat more favorable capital gains treatment in Japan should have much of an effect on net stock accumulation and even less on total saving by households.

Parenthetically, it should be pointed out that a regression of savings ratios across countries, even if done correctly, may have little connection with the relationship to saving of after-tax return on capital income. Thus, in Japan interest rates paid on bank deposits have historically been below the interest rates available in the United States and below a comparable market rate because of the quasi-monopolistic control of the banking system by a few large institutions.[24] A similar situation apparently characterizes some European nations. If properly analyzed and compared to the U.S., such countries might point to higher saving rates associated with lower after-tax rates of taxation on capital income, though there may be no causal relationship between the two variables in view of significant differences in before-tax risk-adjusted rates of return. There are of course many other institutional differences among countries which may cast serious doubt on any cross-sectional country analyses of saving and after-tax rates of return.

In spite of the difficulties involved and the need for special care in analyzing the saving experience in foreign countries to obtain insights which may be useful in the United States, I think there is potentially a substantial payoff in analyzing time-series data within a number of foreign countries to investigate the apparent effect on saving of major changes in their tax laws. A large number of changes in the tax laws of these countries have taken place in the post–World War II period, many with the avowed purpose or theoretical potential of stimulating saving, but to my knowledge there has been no systematic inquiry into the end results.[25]

Improvement in Quality of Saving

Since the main intent in stimulating saving is presumably to increase the nation's productivity and economic growth, it should be pointed out that such an objective would be furthered by appropriate changes in the flow of saving as well as in its total. One tenable approach to this end would be to eliminate or at least greatly reduce the tax preference available for owned homes by equalizing the tax burden between investment in housing and investment in plant and equipment. Another would be to eliminate or at least greatly reduce the disparities in the taxation of business plant and equipment and in the taxation of investment in different industries, thus contributing to allocational efficiency. Such measures are integral parts of the flat-tax proposals mentioned earlier in this chapter, especially the Bradley–Gephardt proposal and, to a less extent, the Treasury and administration proposals.

At a more general level, on grounds of both efficiency and equity, the same tax rates should apply to all sources of economic return, whether the return comes from investment in housing or plant and equipment, from stocks or bonds, from capital gains or ordinary income, from deposits in commercial banks and other depository institutions, or from policies in life insurance companies. This does not mean that there may not be products or periods when national policy considerations would lead to differential taxation on different forms of economic activity, for example, the consumption of cigarettes, liquor, or gasoline. However, such exceptions should be kept to a minimum and should require a strong justification.

One other change in the composition of investment frequently advocated to raise productivity is to increase the proportion of business plant and equipment outlays flowing into risky investment. The rationale for this position is that the expected return on risky investment is higher than that on less risky investment. There is, however, no strong evidence that the return on unseasoned stock is significantly different from the return on seasoned or less risky equities or that any risk premium required by the market on the riskier equities is excessive or high.[26]

Summary and Conclusions

This chapter indicates that it is extremely difficult to point to measures which can be depended on to significantly increase national saving or saving-income ratio by raising private saving. Measures frequently advocated for this purpose have no firm support, either theoretical or empirical, backing their alleged effect on saving. They also raise serious problems of both distributional equity and efficiency—for example, difficulties rising from the increased burden of taxation on labor income associated with decreased taxation of capital income.

Probably the most important step that could be taken to increase national saving would be the immediate enactment of a substantial reduction in the current federal government deficit and eventually the elimination of such deficits in boom periods. Obviously, in a period of cyclical depression, stimulative government policies might be required both to preclude excessive unemployment and underutilization of other economic resources and to avoid the related decline in national income and national saving.

Another step which the government might take to increase the national saving would be to institute over a suitable period of time a completely funded social security system. The stimulation of private pension or retirement funds might also be justified, assuming that equity among taxpayers is maintained, since such savings like social security seem to result in a significant net addition to total saving.

Since greater availability of consumer debt stimulates consumer spending, especially on consumer durables, and increased expenditures on consumer durables seem largely to be associated with decreased saving in financial assets rather than decreased consumption of nondurables, a decline in the availability of consumer debt would also be expected to enhance saving. This might be accomplished by making consumer credit more costly through elimination of the income tax deductions available for interest paid on credit purchases of consumer goods, or by making it less freely available through appropriate actions of the monetary authorities. More broadly, interest deductions on loans should generally be allowed for income tax purposes only to the extent that the returns from the assets financed are included in taxable income.

There is no scientific support for a strong or even a significant negative after-tax interest elasticity of desired or realized saving. Even if such an effect is assumed as a matter of faith, there is no reason to believe that the implied increase in saving incentives, which would be associated with a reduction in taxes on capital income, would not be accompanied by a corresponding decrease in labor incentives as a result of the higher taxes on labor income required to maintain the same level of total tax income. Moreover, such changes in the tax structure cannot go very far without introducing regressivity into the incidence of taxes.

The fact that there is no convincing evidence supporting a significant deterrent effect of income tax on saving does not mean that those interested in saving policy should be indifferent to the structure of taxes. If income taxes do depress saving and labor incentives, it is the marginal rather than the average tax rates which are relevant. An obvious way to cut down any depressive effects on both capital and labor of a given total of taxation would be to minimize the marginal rates, keeping them consistent with a desired rate of progressivity in the average tax-income ratios. Several flat-tax proposals of recent years—including the Bradley–Gephardt, Kemp–Kasten, and 1984 and 1985 Treasury and administration proposals—are substantial improvements in this respect over the present tax structure.

The substitution of progressive consumption taxes for progressive income taxes would probably result in some net stimulation of saving, but it would raise substantial transitional, enforcement, and other problems. The substitution of flat consumption taxes for income taxes in our tax structure might have a larger stimulating effect, but only at the price of strongly regressive changes in the tax structure and a more negative effect on labor supply.

The apparent paucity of noncoercive economic measures which could be taken by the government to increase household or private saving may seem strange in view of the extremely large observed differences in the underlying saving-income ratios for different countries. Although these differences have not been satisfactorily explained in the literature, it is my judgment that to a major extent they represent cultural differences or differences in tastes (perhaps like those reflected in the Puritan ethic). As a consequence, it may be possible to increase private saving more effectively through noneconomic means than through economic policies. Such noneconomic methods were not considered to be within the province of this chapter.

While acceptable changes in economic policies seem to have limited scope for improving the nation's productivity by increasing private saving, there is substantial scope for improving allocational efficiency and hence productivity by insuring that, except for unusual circumstances, the same tax rates apply to all measures of economic return. This should generally be true whether the return comes from investment in housing or plant and equipment, from stocks or bonds, from capital gains or ordinary income, from deposits in banks and similar institutions, or from policies in life insurance companies.

Notes

1. Marshall E. Blume, Jean Crockett, and Irwin Friend, "Stimulation of Capital Formation: Ends and Means" in *Towards a New Industrial Policy*, ed. Michael L. Wachter and Susan M. Wachter (Philadelphia: University of Pennsylvania Press, 1981).

2. Martin S. Feldstein, "Tax Incentives, Corporate Saving and Capital Accumulation in the United States," *Journal of Public Economics* 2 (1973); Martin Feldstein and George Fane, "Taxes, Corporate Dividend Policy and Personal Saving: The British Postwar Experience," *Review of Economics and Statistics*, November 1973; Paul David and J.L. Scadding, "Private Savings, Ultra-Rationality, Aggregation and Denison's Law," *Journal of Political Economy*, March–April 1974; Philip Howrey and Saul H. Hymans, "The Measurement and Determination of Loanable Funds Saving," *Brookings Papers on Economic Activity* 3 (1978); J. Ernest Tanner, "Fiscal Policy and Consumer Behavior," *Review of Economics and Statistics*, May 1979; and Marshall Blume and Jeremy Siegel, "Personal Saving: Theory and Evidence" in *Saving, Investment and Capital Formation in an Inflationary Economy*, ed. Marshall Sarnat and Giorgio Szego (Cambridge, Mass.: Ballinger, 1982).

3. A more definitive analysis of the relation between household and corporate saving is possible on the basis of available household survey data, but such an analysis has yet to be carried out.

4. For the six countries for which the data were readily available (Great Britain, France, West Germany, Italy, Japan, and the United States) the simple cross-section correlations between the government saving—income and the personal and private saving—income ratios were not significantly different from zero in the two years 1970 and 1980 (and were insignificantly positive in both years). When a cyclical variable—the rate of change in real GNP to initial GNP—was added to the regression, the results were not changed.

5. For the decade ending in 1984, the correlations between the annual U.S. ratios of personal saving to personal disposable income, or private saving to income, or government saving (either federal or federal, state, and local combined) to revenue were again not significantly different from zero (insignificantly negative for personal saving and insignificantly positive for private saving). The correlation (adjusted for degrees of freedom) between the personal saving—income ratios and the corporate saving—income ratios (adjusted for inventory and depreciation revaluations) was −.34. However, when a cyclical variable—relative change in real GNP—was added to the regression, the partial correlation between the personal and corporate saving—income ratios also became insignificant.

6. For example, see Martin Feldstein, "Social Security, Induced Retirement

and Aggregate Capital Accumulation," *Journal of Political Economy*, September-December 1974.

7. Robert Barro, *The Impact of Social Security on Private Saving* (Washington, D.C.: American Enterprise Institute, 1978); Dean Leimer and Selog Lesnoy, "Social Security and Private Saving," *Journal of Political Economy*, June 1982. Also see reply by Feldstein in the same issue of the *JPE* and further comments by Leimer and Lesnoy in "Social Security and Private Saving: An Examination of Feldstein's New Evidence," ORS Working Paper no. 31 (Social Security Administration, U.S. Department of Health and Human Services, October 1983), and in "Social Security and Private Saving: Theory and Empirical Evidence," *Social Security Bulletin*, January 1985.

8. For example, see Alan S. Blinder, Roger Gordon, and Donald E. Wise, "Social Security, Bequests, and the Life Cycle Theory of Saving: Cross-Sectional Tests" in *The Determinants of National Saving and Wealth*, ed. F. Modigliani and R.E. Hemming (New York: St. Martin's Press, 1983); Peter A. Diamond and Jerry A. Hausman, "Individual Retirement and Savings Behavior," *Journal of Public Economics*, February-March 1984; M. King and L. Dicks–Mireaux, "Asset Holdings and the Life Cycle," *Economic Journal* 92 (1982); George Kopits and Padma Gotur, "The Influence of Social Security on Household Saving: A Cross-Country Investigation," *International Monetary Fund Staff Papers* (March 1980); Erkki Koskela and Matti Viren, "Social Security and Household Saving in an International Cross Section," *American Economic Review*, March 1983; Mordecai Kurz, "The Life-Cycle Hypothesis and the Effects of Social Security and Private Pensions on Family Saving," Institute for Mathematical Studies in the Social Sciences Technical Paper no. 335 (Stanford University, 1981); Franco Modigliani and Arlie Sterling, "Determinants of Private Saving with Special Reference to the Role of Social Security—Cross-Country Tests" in *The Determinants of National Saving and Wealth*, op. cit.

9. Albert Ando, *Microeconomic Study of Household Savings Behavior in Japan, 1974–1979*, to be published by the Economic Planning Agency, Government of Japan, 1985.

10. Additional details on a number of the subjects discussed in this chapter appear in Albert Ando, Marshall Blume, and Irwin Friend, *The Structure and Reform of the U.S. Tax System* (M.I.T. Press, 1985).

11. Joseph A. Pechman, *Who Paid the Taxes, 1966–1985?* (Brookings Institution, 1985).

12. There are of course numerous studies which show either small positive or negative after-tax rates of return effects on saving, but these give little indication for useful saving policy. One recent unpublished analysis made available to me by Lawrence Klein points to a long-run interest rate elasticity of per capita personal consumption expenditures of $-.04$, which, though statistically significant, is economically inconsequential. It is not clear how this result is affected by the absence of a net-worth variable (though the use of a number of lagged-income variables may serve as a partial substitute) or by the inclusion of investment in durables as part of consumption.

13. Marshall Blume and Irwin Friend, "The Effect of a Reduction in Corporate Taxes on Investment in Riskfree and Risky Assets," Rodney L. White

Center for Financial Research Working Paper no. 3-84 (University of Pennsylvania, 1984).

14. Irwin Friend and Joel Hasbrouck, "Comment on Inflation and the Stock Market," *American Economic Review,* March 1982.

15. Mervyn A. King and Don Fullerton, "The Taxation of Income from Capital: A Comparative Study of the U.S., U.K., Sweden and West Germany— Comparisons of Effective Tax Rates." New York: National Bureau of Economic Research Working Paper no. 1073 (February 1983).

16. The substitution of consumption for income taxes raises many equity issues totally apart from regressivity. One is the question of the basis on which the burden of financing public goods (for example, defense) should be allocated.

17. For example see Peter Diamond and Jerry Hausman, "Individual Retirement and Savings Behavior," *Journal of Public Economics,* February–March 1984; Mordecai Kurz, "The Life-Cycle Hypothesis and the Effects of Social Security and Private Pensions on Family Saving," Institute for Mathematics and the Social Sciences Technical Paper no. 335 (Stanford University, 1981); and Albert Ando, "Microeconomic Study of Household Savings Behavior in Japan, 1974–1979," to be published by the Economic Planning Agency, Government of Japan, 1985.

18. R. Glenn Hubbard, "Do IRAs and Keoghs Increase Saving?," *National Tax Journal* (March 1984). Some of the problems with this analysis are: the variable analyzed is household net worth (which includes capital gains); the results may reflect differences in saving tastes and saving capacity between households with IRAs and Keogh plans and other households; and only three classes are used to draw conclusions about the joint effects of IRA- and Keogh-eligibility and tax bracket on net worth (and inferentially on savings).

19. See Irwin Friend and Robert Jones, "The Concept of Saving" in *Consumption and Saving,* Vol. II, ed. Friend and Jones (University of Pennsylvania, 1960).

20. Since I was not able to obtain such information from readily available literature, I relied on the testimony of academic colleagues from these countries. It might be noted that these countries also seemed to be less permissive in their tax treatment of interest paid on other forms of personal debt, notably home mortgage loans, where caps or other constraints were imposed on the amount of interest paid which was tax deductible.

21. Harry Galper and Eugene Steuerle, "Tax Incentives for Saving," *The Brookings Review,* Winter 1983.

22. According to *U.S. Economic Performance in a Global Perspective* (New York Stock Exchange, February 1981, p. 24), dividend income was taxed somewhat more in the United States while interest income was taxed somewhat more in Japan during the period covered, which apparently was the late 1970s. It might be noted that the taxation of capital income in the United States has declined somewhat since that time.

23. See Irwin Friend and Joel Hasbrouck, "Comment on Inflation and the Stock Market," *American Economic Review,* March 1982, and Martin Feldstein, "Inflation, Tax Rules and the Stock Market," *Journal of Monetary Economics,* July 1982.

24. I understand that this has begun to change in recent years. For recent interest rates in Japan, see *Economic Statistics Monthly,* December 1984 (Research and Statistic Department, The Bank of Japan, pp. 109–10). The fact that interest rates are lower in Japan than in the U.S. is of course partly attributable to Japan's lower rate of inflation.

25. A more satisfactory analysis of the relationship of tax policy to saving experience in foreign countries is now under way at the Rodney White Center for Financial Research of the Wharton School, University of Pennsylvania.

26. Irwin Friend, "Economic and Equity Aspects of Securities Regulation" in *Management under Government Intervention: A View from Mount Scopus,* ed. R.F. Lanzillotti and Y.C. Peles (Greenwich, Conn.: JAI Press, 1984).

References

Ando, Albert, *Microeconomic Study of Household Savings Behavior in Japan, 1974–1979.* Tokyo, Japan: Economic Planning Agency, Government of Japan, forthcoming 1985.

Ando, Albert, Marshall Blume, and Irwin Friend, *The Structure and Reform of the U.S. Tax System.* Cambridge, Mass.: MIT Press, 1985.

Barro, Robert, *The Impact of Social Security on Private Saving.* Washington, D.C.: American Enterprise Institute, 1978.

Blinder, Alan S., Roger Gordon, and Donald E. Wise, "Social Security, Bequests, and the Life Cycle Theory of Saving: Cross-Sectional Tests" in *The Determinants of National Saving and Wealth,* ed. F. Modigliani and R.E. Hemming. New York: St. Martin's Press, 1983.

Blume, Marshall E., Jean Crockett, and Irwin Friend, "Stimulation of Capital Formation: Ends and Means" in *Towards a New Industrial Policy,* ed. Michael L. Wachter and Susan M. Wachter. Philadelphia: University of Pennsylvania Press, 1981.

Blume, Marshall and Irwin Friend, "The Effect of a Reduction in Corporate Taxes on Investment in Riskfree and Risky Assets." Rodney L. White Center for Financial Research Working Paper #3–84. Philadelphia: University of Pennsylvania, 1984.

Blume, Marshall and Jeremy Siegel, "Personal Saving: Theory and Evidence" in *Saving, Investment and Capital Formation in an Inflationary Economy,* ed. Marshall Sarnat and Giorgio Szego. Cambridge, Mass.: Ballinger, 1982.

David, Paul and J.L. Scadding, "Private Savings, Ultrarationality, Aggregation and Denison's Law." *Journal of Political Economy,* 82 (March–April 1974).

Diamond, Peter A., and Jerry A. Hausman, "Individual Retirement and Savings Behavior," *Journal of Public Economics,* February–March 1984.

Economic Statistics Monthly, December 1984. Tokyo, Japan: Research and Statistic Department, The Bank of Japan, pp. 109–110.

Feldstein, Martin, "Inflation, Tax Rules and the Stock Market." *Journal of Monetary Economics,* July 1982.

———, "Social Security, Induced Retirement and Aggregate Capital Accumulation." *Journal of Political Economy,* September–December 1974.

————, "Tax Incentives, Corporate Saving and Capital Accumulation in the United States." *Journal of Public Economics* 2 (1973).

———— and George Fane, "Taxes, Corporate Dividend Policy and Personal Saving: The British Postwar Experience." *Review of Economics and Statistics,* November 1973.

Friend, Irwin, "Economic and Equity Aspects of Securities Regulation" in *Management under Government Intervention: A View from Mount Scopus,* ed. R.F. Lanzillotti and Y.C. Peles. Greenwich, Conn.: JAI Press, 1984.

Friend, Irwin and Joel Hasbrouck, "Comment on Inflation and the Stock Market." *American Economic Review,* March 1982.

Friend, Irwin and Joel Hasbrouck, "Saving and After-Tax Rates of Return," *Review of Economics and Statistics,* November 1983.

Friend, Irwin and Robert Jones, "The Concept of Saving" in *Consumption and Saving,* Vol. II, ed. Friend and Jones. Philadelphia: University of Pennsylvania, 1960.

Galper, Harry and Eugene Steuerle, "Tax Incentives for Saving." *The Brookings Review,* Winter 1983.

Howrey, Philip and Saul H. Hymans, "The Measurement and Determination of Loanable Funds Saving." *Brookings Papers on Economic Activity* 3, Washington, D.C., 1978.

Hubbard, R. Glenn, "Do IRAs and Keoghs Increase Saving?" *National Tax Journal,* March 1984.

King, M. and L. Dicks–Mireaux, "Asset Holdings and the Life Cycle." *Economic Journal* 92 (1982).

King, Mervyn A., and Don Fullerton, "The Taxation of Income from Capital: A Comparative Study of the U.S., U.K., Sweden and West Germany—Comparisons of Effective Tax Rates." Cambridge, Mass.: National Bureau of Economic Research Working Paper no. 1073, February 1983.

Kopits, George and Padma Gotur, "The Influence of Social Security on Household Saving: A Cross-Country Investigation." *International Monetary Fund Staff Papers,* Washington, D.C., March 1980.

Koskela, Erkki and Matti Viren, "Social Security and Household Saving in an International Cross Section," *American Economic Review,* March 1983.

Kurz, Mordecai, "The Life-Cycle Hypothesis and the Effects of Social Security and Private Pensions on Family Saving." Institute for Mathematical Studies and the Social Science Technical Paper no. 335. Palo Alto: Stanford University, 1981.

Leimer, Dean and Selog Lesnoy, "Social Security and Private Saving." *Journal of Political Economy,* June 1982.

————, "Social Security and Private Saving: An Examination of Feldstein's New Evidence." ORS Working Paper no. 31. Washington, D.C.: U.S. Department of Health and Human Services, Social Security Administration, 1983.

————, "Social Security and Private Saving: Theory and Empirical Evidence." *Social Security Bulletin,* January 1985.

Modigliani, Franco and Arlie Sterling, "Determinants of Private Saving with Special Reference to the Role of Social Security—Cross-Country Tests" in *The Determinants of National Saving and Wealth,* op. cit.

Pechman, Joseph A., *Who Paid the Taxes, 1966–1985?*. Washington, D.C.: Brookings Institution, 1985.

Tanner, J. Ernest, "Fiscal Policy and Consumer Behavior." *Review of Economics and Statistics*, May 1979.

U.S. Economic Performance in a Global Perspective. New York Stock Exchange, February 1981, p. 24.

4

Issues in National Savings Policy

Lawrence H. Summers

T
he allocation of resources between present and future consumption or savings is perhaps the most fundamental choice facing any economy. Just as an economy faces a choice between guns and butter today, it faces a choice between consumption today and consumption in the future. The stakes involved in this choice are extremely large. Most of national wealth will be spent on future as opposed to present consumption. The rate of savings determines the rate of economic growth a country can enjoy. As we will see, it can also have an important influence on a nation's competitiveness in international markets.

The protection of generations yet unborn is often held to be one of the most fundamental roles of government. Public policy affects the national savings decision in many ways: through direct public saving or dissaving, through the effects of taxation on the rates of return available to private savers, through the effects of financial regulations on the public's ability to dissave and borrow, and through the effects of social insurance programs on incentives to self-insure through private savings, to name just a few of the most important examples. In many areas of economic policy, it is possible for the government to be neutral, leaving the private economy to determine the allocation of resources. In the context of savings policy, this is impossible. Any set of tax and spending rules must necessarily influence the rate of savings. There is no natural benchmark of neutrality.

This chapter surveys some of the issues that are critical in thinking about national savings policy. A major theme of much of the analysis is the importance of thinking not just about the level of national savings but also about its allocation. While increases in national savings and increases in productive plant and equipment are often equated in popular discourse, there is a substantial difference. National savings go to finance residential investment, spending on consumer durables, and net foreign investment as well as plant and equipment investment. Only a relatively small share of any increase in national savings, perhaps one-fourth, is

I am indebted to James Poterba and Andrei Schleifer for valuable discussions.

likely to go into plant and equipment investment. Thus if the goal of policy is to increase productivity, measures directed at the allocation rather than the level of savings are likely to be more effective.

Of course, there are other reasons for advocating increases in national savings besides raising plant and equipment investment. Residential investment also provides for the future. The accumulation of foreign assets, or reductions in the rate at which foreigners accumulate U.S. assets raise the level of attainable future consumption and may serve more general foreign policy goals. Since the current and capital accounts must sum to zero, changes in the rate of net foreign investment have direct effects on the performance of the economy's traded goods sector. The level of national savings and its susceptibility to influence by policy therefore remain important issues. The question of what policy instruments should be used to attain any given target for national savings is significant.

The chapter is organized as follows. The first section briefly examines the current level of savings in the U.S. from both historical and international perspectives. By historical as well as international standards, the rate of saving in the United States is rather low, though the reasons why are far from clear. The second section examines the various channels through which public policy may influence the savings rate. The most potent and reliable instrument the government can use to change the national savings rate is alterations in its own savings rate through changes in deficit policy. There also appears to be some scope for policy interventions to affect the savings rate through reforms which move us from an income tax toward a consumption tax.

The third section considers the allocation of incremental savings. Presumably a judgment about where incremental savings will be allocated is central to any analysis of the desirability of policy measures directed at increasing national savings. Both reduced-form estimates of the effects of government deficits and econometric model simulations suggest that incremental savings are likely to be allocated about evenly between business investment, housing investment, consumer durables, and net foreign investment. These empirical results are consistent with available data on the allocation of existing national wealth. The concluding section considers the strength of the case for major policy initiatives to increase national savings. Both the current situation and longer-term issues are examined.

National Savings in Perspective

Table 4–1 presents estimates of the net and gross savings rate in the United States over the post–World War II period. Information on the

Table 4–1
U.S. Savings Behavior 1950–1984

	Gross Savings	Gross Private Savings	Net Savings	Personal Savings	Corporate Savings	Government Savings
				GNP		
1950–1954	15.4	15.4	7.0	4.7	2.3	– .1
1955–1959	16.3	16.5	7.1	4.8	2.6	– .2
1960–1964	15.7	15.8	6.9	4.1	2.8	– .2
1965–1969	16.4	16.7	8.1	4.9	3.6	– .2
1970–1974	15.9	16.4	6.9	5.5	1.9	– .6
1975–1979	16.0	17.3	5.7	4.6	2.4	–1.3
1980–1984	14.7	17.3	3.4	4.2	1.8	–2.7
1984	15.1	18.4	4.1	4.3	3.1	–3.4

Source: National Income and Product Accounts.

components of national savings is also presented. The data are drawn from the national income accounts and so are subject to a number of problems. All government spending and consumer spending on durable goods are excluded from savings. No adjustment is made for the effects of inflation on nominal interest payments. This leads to an understatement of the saving of the government and corporate sectors, since they are net debtors, and to an overestimate of personal savings since the household sector is a net creditor. It does not, however, affect the calculated level of national savings.

The data in table 4–1 suggest several conclusions. First, the share of depreciation in GNP has increased substantially through time, causing the trends in gross and net savings to diverge. This is a consequence of the rising capital output ratio in recent years that has resulted from the slowdown in productivity growth, and a shift in the composition of investment toward short-lived assets. In recent years, gross private savings have been relatively high by historical standards whereas net private savings have been relatively low. Second, as has been emphasized in the policy debates of recent years, there has been a dramatic increase in the rate of dissaving by government. This is wholly the result of federal deficits since state and local saving actually increased as a share of GNP between 1981 and 1984. Third, during the strong recovery of 1984, the net private savings rate rebounded strongly, reaching its highest level since 1975 when it was inflated by the large temporary tax reductions granted to households. It is too early to tell whether the strength of the savings rate observed in 1984 is likely to persist.

It is important to note that U.S. savings rates are rather low in long-term historical perspective. Feldstein (1976), drawing on the work of Simon Kuznets, presents some estimated savings rates for the pre–World War II period. He finds relatively substantial decreases in savings. Compared to an average net private savings rate of 6.3% for 1950 to 1984, Feldstein reports a net capital formation of 13.2% for the decade of the 1890s and 10.1% for the 1920s. This finding is perhaps surprising. Much modern theory emphasizes the role of saving for retirement. Yet retirement was an almost nonexistent phenomenon in the early part of the twentieth century. This may be taken as weak evidence in favor of the argument of Kotlikoff and Summers (1981) that bequests are a dominant motive for savings.

Just as current U.S. savings rates appear relatively low in historical perspective, so do they appear relatively low in international perspective. Table 4–2 presents national savings rates for the United States, the European members of the OECD, and Japan. The data do not agree exactly with those in table 4–1 because table 4–2 is based on the United Nations system of national accounts. The data in table 4–2 show that the Amer-

Table 4–2
International Comparison of Net National Savings Rates

	United States	European Members of the OECD	Japan
1955–1959	9.8	NA	21.5
1960–1969	10.5	17.3	17.0
1970–1979	8.0	15.1	25.5
1980–1981	5.0	11.0	21.3

Source: Lawrence Kotlikoff, "Taxation and Saving: A Neoclassical Perspective," *Journal of Economic Literature,* 22, no. 4 (1984):1584.

ican savings rate lags far behind those of Europe and Japan. During the 1970s, the national savings rate in the U.S. was only 53% of Europe's and 31% of Japan's. The only major European country with a savings rate as low as that of the United States was the U.K., which like the United States enjoyed a very low rate of productivity growth.

Why are there such large differences in savings rates across developed economies? The question has been investigated, but is far from resolved. Differences in rates of economic growth which lead to differences in the relative affluence of young savers and older dissavers may well be part of the story. Differences in social security systems may also provide a partial explanation. But at this point, economists are forced to fall back on the weak explanation of differences in tastes for savings. These tastes may not be wholly exogenous. Under the lingering influence of Keynes, concern about stagnation due to oversaving has perhaps had more influence on national attitudes toward savings in the U.S. and U.K. than in Japan or on continental Europe.

By the standards of both history and other nations, current U.S. savings rates are very low. Whether they are too low is another question to which we return in the latter part of the chapter. The comparisons presented in this section are disquieting, especially given the disappointing performance of the U.S. economy over the past decade and a half. In the next section we turn to an investigation of what policies could be undertaken to increase national savings. Then we turn to an evaluation of whether or not the U.S. savings rate is too low.

Public Policy and National Savings

This section considers the efficacy of possible policy approaches to increasing national savings. The problem of how to increase national savings is very different from the problem of isolating the cause of our low national savings rate. Just as we do not reinflate the leaky part of flat tires, there is no reason why the cause of low savings rates need be associated with policies to increase savings. Moreover, many potential determinants of the savings rate (such as the age structure of the population and the rate of technical change) are not readily alterable through public policy. Nor is the problem one of merely finding the most potent policy lever for increasing national savings.

The theory of economic policy suggests that policy targets should be assigned to instruments which can influence them significantly, without incurring substantial collateral costs. It would be inappropriate, for example, to try to manipulate the savings rate by abolishing life insurance contracts because of the collateral costs involved, even though the policy might be quite effective. So too, measures such as the issuance of savings bonds cannot play a major role, because while they do not have large collateral costs, they do not have much effect on savings either. The problem of savings policy is to find policy measures which can be carried far enough to significantly increase national savings without giving rise to significant costs.

Public Saving and Dissaving

The most direct tool at the government's disposal for altering the national savings rate is changes in the level of public saving or dissaving. As we saw in the previous section, public saving is one of the three components of national saving.

Except for the possibility that increases in public saving directly cause decreases in private saving, growth in public saving will translate dollar for dollar into increases in national savings. Moreover, the level of public saving is subject to direct public control through changes in the level of taxation and government expenditure. The effects of given policy changes can be gauged with a great deal of precision.

The potentially direct linkages between the rate of public saving and the level of national saving suggest that if altering the rate of national saving is a policy goal, this goal should be assigned to deficit policy. Indeed, if the deficit can be altered without collateral costs, and its effects on national saving can be gauged accurately, the theory of economic policy as described by Brainard (1967) and Theil (1971) suggests that it alone should be used to influence the level of national savings. Other instruments should be set to achieve other goals without regard to their effects on the level of national savings. Any adverse effects on savings that might result from their setting can be mitigated through changes in public deficits.

Thus there are two critical questions that must be addressed before concluding that debt policy should be assigned to the goal of setting capital intensity. First, do changes in public savings have a significant and easily predictable effect on national savings? Second, do movements in the public savings rate have other significant economic effects? The two questions interact to some extent. If changes in public savings have only a small impact on national savings, extreme movements in public savings may be necessary to achieve given goals, and extreme movements are more likely to have other effects than are more moderate changes.

In standard Keynesian macroeconomic models, there is a clear and direct linkage between national savings and public savings. Consider for example a personal tax increase which reduces the government budget deficit. If government spending is kept constant, public savings is increased by the revenue raised through the tax increase. Private savings declines only to the extent that the reduction in disposable income caused by the tax increase reduces private savings. As long as the household sector's marginal propensity to save is low, this offsetting effect is likely to be minor.

This view of the effects of budget deficits on national savings has been challenged in recent years by Robert Barro (1974) and a number of other authors. Their argument runs as follows. In the long run, the present value of the government's tax receipts must equal the present value of its expenditures. Increases in taxes today, with expenditures held constant, entail reductions in taxes tomorrow. The present value of the taxes that will be collected from consumers is unaffected by a tax change. This means that their wealth is unchanged and therefore that they should not alter their consumption decisions. Hence a tax increase should have no effect on national savings. The argument may be stated another way. In Barro's view, which is often referred to as the Ricardian equivalence view, government debt is not net wealth. The value of the government bonds that consumers hold is exactly offset by their knowledge of the tax liabilities that will ultimately be borne to service or pay off the national debt. Changes in government debt, because they cannot affect consumers' wealth, cannot affect their spending decisions, and so cannot have any impact on the level of national savings.

Thus the Ricardian equivalence argument suggests that policies which change public savings while having no effect on the level of public spending can have no impact on the national savings rate. This argument limits severely the efficacy of deficit policy as a tool of savings policy. Is it valid? This has been the subject of a raging controversy over the past decade. Much of the debate has revolved around the commonplace observation that consumers have finite lifetimes. Therefore, holds the Keynesian argument, some of the tax liabilities engendered by the national debt will be borne by future generations. Those alive at present will spend more because they are wealthier on account of the government bonds they hold. Persons yet unborn can hardly save in anticipation of their tax liabilities. As a result, increases in government debt boost private consumption and thereby reduce national savings. Proponents of the Ricardian equivalence view dispute this analysis, holding that those alive today are likely to adjust their bequests to reflect any tax liabilities that are foisted on their descendants.

While the Ricardian equivalence debate has generated a great deal of interest in the determinants of intergenerational transfers, it seems unlikely that the nature of bequest motives is really of fundamental importance in determining the effects of government budget deficits on national savings. The typical adult consumer has an expected future life span of about thirty-five years. If the debt is increased, most of the burden of servicing or repaying the debt will be borne within his or her lifetime. The present value of the debt burden that can be avoided by passing it on to offspring is small. The case for the view that government savings influences national savings must rest on some grounds other than the finiteness of individual lifetimes.

My reading of the evidence suggests that changes in government deficits are likely to have important impacts on national savings. They affect the level of national savings because consumers appear not to consider the effects of future tax policies when they determine their consumption decisions. Even when future tax changes have been legislated, consumers appear not to be much affected. This is illustrated by recent experience. In the summer of 1981, a three-year program of substantial reductions in income taxes was enacted. If consumers acted in a forward-looking way, one would have expected consumption to surge immediately and then not to change much at all when the tax cuts actually took place. This is not what has occurred. Personal consumption expenditures rose at a 1.7% rate during 1981 when the tax cut was enacted, at a 2.5% rate in 1982 when it began to take effect, and at a 5.1% rate in 1983 when it fully came on stream. The savings rate was higher in 1981 before the tax cuts than in 1982 or 1983 after the tax cuts. Similar patterns may be observed in other cases where tax policies have been announced in advance.

Recall the Ricardian equivalence proposition that consumers internalize not only announced tax changes but also the yet unannounced changes that will ultimately be needed to balance the government budget. Imputing this degree of rationality to consumers strains credulity. Of course, in many cases even if households foresaw future tax changes, they would not change their behavior in anticipation of them. Many households are liquidity-constrained and essentially spend all of their current disposable income. Movements in expected future income cannot affect their consumption or saving since they do not save and cannot borrow. On balance it seems reasonable to conclude that increases in current taxes will have a substantial influence on the level of national savings. Any offset due to reduced private savings because of reduced future tax liabilities seems likely to be small.

The analysis here has concentrated on the effects of changes in taxes which leave government spending unaffected. Quite obviously, even with the Ricardian equivalence view, changes in government spending might affect national savings. But such changes also alter the mix between private and public consumption. They are thus not very suitable as a policy instrument for manipulating the national savings rate.

It appears that through its debt policy the government can systematically and fairly predictably manipulate the level of national savings. The question of collateral costs remains. Before assigning the target of the national savings rate to debt policy, it is necessary to consider whether increases in public savings to raise national savings might have other adverse consequences which would make them infeasible. An obvious risk is the Keynesian fear that increases in public savings will lead to stagnation due to insufficient aggregate demand.

Whatever the merits of this argument in the context of the post-Depression period, the fear of excessive savings is not an important one today. The ability of monetary policy to stimulate aggregate demand has been amply demonstrated. Any reductions in demand due to increased government savings can easily be offset by expansionary monetary policies. Indeed, using the plausible view that monetary policy targets nominal GNP de facto, increases in government savings will have no effect on national savings even without changes in monetary policy. Moreover, as Greg Mankiw and I (1984) have argued, increases in taxes may actually raise aggregate demand if the marginal propensity to hold money for consumption exceeds that for other components of GNP.

There are three other potential problems with dedicating deficit policy to the achievement of a national savings target. First, raising taxes to increase public savings involves excess burden. In the real world, all taxes involve some distortion of economic behavior and therefore impose costs on the private sector in excess of the revenue collected. Of course increased taxes at present cut government interest payments, reducing the need for tax revenue in the future. Nonetheless, using tax policy as an instrument for controlling public savings is likely to require that taxes be varied in a way which causes distortions, and this is a collateral cost. Second, if increases in public savings were used to achieve a major increase in national savings to levels anywhere near those observed in Europe, the national debt would be eliminated. It would then be necessary for the government to invest directly in the private sector, which might pose political problems of different sorts. Third, it might be politically impossible for the government to run chronic budget surpluses in an effort to increase national savings. The fiscal situation of the government has an important impact on public spending decisions. Chronic surpluses may well be impossible because of the pressures they create for new spending programs. In this case, it will be infeasible to increase national savings greatly through raising public savings and it might be undesirable as well.

In spite of these potential problems, the analysis in this subsection suggests that the public savings rate should be the principal policy tool used to achieve any given national savings target. Increases in public savings have a predictably potent effect on national savings. And at least some changes in national savings could be achieved without significant collateral costs. However, achieving large increases in national savings to levels even approaching those observed in Europe through raising public saving might not be feasible. Moreover, policymakers appear unwilling to use deficit to achieve a national savings target. It therefore is useful to examine other possible policy instruments for affecting the national savings rate.

Tax Reform

In recent years, many public finance experts have advocated that our current income tax system be replaced with a consumption tax. One of the arguments advanced in favor of a consumption tax is that it would promote saving at the expense of consumption, while more generally, it has been argued that the tax system should be reformed to encourage saving at consumption's expense. These ideas have found legislative expression in the IRA provisions of the 1981 tax act, in the reductions in top marginal rates, and in the generous tax treatment of private pensions. Nonetheless, the argument that tax reform can significantly affect the level of national savings is far from universally accepted. Many experts believe that savings decisions are not sensitive to rates of return and that tax reforms can therefore have only limited effects on the national savings rate. Until quite recently this pessimistic view of the potential for tax policy to increase national savings was generally accepted.

The conventional wisdom that changes in the rate of return to savers caused by tax policy are unlikely to have much impact on the savings rate is buttressed by both theoretical and empirical arguments. The theoretical argument is that increases in the rate of return available to savers have two potential effects. On the one hand, they make saving more attractive. On the other, they reduce that amount that must be saved to hit any given future wealth target. In economists' jargon, substitution and income effects conflict. The empirical argument is that studies which add interest rate variables to aggregate consumption functions typically find those variables to have little impact and not to enter in a statistically significant way.

Elsewhere (Summers 1981, 1982, 1984), I have considered these arguments in detail. My conclusion is that they are not valid. Increases in the rate of return to savings such as might be achieved through tax reforms, would be likely to have a significant effect on the private savings rate. The standard theoretical argument summarized above, by assuming that all labor income is received in the first of two periods, neglects the human wealth effect of increases in rates of return.

Just as increases in real interest rates reduce the value of financial assets by reducing the present value of the income streams that they generate, they also reduce human wealth—the present value of the future labor income that a consumer can expect to receive. These wealth effects lead consumers to reduce consumption and increase savings in the face of higher after-tax rates of return. Furthermore, the standard argument considers the effect of uncompensated changes in rates of return. Compensated increases in rates of return, such as would be associated with the shift from income taxation toward consumption taxation can be shown to unambiguously increase savings. It is also important to recall that even in the standard theory, increases in the rate of return have an unambiguously negative effect on borrowing. This point is empirically significant. In 1981, interest deductions reported on personal tax returns exceeded interest income. Reductions in borrowing have exactly the same effect on national savings as increases in personal savings.

As critics frequently point out, standard analyses of the rate of return's effects on savings ignore risk and uncertainty. Taking account of risk would reinforce the conclusion that capital taxes reduce savings. Capital taxes shift some of the risk associated with savings to the government. This reduction in uncertainty will reduce consumers' precautionary demand for savings.

Nor is there strong empirical evidence in favor of the view that rates of return have negligible effects on savings. The historical experience reflects largely transitory changes in rates of return which would be expected to have much smaller effects on savings than the permanent changes associated with structural tax reforms. There are also important methodological difficulties with existing studies of consumption functions. These include their failure to take account of human wealth effects and their maintained assumption that changes in rates of return have no effect on either disposable income or wealth. The empirical work reported in Summers (1982), which makes use of several alternative techniques that are free of these difficulties, suggests that changes in rates of return might well have significant effects on private savings.

In addition to their effects on rates of return available to private savers, there are a number of other channels through which changes in tax policy might affect private savings. Reductions in corporate taxes which raise corporate cash flow will increase corporate savings unless, as seems unlikely, dividends are adjusted rapidly. It is an open question whether, and over what horizon, households adjust their saving to offset the saving done on their behalf by corporations. Unless they adjust fully and immediately, reductions in corporate taxes will raise national savings.

An alternative example is provided by IRAs. There is a saying that life insurance is sold and not bought. One wonders whether the same is not true of retirement savings. It seems likely that a tremendous volume of advertising inducing consumers to open IRAs, which has become a sure sign of springtime in America, has at least some effect on some savings decisions.

On balance, it seems likely that tax reforms could well increase the national savings rate. This of course does not mean that they should be used for such a purpose. Tax reforms have a host of effects on both economic efficiency and equity, with their impact on national savings not necessarily being the most important. If the desired national savings rate can be achieved through public savings, there is no reason to manipulate the tax system toward this end. Rather, the tax structure should be selected to maximize efficiency and equity goals. If, however, public savings cannot or will not be used to achieve a target rate of national savings, there is a case for tax reforms to encourage national savings.

Social Insurance

Beyond the effects of direct public savings and the tax system, government influences the level of national saving through its expenditure policies. The most obvious example is the Social Security system. Social Security promises citizens support after they retire. It is natural to conjecture following Feldstein (1974) that Social Security thereby reduces private savings. Indeed, Feldstein originally estimated that the existence of Social Security might cut the private savings rate in the United States by as much as 50%. This argument has generated a large literature over the past decade. Theoretical work has emphasized that promised Social Security benefits are unlikely to reduce private savings dollar for dollar. Unlike private savings, Social Security provides support for retirement in indexed annuitized form. Social Security's effects on savings may be offset by its tendency to encourage early retirement, or by its effects on bequest behavior. Empirical work using time-series data, international cross-section evidence, and data on individual households has been somewhat inconclusive as well.

The significance of this debate is unclear. If, as seems likely, Social Security has had the effect of reducing national savings, it is not clear what policy response is appropriate. The program exists because of a social desire to make transfers to the elderly and to provide certain types of insurance. The provision of these types of insurance and transfers may affect the national savings rate. But as long as these effects can be offset with other policy instruments without undue costs, there is little reason to interfere with the provision of insurance in order to influence the national savings rate.

Of course, Social Security reform may be appropriate on its own terms. But, unless increasing national savings is seen as an urgent goal, and no other policy instrument is available, there is no case for Social Security reform on the grounds of national savings. Social Security policy should be directed at goals other than national savings. Its effects on national savings are uncertain, and there are large collateral consequences associated with using it to alter national savings.

A similar argument applies to most other public policies that impact on national savings. The recent reform of regulations on interest rates that financial institutions are allowed to pay, for example, might influence national savings. But it seems inappropriate to base decisions on these reforms on considerations of national savings, given the multiplicity of instruments available to influence national savings and the paucity of other tools available for regulating financial institutions. This is not to endorse deposit ceilings. Rather, the argument is that they should be set on other grounds.

Summary

The theory of economic policy dictates that policy instruments should be assigned to targets if their effect on the target is relatively predictable, and if changes in the use of an instrument do not involve large collateral costs, either because they have minor effects, or because the effects can be offset through the use of other policy instruments. These criteria suggest that the primary instrument of national savings policy should be public savings. Increases in public savings are likely to translate fairly directly into increases in national savings with relatively little uncertainty. Changes in the rate of public savings are not likely to have important collateral costs.

Tax reform is also likely to influence the national savings rate, but it is not clear that it should be used for this purpose unless increases in public savings are infeasible. It is probably not appropriate to give national savings much weight in making policy in other areas.

The Effects of Increased National Savings

Any policy judgment about the desirability of increasing national savings must depend on a judgment about the allocation of increments to national savings. This issue is particularly important given the growing integration of world capital markets. Consider the case of a small open economy in a world where capital was perfectly mobile. Growth in national savings would have no effect on the domestic capital stock. Since capital mobility would equalize returns around the world, any incremental savings would be spread thinly across the various nations. Increases in domestic savings would not tend to raise domestic investment. Such an analysis is clearly appropriate in considering increases in saving within a single U.S. state, since capital is mobile across state boundaries and any state is small relative to the U.S. economy. It is less clear how relevant the analysis is to the U.S. economy, which is large relative to the world economy, and whose savings may not be completely mobile internationally.

Even apart from the international allocation of incremental savings, there is also the question of where savings which increase the domestic capital stock will go. Many of the arguments adduced to support increased capital formation do not really apply if extra savings do not lead to extra investment in plant and equipment. Other forms of capital formation are not penalized by the tax system and are less likely to promote technological innovation. This section considers first the implications of the U.S. economy's openness for savings policy, and then examines the likely allocation of increases in domestic capital formation. Finally, it presents estimates of the effects of reduced budget deficits on the composition of output based on both reduced-form equations and econometric simulations.

International Capital Mobility

Assessing the degree of international capital mobility is crucial in judging the effects of an increase in national savings. If capital is perfectly mobile, one would expect that only a share of increased savings equal to the U.S. share of the world economy would go to domestic capital formation. The remainder would be used to finance investment abroad, or equivalently to purchase capital in the United States now held by foreigners. The United States accounts for about one-third of the output of the world's capitalist economies. Thus, if capital is perfectly mobile, most of any increase in national savings will go to finance foreign investment.

Increased U.S. financing of foreign investment has a necessary concomitant. The balance of payments identity holds that the current and capital accounts must sum to zero. Increased capital outflows or reduced capital inflows must necessarily be balanced by improvements in the trade balance. Exports must rise and imports must fall, improving the competitiveness of U.S. industry. The mechanism through which these changes will occur is simple. Increased savings will reduce the return available on U.S. assets, making them less attractive to foreigners and reducing the demand for dollars. This will lead to an exchange rate depreciation which in turn improves U.S. competitiveness. Thus if capital is internationally mobile, a major effect of any increases in U.S. savings will be an improvement in U.S. competitiveness, or, in other words, a deterioration in our terms of trade.

Alternatively, if capital is not internationally mobile, increases in U.S. savings will lead to equal increases in U.S. capital formation. The extent of international capital mobility then becomes a critical issue. My views on this question are presented in some detail in Summers (1985), so I will just summarize them here. Evidence can be marshalled in support of various positions about the degree to which capital is internationally mobile. The flourishing Eurodollar market, the large U.S. current account deficit, and the substantial international flows of gross investment belie the view that capital is inherently immobile.

On the other hand, as Feldstein and Horioka (1980) have emphasized, the correlation across countries between rates of savings and investment is extremely high. High-savings countries are also high-investment countries on a consistent basis. This proposition is illustrated in table 4–3, which presents 1963–1981 national savings and investment rates for a number of countries. While the long-run average savings rate across countries varied between 17.3% and 34.9%, the largest average current account deficit was only 4.4% and the largest surplus was only 1.7%. The correlation between domestic savings and investment rates was .91. For various sample periods, regressions consistently suggest that the propensity to invest out of domestic savings exceeds .8.

It is not clear how the observed high correlation of domestic savings and investment rates can be reconciled with the high degree of capital mobility that seems apparent. Surely, it is unlikely that coincidence leads to the strong association of savings and investment rates. In Summers (1985), I argue that the observed association between savings and investment rates is a reflection of national economic policies. For reasons that are not entirely clear, nations are unwilling to accept large current account imbalances for sustained periods. This leads them to use the

Table 4–3

Savings, Investment and Current Accounts, 1963–1981

	Savings/GDP	Investment/GDP	Current Account/ GDP
Japan	34.9	34.5	0.5
Switzerland	29.7	28.0	1.7
Austria	27.5	28.2	−0.7
Norway	26.9	29.9	−3.0
Portugal	25.7	27.7	−2.0
Netherlands	24.9	24.5	0.5
West Germany	24.9	24.5	0.5
Iceland	24.9	28.2	−3.3
Finland	24.6	26.5	−1.9
Greece	24.3	26.7	−2.4
France	24.1	24.6	−0.5
Australia	23.8	25.9	−2.1
New Zealand	22.8	25.5	−2.7
Italy	22.6	22.0	0.6
Spain	22.6	23.6	−1.0
Sweden	22.5	23.1	−0.6
Canada	22.3	23.4	−1.1
Belgium	22.3	22.5	−0.2
Denmark	20.7	23.5	−2.8
Ireland	20.7	25.1	−4.4
United States	19.4	19.2	0.2
United Kingdom	18.7	18.9	−0.2
Turkey	17.3	19.5	−2.2

Source: Caprio and Howard (1984).

levers of economic policy to achieve external balance. This leads to a close association between national savings and investment rates. For example, it appears that within the OECD, nations where private savings exceed domestic investment tend to run budget deficits on average, while nations where private savings fall short of investment tend to run surpluses on average.

This interpretation of the data suggests that nations are unlikely to pursue policies which substantially increase national savings without also attempting to stimulate national investment. However, it suggests that if such a policy were attempted, the result would be only small increases in capital formation, and a large effect on the trade balance. In a sense, the United States has pursued this policy in reverse in recent years, as the federal budget deficit has mushroomed. The result has been large capital inflows from abroad which have enabled domestic investment to be extremely strong on a cyclically adjusted basis.

If the primary effect of increases in national savings is to reduce capital inflows or increase capital outflows with relatively little impact on national investment, the question arises as to whether or not they are desirable. This depends on why they are being advocated. Investment abroad will not increase the productivity of U.S. workers. Nor does the tax system create a wedge between the private and American social return to foreign investment. On the other hand, increased foreign investment does pass wealth on to future generations and in this sense may be beneficial. Furthermore increased capital outflows or reduced capital inflows will be associated with improvements in the competitiveness of domestic firms on world markets.

The Domestic Allocation of Capital

The analysis in the preceding section suggests that a large part of any increase in domestic savings would flow abroad. What about the component that would finance investment in the United States? One reasonable first approximation is that it would be spread relatively evenly across the components of national wealth. Information on the asset composition of national wealth may be gleaned from the National Balance Sheets prepared by the Federal Reserve System. They reveal that at the end of 1983, the net worth of the United States was $11.4 trillion. This $11.4 trillion was comprised of $3.9 trillion in residential structures and consumer durables, $3.1 trillion in plant and equipment, $3.3 trillion in land, and $.8 trillion in inventories as well as a small positive claim on foreigners.

Despite the natural tendency to think of plant-and-equipment spending as the principal disposition of savings, less than 30% of national wealth is held in this form. At market value rather than replacement cost, the share of plant and equipment would be even lower. Even among reproducible assets, the share of plant and equipment is less than half. It seems likely, therefore, that much of any increase in national savings brought about by public policy would be allocated to residential structures and consumer durables. In addition, the reduced interest rates that would be associated with increases in savings would lead to increases in the value of nonreproducible assets like land. The resulting growth in wealth would then tend to boost consumption, partially offsetting the initial rise in savings.

This analysis suggests that on the basis of a priori reasoning, one should anticipate that increases in national savings will have only a relatively minor effect on plant and equipment spending. Much of any growth in saving will go to finance increases in foreign investment. And savings allocated domestically will go in substantial part to raise the value of land, and to investment in residential structures. Below, I test these ideas by examining the relationship between changes in federal budget deficits and the composition of national output. Changes in federal budget deficits to a large extent represent exogenous changes in national savings. By examining their impact on the composition of output, we can gauge the likely allocation of incremental national savings.

Federal Deficits and the Composition of National Output

The starting place for our analysis is the national income identity:

$$D = G_f - T_f = PS + (T_s - G_s) + NFI - I \qquad (4.1)$$

where D represents the federal deficit, PS is private saving, $G_s - T_s$ the deficit of nonfederal governments, NFI is net foreign investment and I is domestic investment. In the absence of official reserves transactions, NFI will be just the negative of the current account balance. This identity demonstrates that with GNP held constant, reductions in federal savings must raise private savings, increase state and local surpluses, draw funds in from abroad by crowding out net exports, reduce investment, or have some combination of these effects.

I estimate the effects of increases in federal savings on the composition of national output by fitting reduced-form equations of the type:

$$\frac{Z_{it}}{GNP_t} = a + b_i \frac{D_t}{GNP_t} + c_1 Cycle_1 + c_2 Cycle_2 + U \qquad (4.2)$$

where Z_i represents components of GNP and $Cycle1_t$ and $Cycle2_t$ are variables intended to control for cyclical conditions. The coefficient b_i measures the extent to which deficits affect each national income component. All estimated equations were corrected for first order serial correlation. In alternative specifications, current and lagged capacity utilization and its lagged value, and real GNP growth rates were used to proxy for cyclical conditions. Equations were estimated using both the standard deficit as reported in the National Accounts and an inflation-adjusted deficit which accounts for inflation's erosion of the real value of outstanding debt. The sample period was 1949–1982 except in the case of the net foreign investment equation which was estimated over the 1973–1982 period to allow for the effects of the shift to floating exchange rates. Results are shown in table 4–4.

The results differ somewhat across equations but several reasonably robust conclusions emerge. Budget deficits call forth increased private saving. Such saving rises by about thirty cents for each dollar of federal deficits. This extra saving reflects the effects of increased disposable in-

Table 4–4
The Effects of Federal Deficits on the Composition of GNP

Deficit Concept	Standard	Standard	Inflation-Adjusted	Inflation-Adjusted
Cyclical Variable	GNP Growth	Capacity Utilization	GNP Growth	Capacity Utilization
Net Private Savings	.204	.233	.440	.464
	(.108)	(.126)	(.099)	(.098)
State and Local Saving	.058	.051	.062	.018
	(.030)	(.040)	(.025)	(.031)
Net Foreign Investment	.270	.684	.256	.236
	(.661)	(.749)	(.175)	(.112)
Net Investment	−.624	−.602	−.380	−.423
	(.086)	(.117)	(.074)	(.086)
Net Nonresidential Investment	−.235	−.129	−.172	−.099
	(.067)	(.049)	(.061)	(.031)

Note: Estimates refer to b_i in equation (4.2). Numbers in parentheses are standard errors. Except where noted estimates refer to the sample period 1949–1982. All equations were estimated with correction for first order autocorrelation.

come for consumers, the effects of increases in rates of return caused by federal borrowing, and possibly the effects of anticipated tax liabilities. Each dollar increase in federal dissaving appears to increase state and local saving by about five cents. This may reflect substitution of local for federal activity on either the tax or spending side.

The results confirm the prediction that increased deficits crowd out net exports by attracting foreign capital inflows. It is reasonable to expect that this result should occur much more rapidly with fixed than with floating exchange rates so we focus on estimates for 1973–1982. This makes it difficult to pin down the effects of deficits on net foreign investment with any precision. The equations tend to suggest that each dollar of deficits calls forth about twenty-five cents in increased net foreign investment and so crowds out an approximately equal amount of net exports. In all likelihood, reestimation including the past two years (1984–1985) when both budget and current account deficits have ballooned would suggest a significantly greater effect of budget deficits on net foreign investment.

Finally, the estimates suggest that each dollar of federal deficits crowds out about forty cents of net investment. The average estimate in the table is somewhat greater than this but neglects the effects of deficits on foreign capital inflows which have only become important in the past decade. The estimates in the final row of the table indicate that a little less than half of the crowded-out investment is plant and equipment with the remainder being inventories and housing. An extra dollar of federal saving, according to these estimates, will only generate about twenty cents in extra plant and equipment investment.

There are a number of possible problems with these types of reduced forms. Movements in the budget deficit may not be exogenous. Variables affecting the composition of national output may have been omitted. An alternative approach to estimating the effect of changes in federal saving on the composition of national output is through simulation of a large econometric model. To this end, table 4–5 reports the results of some recent DRI simulations of the effects of a deficit reform package. The deficit reform package which DRI considered reduced the federal deficit as a share of GNP by 3.5% over the 1986–1989 period through a balanced combination of tax increases and spending cuts. DRI also estimated the effects of its package on the components of GNP.

The results in table 4–5 tend to corroborate the estimates just presented. About one-third of the effects of deficit reduction is offset by decreases in private saving. A little less than a third is offset by increased state and local surpluses and reduced net foreign investment. Just over a third of deficit reductions flow into increased net investment, with about two-thirds of this total devoted to residential investment. This means that each dollar of deficit reduction leads to about a fifteen-cent increase in net plant and equipment investment. It is encouraging that these large econometric model estimates are so close to those obtained from reduced forms. While each methodology has its problems for an exercise of this sort, the errors should be relatively independent.

On balance, these empirical exercises confirm the hypotheses sketched at the beginning of this section. Increases in national saving are likely to have a variety of effects. In part, exogenous increases will be offset by the effects of lower interest rates, net foreign investment will decline, and residential and nonresidential investment will increase. As a very rough approximation, these four responses will occur to about an equal extent.

Table 4–5
DRI Econometric Model Estimates of the Effect of a Reduced Deficit on the Composition GNP

	Baseline	Reduced	Difference	Share
Federal Deficit	5.9	2.4	3.5	100
Net Private Saving	7.0	5.8	1.2	34
State and Local Saving	1.5	1.2	.3	9
Net Foreign Investment	2.0	1.3	.7	20
Net Investment	4.6	5.9	1.3	37

Source: All figures calculated by author from data in the *DRI Review* (November 1983). All figures are percentages of GNP.

The conclusion is that increases in national saving are a relatively ineffective way of stimulating business investment. This conclusion would be reinforced if Keynesian effects of increased savings on aggregate demand were considered, or if more weight were given to the current episode of strong investment performance in the face of large budget deficits. The next section considers the implications of these results for policy.

Conclusions

The analysis in this chapter suggests that public policy could be used to increase the level of national savings. Reductions in government borrowing would raise national savings without major associated costs. The remaining question is whether sustained increases in national savings would be desirable in the longer run.

There can be little doubt that reduction of current large federal deficits should be a high priority. Government budget deficits of 5% of GNP loom over any foreseeable horizon. It seems inconceivable that economic growth will generate enough revenues to substantially reduce these deficits. Indeed, most deficit projections such as those of the Congressional Budget Office are based on the assumption that steady economic growth will continue until 1990. It seems much more likely that these projections will prove too optimistic than too pessimistic. Current large deficits do not permit us to avoid the burdens of taxation. They only postpone and increase those burdens through the accumulation of interest.

The choice is not between deficits and tax increases; it is between deficits with tax increases in the future, and tax increases today. There seems little reason not to favor the former course. U.S. budget deficits are having a disastrous impact on the traded goods sector of the economy, and are greatly complicating worldwide economic recovery. Large trade imbalances threaten free-trade policies. The United States is now or soon will be a debtor nation. If foreign capital flows dry up, domestic investment rates will fall dramatically even relative to their historically low levels. Unless an argument can be constructed for substantially reducing the national savings rate below its historical level, there is a clear case for reducing projected federal deficits.

The appropriate stance for policy in the long run is less clear. Feldstein (1976) argues that policy should be used to substantially increase the national savings rate. His argument is that the available rate of return, which he estimates at 12%, is great enough that more savings are desirable unless we discount the utility of future consumption at a very high rate. The estimated 12% return is based on the observed profit rate of nonfinancial corporations. There are a number of reasons to believe that it substantially overstates the return to incremental national saving.

First, the rate of profit has declined dramatically in recent years. A more reasonable current estimate would be in the 9% range. Second, as I have emphasized, most incremental savings would not flow into the corporate sector. There is every reason to expect that return on other uses of saving is lower than the return on corporate investment. Americans receive only the after-tax return on foreign investment. Corporate capital is taxed more heavily than housing or consumer durables. Third, some part of the rate of profit represents a risk premium. One plausible measure of the certainty equivalent return on extra savings is the real return on nearly risk-free investments such as Treasury bills. While this figure is perhaps 5% at present, it has averaged less than 1% over the past forty years. On balance, it seems likely that the current risk-adjusted social return to increased savings is probably well below 9%, and perhaps is less than the economy's growth rate.

At such rates, it is not clear that increased national savings should be a major priority. There does not seem to be a compelling case for raising investment in houses or the value of land. Nor, except for current exigencies, is there a clear case for reducing net foreign investment in the United States. While there is a case for increased investment in plant and equipment, raising national savings is a very indirect way to bring it about.

The third section's arguments about the allocation of incremental savings suggest the desirability of policies directed specifically at stimulating domestic plant and equipment investment. All the analysis implies that the supply of savings to the corporate sector is very elastic. Even if savings do not respond sharply to increases in the rate of return, there is substantial scope for portfolio reallocations to finance increases in business investment. Hence, measures which stimulate investment are unlikely to be crowded out by rising interest rates. The returns to private investment in plant and equipment exceed those on other investment. And there is at least some reason to think that there may be substantial technological externalities associated with plant and equipment investment. The extremely high correlation between national rates of growth and national investment rates may well reflect the embodiment of technical change or learning-by-doing effects.

The most obvious policy measure available for encouraging plant and equipment investment is corporate tax reform. By increasing the investment tax credit (ITC) or accelerating depreciation allowances, it is possible to stimulate investment without conferring windfall gains on the owners of existing capital. From this perspective, the recent Treasury tax proposal is rather unsatisfactory. It reduces the tax burden on old capital by cutting the corporate tax rate and offering dividend relief, and it increases the tax burden on incremental investment by eliminating the ITC and scaling back depreciation schedules.

There appears to be a much stronger case for measures directed at encouraging plant and equipment investment than there is for measures directed at increasing national savings generally. It should be noted, however, that expanding investment incentives will, other factors being equal, lead to capital inflows. This means a deterioration in U.S. competitiveness, at least in the short run, as the dollar appreciates. This adverse effect of increased incentives for investment can only be offset by rising national savings. There may then be a case for raising savings as part of a policy mix directed at increasing business. But the case for a major policy effort to raise the long-term national savings rate without other policy changes is not very strong.

References

Barro, Robert J., "Are Government Bonds Net Wealth?" *Journal of Political Economy*, November–December 1974: 1095–118.

Brainard, William, "Uncertainty and the Effectiveness of Policy." *American Economic Review*, 1967.

Caprio, G. and D. Howard, "Domestic Saving, Current Accounts and International Capital Mobility." Federal Reserve Board International Finance Discussion Paper no. 244, 1984.

Feldstein, Martin, "National Savings in the United States" in *Jobs and Productivity*. Harvard Institute for Economic Research Working Paper no. 506, 1976.

Feldstein, Martin, "Social Security, Induced Retirement and Aggregate Capital Accumulation." *Journal of Political Economy*, September–October 1974: 905–26.

Feldstein, Martin and C. Horioka, "Domestic Savings and International Capital Flows." *Economic Journal*, June 1980: 314–29.

Kotlikoff, Laurence J., "Taxation and Savings: A Neoclassical Perspective," *Journal of Economic Literature*, December 1984.

Kotlikoff, Laurence and L. Summers, "The Role of Intergenerational Transfers in Aggregate Capital Accumulation." *Journal of Political Economy*, August 1981.

Mankiw, N. Gregory and L. Summers, "Are Tax Cuts Really Expansionary?" Cambridge, Mass.: NBER working paper no. 1443, 1984.

Summers, Lawrence H., "Capital Taxation and Accumulation in a Life Cycle Growth Model." *American Economic Review*, September 1981: 533–44.

Summers, Lawrence H., "Tax Policy and International Competitiveness," forthcoming 1985 in *International Competition* (ed. M. Spence).

————, "Tax Policy, the Rate of Return and Private Savings." Cambridge, Mass.: NBER working paper no. 995, 1982.

————, "The After Tax Rate of Return Affects Private Savings." *American Economic Review,* May 1984.

————, "The Long Term Effect of Current Macroeconomic Policies" in *The Legacy of Reagonomics,* ed. Hulten and Sawhill. Washington, D.C.: The Brookings Institution, 1984.

Theil, H., *The Theory of Economic Policy.* Amsterdam, The Netherlands: North Holland, 1971.

Part II
Savings in the
United States and Japan

5
Savings Rates in Japan and the United States: The Roles of Tax Policy and Other Factors

John H. Makin

Introduction

Saving behavior is of interest because it represents the portion of current output available to support future consumption. Obviously, if future living standards are to improve, a society must devote some portion of current output to increasing its stock of wealth. That is, net saving—the amount of saving in excess of that required to maintain the current stock of wealth intact—must continue. More precisely then, net saving is the portion of current output devoted to *increasing* future consumption. Unless otherwise noted, references made hereafter to the *savings rate* are to the net savings rate.

When compared to savings rates elsewhere, particularly in Japan, the U.S. savings rate is low. While measurement issues abound, even after adjustments of every conceivable kind, what stands out in cross-sectional surveys is the low level of the U.S. savings rate and the high level of the Japanese savings rate. The wide difference in American and Japanese rates is often viewed with concern. Americans conclude that they may be consuming too much while, interestingly, Japanese sometimes conclude that they may be saving too much. In any case, comparisons of net savings rates are usually followed by comparisons of real growth, productivity growth, and growth of the capital stock. The conclusion is that in these categories, as in the savings rate category, the United States is falling behind other industrial countries. As will become evident, in open economies with unfettered capital flows (trade in saving), the link be-

I wish to thank without implicating John Shoven for helpful discussion and Michael Allison for excellent assistance in estimating the saving equations. I also wish to thank the Japan External Trade Organization for enabling me to discuss saving behavior in Japan with specialists in Tokyo too numerous to mention. Any views expressed or errors committed are my own.

tween national saving and investment may be broken. The link, however, between saving and available increases in future consumption remains intact.

The difference between savings rates in the United States and Japan, along with the economic implications of the difference, are the subjects of this chapter. Particular though by no means exclusive attention is paid to the role played by differences in tax and budget policies in determining saving behavior. To concentrate exclusively on such policies would not constitute a properly controlled experiment in which to test the hypothesis that differences in these policies account for some significant part of the discrepancy between savings rates in Japan and the United States.

At the outset it is useful to keep in mind one glaringly obvious fact when looking at divergent levels of national net savings rates. The United States began the post–World War II period with a huge capital stock intact while the rest of the industrial countries of the world, especially Japan, began the postwar period with a capital stock that was both small absolutely and tiny when compared to its prewar level. While estimates of capital stock are difficult to obtain, twenty years after the war's end OECD estimates place Japan's 1965 real capital stock per capita at $1,993 in 1975 dollars while that of the United States stood at $14,465 in 1975 dollars. Between 1964 and 1980, the growth rate of Japan's real capital stock was 9.6%, while that for U.S. real capital stock was 3.6%. The ratio of real growth rates of the capital stock is about the same as the ratio of net savings rates.

A similar picture emerges from examination of real per capita income. Based on an index of U.S. real per capita GNP equal to 100 in 1980, Japan's real per capita GNP stood at about 12 before World War II and fell to half that level after the war. Over the same period the figure for the United States rose from about 50 to about 65. By 1980 Japan's real per capita GNP had reached 70% of the U.S. level. That kind of catch-up describes a high rate of saving and capital formation but does not explain it. Part of the explanation is twofold: first, Japan's strong desire to restore the prewar level of living standards, and second, a resumption of the prewar effort to raise Japanese living standards to those of the major western industrial economies.

A nation that possesses a large stock of real capital is not likely to desire to add to it as rapidly as one which, having possessed a large capital stock, has seen half of it destroyed. An interesting question is whether private-sector saving decisions would have yielded a net savings rate as high as the 25 to 30% that characterized postwar Japan or whether the heavy role actually played by the government was necessary to engineer the Japanese economic miracle of the 1960s. A comparison with postwar savings rates in Europe (whose rates equalled Japan's until the

1970s even though forced-saving measures were less severe) suggests that the private sector responds to saving incentives.

While destruction of over half a nation's capital stock can result in a much higher incentive to save on net, to *raise* the portion of output available to support an *increase* in future consumption, it seems reasonable to suppose that a nation like the United States having a large extant capital stock should not expect to duplicate the net savings rate of Japan. It is important to bear these secular considerations in mind when comparing levels of the net savings rates in Japan and the U.S.

A number of other general considerations deserving attention will be taken up here. If saving is aimed largely at consumption-smoothing and bequest motives, the age profile of the population together with its government and private pension programs will heavily affect household saving. Since the major asset of most households in both the United States and Japan is a house, the factors affecting purchase and financing of homes are important. Finally, if leisure time and consumption are viewed as complements, average workweek statistics are relevant to decisions about consumption and saving, as are prospects for the length of the future workweek. It hardly makes sense to duplicate Americans' capital-intensive leisure activities if little time exists to spread the unit-leisure-time costs of expenditure.

A final important consideration to remember when examining widely divergent saving behavior between nations is the degree of openness of capital and commodity markets. Since the December 1981 liberalization of its foreign exchange laws, Japan's net long-term capital outflows (its net exports of savings) have totaled over $92 billion. Over the same period U.S. net capital inflows (net imports of saving) totaled more than $140 billion. When a nation imports saving, the identity between its total net saving and its total net investment is broken. Part of net investment is financed by imported saving and thus is available to support future consumption by nonresidents.

In 1984 U.S. gross saving of $675 billion was absorbed by about $645 billion in private investment ($400 billion of which was capital consumption) and $125 billion in net federal, state, and local government deficits. The shortage of $95 billion was financed by imported saving. Viewed in another way, U.S. 1984 net capital formation of $245 billion will not support much of an increase in future American consumption since the bulk of it will either have to yield returns to pay interest on government debt (via future taxes) or to pay interest to the foreigners who have increased their holdings of claims on future U.S. output.

The remainder of this chapter is organized as follows. The next section examines Japanese and U.S. net savings rates since 1960 and identifies their general outlines in terms of level, trend, and deviations from trend. The third section discusses the theory of saving behavior and then examines its implications in the light of demographic (life-cycle) trends, government and private pension programs, shocks to real income, and behavior of real, after-tax interest rates in Japan and the United States. The fourth section focuses on the role of tax-policy incentives for home ownership and saving behavior. Estimated saving equations for Japan and the United States are examined in the next section, while the sixth contains a brief summary and some concluding remarks.

An examination of Japanese saving behavior before we fully understand American saving behavior may seem premature. Disagreement among analysts of the American saving/investment process continues in a number of important areas including the size of the interest elasticity of saving, the impact of government pension programs on private saving, the role of the bequest motive, a myriad of measurement issues, and of course the role of the tax system. Even though these and other issues are hardly settled in the American context, the time may have come to look carefully at a new set of data and a new set of pension, tax, and demographic characteristics. At the very least we can expect, based on an expanded look at Japanese behavior, to better employ the considerable knowledge about saving behavior already in hand in order to assure greater coordination of budget and tax policy between the two largest industrial economies operating within an increasingly open and interdependent world economy.

Overview of Net Savings Rates

Among industrial countries the largest difference in the level of net savings rates exists between Japan and the United States. Though many adjustments to the measurement of saving are possible, and important differences remain among analysts regarding the correct measure of saving, the System of National Accounts (SNA) adopted by the United Nations and employed by the OECD is employed throughout this chapter as a basis for measuring saving. Those interested in a full discussion of alternative measures of saving should read the excellent studies by Blades (1983) and Blades and Sturm (1982).

Figure 5–1 presents an overview of 1955–1983 net savings rates in Japan and the United States. Figure 5–2 gives an overview of 1983 net savings rates for industrial countries. The net savings rate is defined as the ratio of saving less capital consumption to national disposable income. National disposable income is GNP less capital consumption less net transfers to the rest of the world. Three bases for comparison of net

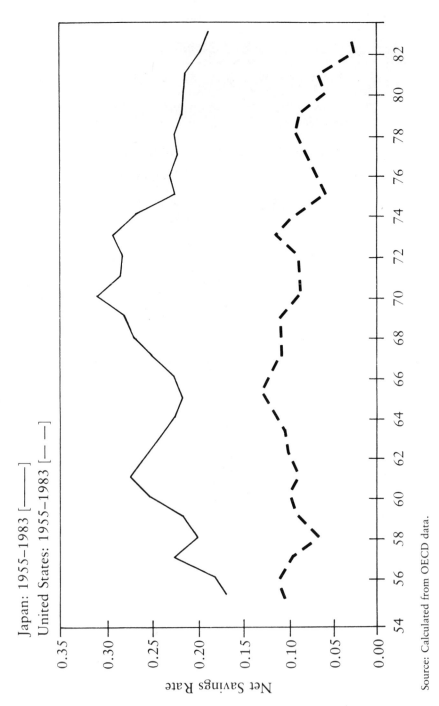

Figure 5-1. Net Savings Rates—Japan and United States

Source: Calculated from OECD data.

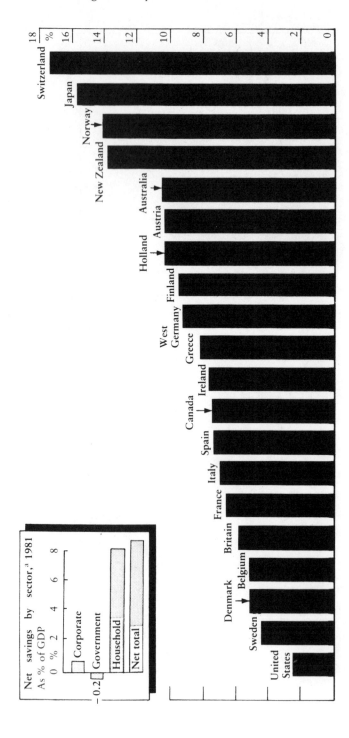

Figure 5–2. OECD Countries' Net National Savings Ratio, 1983 *(as percentage of GDP)*

savings rates are level, trend, and deviation from trend. The time period is largely determined by the availability of reliable, comparable data for the countries studied.

The level of Japan's net saving rate is two and one-half to three times that for the United States. Both series have a slight negative trend without a pronounced difference in slope except for the possible effect of the very low U.S. net savings rate during 1982 and 1983. One might have expected that given diminishing returns, as Japan's capital stock per capita approached that of the United States, the secular trend in its savings rate would become more sharply negative than that for the United States. This is not apparent from figure 5–1, perhaps due to the operation of other factors or perhaps due to a sample period too short to display such a gradually evolving phenomenon. Still, both Japan and the United States are advanced industrial economies having gradually declining net private savings rates. A number of possible explanations of this phenomenon, particularly the growth of government pension programs from 1960 to 1983, will be considered later. Life-cycle, consumption-smoothing considerations, tax treatment of saving and the real return on saving, available leisure time, and other factors may cause part of the difference in levels of private net savings rates.

Deviations from the negative trend line of the private net saving rate in Japan can be grouped into three episodes. During the first half of the 1960s the Japanese savings rate trended downward rather sharply and then rose to hover around 30% until the first oil shock late in 1973. Subsequently the savings rate dropped sharply, as consumption-smoothing behavior would suggest but, inconsistently with that explanation of the initial sharp drop in 1973, the rate has not yet recovered and continues to trend downward. Part of the explanation may lie with faster capital consumption after the oil shock, which would depress net saving faster than disposable income.

American savings rate deviations from trend are less sharply episodic than those for Japan. The rate moved inversely with the Japanese rate during the 1960s, peaking in about 1966 just as the Japanese rate was bottoming. It fell slightly until 1972 and then rose sharply just before the first oil crisis, dropping sharply thereafter in tandem with the Japanese rate. Unlike Japan's, the American savings rate recovered after the oil crisis, though not quite to its earlier level, and peaked in 1979 before dropping sharply to unprecedented low levels during the early 1980s. It is interesting, if somewhat disquieting, to note that the anemic recovery of the American savings rate after 1976 coincided with a period of negative real after-tax interest rates on a negative trend, while the subsequent collapse of the savings rate coincided with the sharpest rise in after-tax real interest rates since the Civil War.

Needless to say, a good deal remains to be explained concerning behavior of both Japanese and American savings rates in absolute terms and relative to one another. We shall turn in the fifth section, "Estimation of Japanese and United States Aggregate Saving Equations," to a systematic empirical examination of the two nations' postwar saving. The theory of saving behavior will help to suggest explanations for differences in the level, trend, and deviations from trend of saving in Japan and the United States.

Saving: Consumption-Smoothing, Bequests, and After-Tax Real Interest Rates

Theory of Saving

The theory of saving is usually developed in a multiperiod model where saving is viewed as future consumption. (Kotlikoff 1984 and Shoven 1984 provide good overviews of saving behavior.) The household or firm spends or does not spend (saves) out of current income based on a desire to maintain a smooth path of consumption relative to some long-run underlying notion of its ability to support a given level of consumption. That underlying notion is usually represented as wealth or permanent income.

During an average lifetime, a person may follow this spending/saving cycle: spending in excess of current receipts or dissaving when he or she is young; accumulating assets and saving during years when earnings exceed spending levels dictated by underlying (permanent-income) considerations; and dissaving again during old age (after retirement) when income drops off sharply. If the saver's horizon is multigenerational so that his or her utility depends on that of heirs, the bequest motive may affect saving behavior relative to measured income.

Once the saver's time horizon extends to a lifetime or beyond, demographics and the existence or absence of a government pension program become potentially important determinants of aggregate saving behavior. Since the aggregate savings rate is a weighted average of savings rates across all income groups, given a life-cycle model, that rate ought to rise as a nation's population profile expands into the maximum saving years and then decline as the share of the retired population rises. Introduction of a government-financed pension program or a significant increase in the real expected present value of government pension benefits ought to reduce discretionary private saving unless a higher prospective tax liability offsets the impact of a higher prospective government pension, which is likely in an intergenerational model with a bequest motive.

In the latter case, an unfunded social security program that taxes the young to pay for pension benefits of retirees may leave private saving unaffected. The forward-looking private saver realizes that a present-value dollar of pension implies a present-value dollar of tax liability, and if a bequest motive is strong, the saver does not cut asset accumulation with the introduction or increase of government pension benefits. This is equivalent to the Ricardo–Barro proposition that government bonds are no more than receipts for future taxes to be levied on current and future generations. Without the concern for taxes on heirs, government bonds are (partially) net wealth just as social security is a (partial) substitute for private saving.

A rise in the after-tax real interest rate lowers the relative price of future consumption. The pure substitution effect therefore induces an increase in saving. In addition, the labor–leisure choice for workers is tilted toward substitution of more current work, since given a higher interest rate, future leisure becomes relatively cheap in terms of the present value of future forgone output. More current work results in higher current income and less current spending due to the drop in complementary leisure time, so saving rises unambiguously.

The effect of higher interest rates on an individual's wealth is ambiguous. If a higher real after-tax interest rate cuts an individual's wealth, the negative impact on saving may outweigh a positive substitution effect and saving may actually fall. It is those who plan to be borrowers who experience a cut in wealth when interest rates rise, the reverse being true for those who plan to be lenders. In a closed economy the aggregate net stock of bonds is zero (*A*'s asset is *B*'s liability), so that the wealth effect of a change in interest rates is zero for the economy as a whole. A zero net-wealth effect, coupled with a positive substitution effect, suggests that aggregate saving in a closed economy ought unambiguously to rise with the after-tax real interest rate in line with Boskin's (1978) empirical findings and Summers's (1981) analytically derived positive and large interest elasticity of saving.

The result is not so clear in an open economy where the aggregate can be a net borrower or a net lender with respect to the rest of the world. In an economy that plans to act as a net lender to the rest of the world, a higher after-tax real interest rate unambiguously raises saving since wealth and substitution effects operate in the same direction. However, a higher after-tax real interest rate's effect on saving is ambiguous in an open economy that plans to be a net borrower, since wealth and substitution effects operate in opposite directions.

It is worthwhile to be very clear on the reason for an aggregate wealth effect from a change in the interest rate, given net lending or borrowing in an open economy. The relevance of this consideration for tax and budget policy in Japan and the United States will become more obvious presently. Take the case of an open economy looking ahead to a role as net borrower. Far-future spending must be lower relative to far-future income than for the net-lending open economy, where far-future spending is higher relative to far-future income. Because higher discounting given a higher interest rate depresses far-future magnitudes by more than near-future magnitudes, net borrowers see the present value of real income fall by more than the present value of real spending, and wealth falls. The reverse is true for net lenders.

Real After-Tax Interest Rates and Trade in Future Consumption

In view of the wealth and substitution effects operating on net lenders and borrowers, consider Japan and the United States after 1981. Sharp tax cuts made the United States a prospective net borrower from the rest of the world. The sharp rise in after-tax real interest rates reduced the present value of real U.S. income by more than the present value of real spending, resulting in a powerful negative wealth effect on saving that may (other factors remaining equal) have outweighed the positive substitution effect. (Shoven 1984 estimates actual dissaving in the United States between 1980 and 1982.)

On the other hand, in Japan (a prospective net lender to the rest of the world, especially in view of the easing of foreign-exchange restrictions in December 1981) and other countries planning to be net lenders, wealth and substitution effects of higher after-tax real interest rates may have operated together to increase saving in response to higher real interest rates. Such behavior is consistent with an observed sharp increase in the flow of capital to the United States from Japan, and with a rapid move toward net debtor status for the United States as capital flowed in from many parts of the world. During 1980 and 1981, net capital outflows from the United States totaled $12.1 billion. Thereafter, the flows reversed sharply with net inflows of $6.6 billion in 1982, $33.9 billion in 1983 and $94.5 billion in 1984.

While a good deal of work remains to trace the international effects of the radical 1981 change in the U.S. macro policy mix to tight money/easy fiscal with tax cuts aimed at enhancing investment, some suggestive results began to emerge by 1985. The United States took aggressive measures (tax cuts) to stimulate investment, making itself a prospective net debtor to the rest of the world. No measures were taken to stimulate saving beyond the prospective rise given elevated incomes. Consequently the sharp rise in real interest rates required to clear asset markets produced only a muted response of American saving in view of the tendency of associated wealth and intertemporal substitution effects to operate in opposite directions. Simultaneously, the higher real interest rates in worldwide markets increased saving rates outside the United States as wealth and substitution effects reinforced each other in net-lending countries.

The incentive to export saving was especially strong in Japan for two reasons. First, controls on capital outflows were reduced in December 1981. Second, because tax treatment of interest income and expense for Japanese households is essentially the reverse of that for U.S. households, after-tax real interest rates in the United States, when viewed from Japan, were higher than even the already high levels from the U.S. perspective. (This is detailed further in the section "Tax Policy and Saving Behavior.") These factors combined to reverse U.S. net capital flows from outflow to inflow so sharply that by the first half of 1985 the United States became a net debtor for the first time in over sixty years. The special factors relative to tax treatment of interest income and expense in Japan, plus, it is likely, the high overall saving rate relative to domestic investment opportunities in Japan turned Japan into the "World's Number One Capital Exporter," to employ the description applied by Salomon Brothers.[1]

We have seen that in the United States (where the increase in debt sharply exceeds real GNP growth, thereby placing upward pressure on real interest rates), debt-financed expansionary fiscal policy is more likely to be financed by foreign than domestic savers. For foreigners, wealth and substitution effects of higher real after-tax interest rates operate together to raise saving, while for the United States the wealth effect tends to cancel the substitution effect. Viewed in this way, sharp changes in fiscal policy become a powerful determinant of international capital flows and exchange rate behavior in a world where forward-looking capital markets adjust more quickly than commodity markets.

It is interesting to ask, in light of this theoretical discussion, what would be the effect of an attempt by the United States to raise domestic saving by cutting or eliminating the tax on interest income. If nominal interest rates were already at a level sufficient to pay an equilibrium after-tax real rate, the only impact would be to lower nominal dollar interest rates, leaving real after-tax interest rates for domestic savers unaffected. The same qualitative result would follow from the Treasury's November 1984 proposal to lower overall tax rates and to exempt from tax part of the inflationary portion of nominal interest.

For foreign savers, facing unaltered domestic tax policy on interest income and unaltered inflation expectations, lower nominal U.S. rates would mean lower after-tax real rates on U.S. dollar instruments and therefore lower rates on domestic instruments. As net lenders their saving would unambiguously fall, causing some dollar depreciation until after-tax arbitrage equilibrium conditions were restored.

Ironically, a reduction in the tax rate on interest income by a net borrower like the United States could result in lower global saving by leaving its own after-tax real interest rate unchanged and lowering it for net lenders elsewhere. If the United States were a net lender, however, the drop in after-tax real rates worldwide following a cut in the tax rate on interest income would see global saving either rise, fall, or remain unchanged, depending on dominance of the wealth, or the substitution effect, or an approximate netting of the two.

Life Cycle and Bequest Factors in Comparison of Saving in Japan and the United States

Stylized facts regarding Japan's retirement practices, government pension programs, demographics, and available leisure time in some cases help to explain the level and trend of its saving rates and, in other cases, make observed saving behavior in Japan harder to explain.

The typical Japanese worker retires from his or her primary "lifetime" job at age fifty-five and often takes on a lower-paying, possibly part-time job until age sixty. Japanese government old-age pensions (social security) begin at age sixty for men and at age fifty-five for women. The Japanese government adopted a comprehensive social security system in 1960. As of 1980–1982 its pension benefits were about 44% of the average wage, which was roughly comparable to the level of benefits in the U.S. and Sweden, slightly below that in the U.K., and slightly above West Germany's. The Japanese ratio will rise to 60% as the full working population moves toward full benefits. Meanwhile some of the newer entrants have not paid in sufficient amounts to receive full benefits.

Japan's population is aging more rapidly than those of most major industrial countries. Figure 5–3 shows the sixty-five-and-over age group's share of the total population in six nations, while Figure 5–4 shows Japan's "population pyramid" for 1920, 1983, and 2025. In Japan the sixty-and-over group is the most relevant for social security while the fifty-five-and-over group is largely in the dissaving range under life-cycle considerations.

Japan's population not only retires earlier and receives full social security benefits earlier than the U.S. population, but it also lives longer. In 1983 life expectancy at birth for Japanese males and females was 74.2 and 79.8 years, compared to 70.5 and 78.1 for Americans (Ministry of Health and Welfare, Japan; U.N. Demographic Yearbook, 1981). In fact, Japan's newborn population became the world's leader in life expectancy

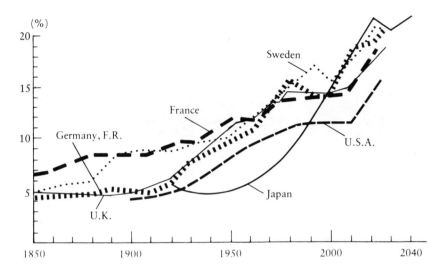

Source: Economic Planning Agency, Japan, *Japan in the Year 2000*.
[a]Based on U.N., *Demographic Indicators by Countries as Assessed in 1980: Medium Variant*.

Figure 5–3. Persons 65 Years Old and Over: Percent of Total Population (1850–2040)[a]

in 1983. This commendable achievement will, however, offset the reduction in future demands on retirement programs that might have come from a recent drop in birth rates.

Japan has promised one of the world's most generous pensions to a rapidly aging population that will retire early and live for a long time by world standards. Regardless of increased life expectancy, which will not become particularly economically relevant until Japan's current well-nurtured newborn population retires, typical retirees receive full government pensions for five years longer than their U.S. counterparts and have five years between age fifty-five and sixty during which some dissaving can be expected in order to maintain living standards.

The experience of Japanese households attempting to purchase housing differs from that of U.S. households in a way that increases observed savings rates for the under-forty population. (This discussion draws heavily on preliminary work by Hayashi, Ito, and Slemrod (1984).) Japanese households, with per capita incomes (as of 1982) at about two-thirds of the U.S. level, face average home prices 10% higher than those in the United States. Japanese self-finance about 40% of the purchase price of a house while borrowing the rest through government-subsidized loans (which are rationed) and loans from relatives. In some cases loans

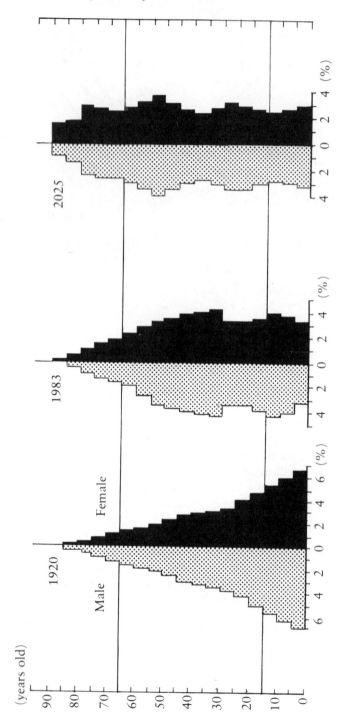

Source: Institute of Population Problems, Ministry of Health and Welfare, Japan.

Figure 5–4. Japan's Population Pyramid (1920–2025)

from employers and relatives may lower the rate of self-financing to 30%. Interest expense for households is not deductible from tax in Japan, even for home mortgage borrowing. As a result, the average age at which the Japanese head-of-household purchases a home is forty, ten years later than the American counterpart.

Compared to the United States, the combination of more costly housing, lower real income, absence of tax subsidies to borrowers, and rationing of government-subsidized mortgage loans implies higher savings rates in Japan, especially for households whose heads are between thirty and forty years old. An important task for researchers is to obtain good age-profile data on savings rates in Japan for comparison with U.S. data in order to isolate the possible effect on savings rates arising from unsubsidized borrowing, more self-financing, and higher real housing costs.

As Blinder (1982) suggested, since U.S. tax law, which subsidizes borrowing while taxing lenders, encourages saving in the form of houses and consumer durables, saving statistics ought to be adjusted for imputed rents on owner-occupied dwellings and durable consumer goods. To some extent, the OECD practice of measuring saving as income less consumption and depreciation may achieve part of this adjustment. As suggested by a comparison of Japanese and American net savings rates in figure 5–1, a large gap remains.

Complementarity between leisure time and consumption spending suggests another reason for a higher rate of saving in Japan. The average work week in Japan was 43.5 hours in 1983, up from about 41 hours in 1975. For the United States, that figure remained in the 37 to 37.5 range between 1975 and 1983, the difference largely stemming from the simple fact that most Japanese work until about three P.M. on Saturdays.

During typical working lives until age fifty-five, Japanese workers have six hours less per week in which to consume the fruits of their labor. As noted earlier, capital-intensive leisure activities in Japan are therefore more expensive per hour (a full twice as expensive if one views Saturday as "shot" for capital-intensive leisure activities) than they are in the United States. Working-age Japanese, enjoying six hours less leisure time per week and contemplating a relatively early retirement, are far more likely to substitute future consumption for expenditure or current consumption. Consumer durables like boats, campers, or recreational equipment are especially costly in view of the scarcity of time to use them and in view of the inability to deduct household interest expense from taxable income. The fact that the interest on roughly two-thirds of household saving in Japan is untaxed raises the opportunity cost of nondeductible borrowing. All of these factors mean that life-cycle, consumption-smoothing considerations suggest a positive relationship between the share of Japan's working-age population in the total population and the average saving rate. The possible role of the bequest motive in the saving behavior of older Japanese is another issue in need of investigation.

Life-cycle, home-financing, and labor-leisure trade-offs are quite different for Japanese households when compared with American counterparts. Between the ages of thirty and forty, typical Japanese heads-of-household have very heavy incentives to save. They work six days a week. Interest income is largely untaxed while interest expense is not deductible. At age forty they will buy houses costing 10% more than those of their American counterparts, given a per capita income two thirds as large. Fifteen years after that, at age fifty-five, they will face compulsory retirement after which a reduced level of income will be available if they take a secondary job until receiving social security benefits at age sixty. Most probably their companies provide no pension benefits, nor do they have an IRA or Keogh plan beyond normal savings on which interest is untaxed but for which additions are not deductible.

For those with multigenerational time horizons, it is possible to contemplate for Japan a rapidly aging population that will place heavy demands on children and children's children if generous, unfunded commitments for government pension benefits are to be honored. In 1981 Japan's social security transfer payments were roughly equal, at 14% of national income, to those in the United States. The ratio will rise as average benefits and the number of recipients increase over the next fifty years and as the ratio of Japan's retired population to its working population rises.

Comparisons of Japanese and American retirement, home financing, demographic, and work/leisure patterns suggest some of the reasons for Japan's higher savings rate. Tax treatment of interest income expense, which along with other tax incentives will be examined in the next section, also encourages saving over acquisition of housing and consumer durables in Japan. In light of some of the necessary reasons for the high savings rate in Japan, it may not be desirable for the United States to attempt to duplicate that country's rate of saving. At the same time it may be worth considering some change in tax subsidies for consumption in the United States.

Life-cycle and intergenerational models carry conflicting implications for the impact of retirement programs and demographic trends on Japan's savings rate. Life-cycle considerations suggest that as the bulge in Japan's population pyramid moves through the working-age years (figure 5–4 shows the bulge spanning ages thirty-five to fifty-five in 1983), the savings rate should rise with the share of the population in the "saving" stage of its life-cycle profile. As is clear from figure 5–1, Japan's savings rate has been on a secular decline since 1970, experiencing a sharp drop after the first oil crisis following which it not only has not recovered but has continued to drift still lower.

The downward trend in Japan's savings rate may be attributed to the rising share of the work force looking forward to full social security benefits. Recall that the program was initiated in 1960 and that Japan's baby-boomers born in the early 1950s have been rapidly entering the work force since the mid-1970s. This life-cycle explanation whereby government pensions offset private saving is inconsistent with the intergenerational view. Under that theory Japan's rapidly aging population and the prospective tax increases required to provide it with generous government pensions ought to have prevented any drop in the savings rate and might even have increased it if current parents wish to shield their children's after-tax disposable incomes from future diminution.

The factors affecting the level and trend of Japan's savings rate are many, and a much more systematic effort will be required to explain it satisfactorily or at least to understand it better. It may be that closer empirical investigation of Japanese saving behavior will help to shed some light on as yet unresolved differences between life-cycle and intergenerational views of U.S. saving behavior.

Tax Policy and Saving Behavior

An Overview of Tax Burdens

It is useful to begin a discussion of tax policy and saving with an overview of tax burdens. This is followed by a brief sketch of the parts of the Japanese tax system most directly related to saving decisions. I shall assume that relevant features of the U.S. tax code are known only too well. Most of the details on Japan's tax system are drawn from *An Outline of Japanese Taxes 1984* published by Japan's Ministry of Finance.

Japanese households and firms are more lightly taxed than their U.S. counterparts, as shown in table 5–1. In 1984 Japan's combined federal and local government revenues were 18.6% of GNP versus 30.9% in the United States. Total 1984 government expenditure in Japan was 27.2% of GNP versus 34% in the United States. At the federal or central government level in Japan, 1984 revenues were 11.7% of GNP versus 19.2% in the U.S., while expenditures were 17.2% of GNP in Japan and 24% of GNP in the U.S.

Japan's overall government deficit at about 9% of GNP appears at first glance to be considerably more burdensome than the 3% gap for the United States. Two qualifications need to be recalled, however. On average Japan's net savings rate has hovered between two and three

Table 5–1
Government Revenue and Expenditure Shares, 1984
(as a percent of GNP)

	Revenue			Expenditure		
	Federal	State and Local[a]	Combined	Federal	State and Local[a]	Combined
Japan	11.7	6.9	18.6	17.2	10.0	27.2
United States	19.2	11.7	30.9	24.0	10.0	34.0

Source: *An Outline of Japanese Taxes* (Tokyo: Tax Bureau, Ministry of Finance, 1984); *Japan, 1984, An International Comparison*, Tokyo: Keizai Koho Center, 1984); *Annual Report of the Council of Economic Advisers*, Office of the President (Washington, D.C.: 1985).

[a]State and local shares exclude transfers from the federal government.

times that of the United States, and during 1982 and 1983 the net savings rate in Japan was almost eight times the U.S. rate. In addition, about 45% of federal government spending in Japan is earmarked for capital formation. Japan's savers have absorbed the sharp increase in government debt since 1975 and have had ample saving left over to export, especially since 1981.

At the federal level (local and state estimates being difficult to obtain), Japanese corporations pay a larger share of income taxes than their U.S. counterparts. (See table 5–2.) In 1984 corporation income taxes were about 32% of revenues while personal income taxes were about 40%. Comparable 1984 figures for the United States were 10% and 44%. The balance was taken up by sales and other indirect taxes and social security contributions. As a share of GNP, 1984 Japanese corporation taxes were about 3.7% versus 1.9% for the United States.

Tax Structure Related to Saving

Japanese households are largely untaxed on interest earnings and capital gains on equity sales, although the former exclusion is the more significant in view of a relatively low level of household participation in equity markets and concentration on postal saving accounts. Individuals with taxable incomes of $40,000 or less (10 million yen) receive a 10% credit on dividends, so that if average tax rates are 10% or below, dividends are tax free. Those with higher incomes are allowed a dividend tax credit of 5%. Overall, although marginal tax rates on individual taxable income rise sharply from 10.5% to 70%, effective tax rates (including local taxes) are lower for households in Japan than in the United States for incomes below $75,000. (See figure 5–5). Most Japanese households therefore enjoy a lower tax burden than their U.S. counterparts while paying little tax on interest earnings on about two-thirds of all assets owned.

The lower tax burden on interest income and nondeductibility of

Table 5–2
Division of Federal Tax Burden: 1984
(percent)

	Personal	*Corporate*	*Indirect and Social Insurance*
Japan	40.4	31.8	27.8
United States	44.1	10.2	45.7

Source: *Japan, 1984, An International Comparison* (Tokyo: Keizai Koho Center, 1984); *Annual Report of the Council of Economic Advisers*, Office of the President (Washington, D.C.: 1985).

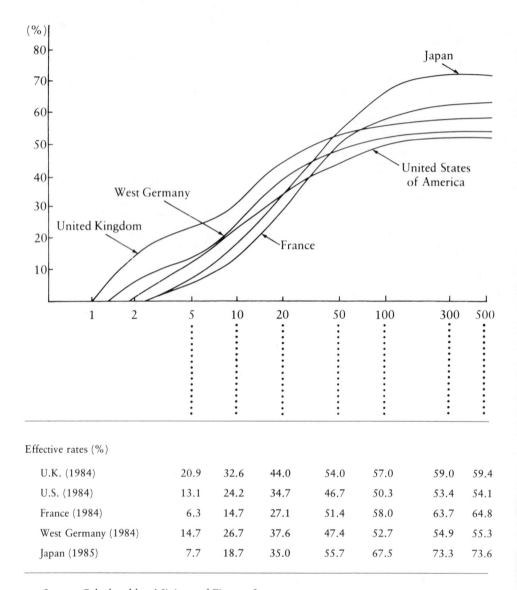

Effective rates (%)

U.K. (1984)	20.9	32.6	44.0	54.0	57.0	59.0	59.4
U.S. (1984)	13.1	24.2	34.7	46.7	50.3	53.4	54.1
France (1984)	6.3	14.7	27.1	51.4	58.0	63.7	64.8
West Germany (1984)	14.7	26.7	37.6	47.4	52.7	54.9	55.3
Japan (1985)	7.7	18.7	35.0	55.7	67.5	73.3	73.6

Source: Calculated by: Ministry of Finance Japan.
Note: Exchange rate (Jan–Jun, 1984): $1 = 239 Yen; £1 = 361 Yen; 1DM = 91 Yen;
1 fr = 30 Yen.

Figure 5–5. **International Comparison of Effective Income Tax Rate (Including Local Taxes)—Standard Household (Man, Spouse and Two Children)**

interest expense are strong incentives for Japanese households to save rather than consume. The structure of Japanese taxes reinforces the impact on saving of life-cycle, demographic, and home-buying burdens discussed earlier. The dividend exclusion and absence of tax on interest earnings go a long way toward elimination of the double taxation over saving implicit in a standard income tax system.

Japanese corporations can exclude from taxable income dividends from domestic corporations (less a portion of interest paid by the corporation on borrowed funds), contributions up to 1.25% of income (0.125 of paid-in capital), and interest on borrowed funds. The tax rate on corporate income is 43.3%. Income distributed as dividends is taxed at 33.3%. Combined with the dividend exclusion for households, the reduced tax rate on dividend distributions probably means that dividend income is less heavily taxed in Japan than in the United States. Still, full deductibility of interest expense makes Japan's highly leveraged corporations more dependent on debt finance.

There do exist special tax measures for Japanese corporations related to depreciation, reserves, and special tax credits. Some such special measures were enacted in 1984 for corporations. The associated total annual revenue loss was estimated at about $1.5 billion by the Ministry of Finance. This of course is very small compared to the annual $50 billion revenue loss linked to accelerated depreciation and investment tax credit measures in the United States.

Corporate depreciation allowances in Japan are modest by U.S. standards. No depreciation of intangible assets is allowed. Depreciation is calculated on a straight-line or declining-balance basis with salvage value at 10%, total write-off of 95% allowed, and expensing for purchases of below $400. No carryover is allowed for unused depreciation.

For Japanese households, these features contribute to a tax code having lower average rates and higher marginal rates than the U.S. code. Individual saving is encouraged by not taxing interest income on about two-thirds of household assets, while nondeductibility of interest expense coupled with burdens of retirement and home-buying tend to discourage consumption.

Japanese corporations pay a larger share of income taxes than their U.S. counterparts and carry a larger tax burden as a share of GNP. This does not mean, however, that on an integrated basis, effective marginal tax rates on capital income as calculated in a comprehensive model like that of King and Fullerton (1984) are higher in Japan than in the United States or other industrial countries. This question is being investigated, and the results should be of considerable interest in view of Japan's strong record of saving and capital formation.

This outline of Japan's tax system suggests only some of the basic differences between its code and that of the United States. A much more detailed analysis will be required, particularly in the important area of effective marginal tax rates, to enable a full understanding of the role, if any, of the Japanese tax system in encouraging high rates of saving and capital formation.

The most striking difference between U.S. and Japanese tax systems to emerge from an initial examination is the reversal of the treatment of household interest income and expense. Japan's system approaches neutrality in the taxation of current versus future consumption, while the United States taxes lenders and subsidizes borrowers by taxing nominal interest as ordinary income and allowing full deductibility of nominal interest expense. As in other areas this distortion rises with inflation, thereby increasing the U.S. tax on saving while raising the subsidy of borrowing for consumption or investment. The Japanese tax code, like the U.S. code, has been largely unindexed, but resulting distortions have been less because on average inflation has been much lower in Japan.

Estimation of Japanese and United States Aggregate Saving Equations

This section presents results of estimating saving equations for the United States and Japan. Overall they suggest that year-to-year changes in aggregate saving have been more consistent with theory in the United States than in Japan, although there appears to have been a significant regime change after 1981 in the United States. When comparing results for the United States and Japan, it is important to remember that until the late 1970s, and still to some extent, Japan's capital markets were heavily regulated and closed internationally. In some cases it is likely that saving behavior reflected a residual decision driven by simple quantity constraints with regard to consumption opportunities.

The saving equations estimated contain a scalar, a consumption-smoothing term, and a measure of the after-tax real rate of interest. For both countries the scalar is the OECD's measure of real physical capital. The consumption-smoothing term is deviations from trend of personal disposable (after-tax) U.S. income and deviations from trend of national disposable (before-tax) Japanese income.[2] The after-tax real interest rate in the United States is the expected rate, measured as the after-tax nominal interest rate on one-year Treasury bills less the yearly average of expected inflation over twelve months as measured by the Livingston survey of inflationary expectations. Effective tax rates on interest income are allowed to vary over time.[3] (See the appendix for full detail on all dates.)

As for Japan, the after-tax real interest rate is the expected real interest rate measured by the call money rate less a forecast of the inflation rate derived from an autoregressive model of Japanese inflation.[4] No adjustment was made for taxation since data were unavailable. A large share of interest earnings is untaxed in Japan and tax rates on the balance have been reasonably stable. Still, a time series on effective tax rates on interest income would be useful.

Equations are estimated by means of both one-stage least squares (OLS) and two-stage least squares (TSLS). Results are reported in table 5–3. TSLS estimates include an investment equation expressed in terms of an accelerator term (growth of real output) and the after-tax real interest rate. The latter is a poor measure of user cost of capital, particularly after 1981 for the United States. This may account for sharp deterioration of performance of the U.S. equation after 1981. Further work is needed to expand the basic model to include effects of tax changes on user cost and thereby on investment.[5] Likewise, a time series on user cost of capital in Japan is needed for proper specification of an investment equation.

The wealth effect on saving operates with a positive sign for the United States and a negative (insignificant) sign for the TSLS equation for Japan. This may reflect a differential impact of wealth and productivity growth on the labor/leisure choice. Postwar Japan was at an earlier stage of development than the United States. Recall that Japan's real capital stock increased three times as rapidly as that of the United States between 1964 and 1980. The rapid increase in wealth resulted in more consumption of both goods and leisure, while the rapid increase in productivity of Japan's labor force caused a substitution effect away from leisure. Therefore, the faster wealth increases relative to productivity, the more likely is rapid development to be accompanied by more consumption of both goods and leisure and thus by a declining, or at least not a rising, level of saving. This phenomenon may be associated with the downward drift in Japan's saving rate since the first oil crisis. (Recall the discussion in the section "Overview of Net Saving Rates.")

In the United States, although productivity growth has been relatively low (about 2.8% annually from 1975 to 1983), wealth growth has been even lower due to a sharply lower saving rate. The slower growth of wealth relative to productivity may have resulted in less of an increase in leisure and more consumption of both current and future goods (saving). Needless to say this explanation is highly speculative. Further investigation should prove interesting, especially in view of the insignificance of the wealth effect in the United States when 1982–1983 observations are added. As usual, an attempt at estimation of "straightforward" equations raises more questions than it answers.

Table 5–3[a]
Estimation of Saving Equations: United States and Japan

	Constant	Wealth	After-tax Real Interest	Deviation from Trend	$\bar{R}^2$	DW
United States						
OLS/1955–1981	17147	0.0187	4278	764.1	0.82	1.90
	(0.86)	(2.35)	(2.53)	(6.47)		
1955–1983	46997	0.0039	1978	895.3	0.75	1.77
	(2.29)	(0.48)	(0.93)	(5.93)		
TSLS/1955–1981	32187	0.0141	7905	759.5	0.80	2.21
	(1.88)	(2.38)	(3.09)	(6.60)		
1955–1983	56331	0.0029	5921	974.1	0.72	1.90
	(2.58)	(0.40)	(1.93)	(6.81)		
Japan						
OLS/1957–1983	3644.89	0.0429	−2.86	0.572	0.97	1.51
	(1.58)	(3.97)	(0.04)	(7.45)		
TSLS/1957–1983	193572	−0.0146	115.2	0.628	0.97	2.03
	(3.07)	(0.69)	(1.85)	(10.77)		

Note: *t* statistics in parentheses. All equations estimated with correction for serially correlated errors.
[a]See appendix for a full description of data.

The sign of estimated impact of after-tax real interest on saving is positive in the United States and marginally positive for Japan in the TSLS case. Recalling our earlier discussion, we found the effect ought to be unambiguously positive for a closed economy where wealth effects net to zero and the substitution effect toward future consumption and more current work both increase saving. In an open economy that plans to be a net lender, both wealth and substitution effects cause higher saving given a higher expected real after-tax rate of interest. This description fits the United States through 1981 before sharp federal tax cuts raised outyear deficits to the $200 billion-plus level. This regime change along with the user cost discussion may account for the sharp deterioration in the fit of the U.S. equation after 1981.

The estimated positive effect of interest on saving in Japan may reflect the operation of a positive substitution effect in an economy where capital markets were largely closed prior to 1981. Since 1981 Japan has been a large net lender and this would lead to the expectation of a positive coefficient on the interest rate. Overall, Japan's financial markets have only begun to be deregulated at home while simultaneously being gradually opened up to the rest of the world. Further, interest rates were heavily controlled during most of the sample period. It may be that good estimates of the interest elasticity of Japanese saving will have to await passage of time sufficient to generate enough sample data that reflect unconstrained behavior responsive to market-determined rates.

It is perhaps worth noting that the implied estimates of the interest elasticity of U.S. saving in table 5–2 are 0.12 (TSLS) and 0.09 (OLS) based on the 1955–1981 sample. While significantly different from zero, these estimates are also significantly below Boskin's (1978) estimates of 0.4 and well below Summers's (1981) inferences of 0.74 to 3.71. The estimated interest elasticity of Japanese saving is very small at 0.02. It will be interesting to see whether Japan's continued role as an international net lender results in estimates of a larger elasticity as post–1981 sample data accumulate.

The consumption-smoothing terms in both American and Japanese saving equations are consistently significant and carry the anticipated sign. It appears that both American and Japanese households and firms use saving as a residual to smooth year-to-year consumption.

The saving equations estimates presented here for the United States and Japan suggest some interesting paths for further investigation. The impact of wealth on saving may be conditional on growth of wealth relative to productivity. This possibility needs to be investigated systematically, particularly in view of divergent trends for these series in Japan and the United States, reflecting the fact that the former economy has been at an earlier, more rapidly developing stage than the latter. The impact on saving of expected real after-tax interest needs to be estimated holding investment constant with a TSLS procedure that involves identification of a good structural equation describing investment. Further investigation of national status as a net lender (borrower) vis-a-vis the rest of the world should prove interesting, particularly in view of the sharp change after 1981 in the outlook for the role of the United States as a new net borrower. Japan's evolution as a net lender may also prove significant in raising the response of its saving to the real interest rate. Longer-run life-cycle and bequest factors also will require more careful investigation.

Summary and Conclusion

The large difference in net savings rates between Japan and the United States suggests that the former is devoting a far greater share of output to increasing future consumption. It is useful to remember, however, that savings rates outside these two countries cluster closer to the rates in Japan than they do to rates in the United States. The more appropriate question to emphasize may be: "Why is the U.S. devoting so little output to increasing future consumption?" rather than "Why are the Japanese devoting so much?" The question regarding the low level of U.S. net saving is even more pressing in the light of its virtual collapse since 1981.

This chapter rejects the notion that the difference between saving rates in Japan and the United States is illusory and essentially a measurement problem. While, as Blinder notes, part of imputed rents from owner-occupied housing and durables in the United States may be counted as saving, even a liberal adjustment for this component while totally ignoring a similar component of saving in Japan will not account for much of the large difference in savings rates. And since unrealized gains in housing value are also untaxed in Japan, some saving component arises from owner-occupied housing there as well. Japan and most other industrial countries are clearly devoting a larger portion of current output to increasing future consumption than is the United States.

Japan's higher level of saving is seen as tied to demographic, life-cycle, home-financing, and tax factors. Japan, during much of the post–World War II period, has been at an earlier stage of development, anxious to resume a rapid increase in living standards underway before the war. Loss of half its capital stock together with forced saving by virtue of severely constrained opportunities to consume coupled with strong incentives to save are underlying reasons for a high rate of saving in Japan. Other facts have tended to keep savings rates high even as real incomes in Japan rose. Japanese workers retire earlier and can expect to live longer than their U.S. counterparts. Private pension plans are scarce. The unfunded social insurance (government pension) plan offers generous benefits approaching 60% of the average working wage, starting at age sixty for men and fifty-five for women, to a rapidly aging population with a rising life expectancy.

Some expectation of higher future federal taxes needed to finance unfunded social insurance benefits may be keeping savings rates high. As of 1984, tax burdens in Japan are low by international standards (11.2% of GNP compared to 19.2% in the United States) and low relative to federal expenditure (17.2% of GNP relative to 24% in the United States).

Japanese families with per capita incomes at about two-thirds of United States levels face housing prices at least 10% higher, larger down payments, rationed mortgage money, and nondeductibility of mortgage interest expense, while most interest income is untaxed. The need and the incentive to accumulate saving to buy housing is far greater in Japan than in the United States, while the fact that the average age of a Japanese household head at date of purchase of a first house is forty (ten years older than his or her American counterpart) is hardly surprising. The under-forty age group in the population at large obviously bears on the measured saving rate in Japan.

While Japan's tax burden is relatively light, the 1984 share carried by corporations is higher (32% of federal taxes and 3.7% of GNP) than in the United States (10% of federal taxes and 1.9% of GNP). While this difference may have little impact on savings rates, it has not constituted an impediment to sustained high growth of output and productivity.

A saving equation expressed in terms of wealth, an after-tax real interest rate, and a consumption-smoothing variable "work" for both the United States and Japan, although the wealth variable for Japan is insignificant in the two-stage least-square formulation, and the estimated interest elasticity of saving is low (0.02) and only marginally significant.

The role of private pension plans in determining measured saving behavior may prove a fruitful line of investigation to follow in studies of saving behavior in Japan and the United States. The higher rate of participation in private pension plans in the United States and the rapid growth of such plans has made pension contributions a large part of personal saving. Bernheim and Shoven (1985) have suggested that for the period after 1981, the rising stock market, lower wage growth, and high real interest rates have combined to reduce the number of underfunded private pension plans. As a result, due to a purely mechanical response to funding rules, corporations have cut pension contributions because higher earnings on pension fund assets have lowered contributions required to meet legal funding obligations. Lower corporate contributions to pension funds may help to explain the sharp drop in post–1981 measured U.S. savings rates, while, of course, the absence of such arrangements in Japan and elsewhere suggests a reason for a sharp rise in imported saving. If such behavior is verified and persists, it raises questions about the design of laws governing corporate contributions to employee pension programs. If pension funds are viewed as net lenders, wealth of the funds does rise with interest rates, but the permanence of such changes may not match the permanence of fund liabilities. More succinctly, the wealth effects may be transitory.

The role of private pensions notwithstanding, a fuller understanding of reasons for different saving rates is important if policy errors related to trade flows in commodities and saving are to be avoided. The high level of Japan's saving rate has led some to suggest that Japan oversaves. This opaque conclusion often comes from discussions of Japan's trade balance surplus. The real complaint is that Japan underconsumes, since that propensity is seen to result in too little Japanese spending on imports.

Such reasoning is seriously flawed as are most descriptions of economic behavior preceded by "over" or "under," such as "overvalued currency." Nations trade in current and future goods. The former transactions are recorded in the current account, the latter in the capital account. Trade results from a difference between domestic and foreign rates of exchange between commodities. The rate of exchange between current and future goods differed sharply enough after 1981 to cause a large, incipient net flow of current goods from Japan to the United States and a large, incipient net flow of future goods from the United States to Japan because high real interest rates in the U.S. made future goods relatively cheap compared to Japan. As a result the United States was a net buyer of current goods from Japan and the rest of the world and a net seller of future goods to Japan and the rest of the world. As already noted, Japan's share of U.S. future goods was enhanced by opposite tax treatment of interest income and expense, coupled with a relaxation of Japanese restrictions on capital outflows.

A fuller understanding of saving behavior suggests that Japanese saving is related to some painful realities regarding need to provide for retirement, financing of lumpy purchases such as homes, and prospective sharp tax increases tied to funding of generous government pensions for a rapidly aging population. Japan has supplied a large share of the shortfall of saving required to finance net capital formation in the United States and, in the process, has enhanced its provision for future consumption, while the reverse has been true for the United States.

Trade in saving (future goods) is governed by forward-looking investors whose expectations may be volatile. Exchange rate volatility reflects this fact. Trade in commodities is in turn affected by exchange rates. The more we understand about savings rates and the role of tax policy and other factors in determining such rates, the better able we will be to avoid policies which imply exchange rates that create serious problems of redundancy for capital in traded goods industries concentrated in the manufacturing sector.

International differences in tax and budget policy are, in the open international capital markets of the 1980s, transmitted through international saving flows. To say that Japan oversaves or underconsumes is no more sensible than to say that the United States has too much food or too many natural resources. Different rates of exchange between commodities create trade in current goods just as different rates of exchange between current and future goods create a pattern of trade flows in current and future goods. To understand this we need to understand saving behavior. A good place to begin is with Japan and the United States, which together account for about a third of the world's economy. I hope the discussion in this chapter provides a start toward understanding differences in saving behavior in these two nations and their implications for observable economic behavior.

Appendix 5A

United States

Real saving in millions of 1967 dollars $= \text{saving}_t/\text{CPI}_t$

> saving_t = net saving in millions of current dollars
> > Source: OECD, National Accounts, Main Aggregates, Vol. I
>
> CPI_t = consumer price index—all items (seasonally adjusted)
> > Source: Council of Economic Advisers, Economic Report of the President

Real after-tax one-year interest rate $= \left[\dfrac{(1 + i_t (1\text{-}t_t))}{(1 + \pi_t^e)} - 1 \right] \cdot 100$

> i_t = yield on Treasury securities at constant maturity of one year, per annum, averages of daily figures, not seasonally adjusted
> Source: Board of Governors of the Federal Reserve System, Statistical Release G.13, Selected Interest Rates and Bond Prices
>
> t_t = marginal tax rate on interest income, weighted by interest income, for taxable returns
> Source: 1955–1982 - Vito Tanzi
> > 1983 set equal to 1982 value
>
> π_t^e = twelve-month CPI forecast, average of semiannual figures
> Source: Livingston Survey, Philadelphia Inquirer.

Deviations from linear trend—real personal disposable income

> $(\text{YD}_t/\text{CPI}_t) - 5.582221 - 0.03179\ (\text{time}_t)$
> (from OLS regression of YD_t/CPI_t on time: 1955–1983)
>
> YD_t = personal disposable income in billions of current dollars
> > Source: U.S. Department of Commerce, Bureau of Economic Analysis, National Income and Product Accounts of the United States
>
> CPI_t—see above
>
> time_t = time trend, 1947 = 1, with increment of 1 per year

Real wealth in millions of 1967 dollars

$\quad$ = 1955–1980: K_t/CPI_t

$\quad$ = 1981–1983: 13.682033 + 0.039256 (time$_t$)
$\quad$ (from OLS regression of K_t/CPI_t on time: 1955–1980)

$\quad K_t$ = total gross capital stock in millions of current dollars
$\qquad$ *Source:* OECD, *Flows and Stocks of Fixed Capital*

$\quad CPI_t$—see above

$\quad$ time$_t$—see above

Percentage change in gross national product
$\quad$ real gross national product in billions of 1972 dollars
$\quad$ *Source:* U.S. Department of Commerce, Bureau of Economic Analysis,
$\quad$ *National Income and Product Accounts of the United States*

Japan

Real saving in billions of 1967 yen
$\qquad$ = 1960–1983: $saving_t^{PS}/CPI_t$

$$= 1957\text{–}1959: \frac{saving_t^{FS}\left(\dfrac{\sum\limits_{t=60}^{65} saving_t^{PS}}{\sum\limits_{t=60}^{65} saving_t^{FS}}\right)}{CPI_t}$$

$\quad$ Saving$_t^{PS}$ = net saving in billions of current yen, using OECD's present system of national accounting
$\qquad$ *Source:* OECD, *National Accounts, Main Aggregates,* Vol. I

$\quad$ Saving$_t^{FS}$ = net saving in billions of current yen, using OECD's former system of national accounting
$\qquad$ *Source:* OECD, *National Accounts, Main Aggregates,* Vol. I

$\quad CPI_t$ = consumer price index
$\qquad$ *Source:* DRI, *U.S. Central Data Base*

Real interest rate

$$= \left[\frac{(1+i_t)}{(1+\pi_t^e)} - 1\right] \cdot 100$$

$\quad i_t$ = call money rate
$\qquad$ *Source:* International Monetary Fund, *International Financial Statistics*

$\pi_t^e = 3.766044 + 0.222625 \, (CPI_{t-1}) + 14.442542 \, (OIL_t)$
(from OLS regression of CPI_t on CPI_{t-1} and OIL_t: 1957 to 1983)

CPI_t—see above

OIL_t = dummy variable = 0 for 1957–1972, 1976–1983
0.5 for 1973, 1975
1 for 1974

Deviations from linear trend—real national disposable income

$$= (NDI_t/CPI_t) + 14910.827148 - 2613.583252 \, (\text{time}_t)$$
(from OLS regression of NDI_t/CPI_t on time: 1957–1983)

NDI_t = 1960–1983: NDI_t^{PS}

$$1957\text{–}1959: NDI_t^{FS} \left(\frac{\sum_{t=60}^{65} NDI_t^{PS}}{\sum_{t=60}^{65} NDI_t^{FS}} \right)$$

NDI_t^{PS} = national disposable income in billions of current yen, using OECD's present system of national account
Source: OECD, *National Accounts, Main Aggregates,* Vol. I

NDI_t^{FS} = national disposable income in billions of current yen using OECD's former system of national account
Source: OECD, *National Accounts, Main Aggregates,* Vol. I

CPI_t—see above

time_t—same as for U.S.

Real wealth in billions of 1975 yen

1964–1980 = K_t
1957–1963 = $K_{64} \, (GNP_t/GNP_{64})$
1981–1983 = $K_{80} \, (GNP_t/GNP_{80})$

K_t = real gross capital stock in billions of 1975 yen
Source: OECD, *Flows and Stocks of Fixed Capital*

GNP_t = real gross national product in billions of 1975 yen
Source: International Monetary Fund, *International Financial Statistics*

Percentage change in real gross national product
real gross national product—see above

Data Relevant to Table 5–3: United States

	Real Saving	Real Wealth	Real After-Tax Interest Rate	Deviation from Trend	Growth of Real Output
1955	45040	1344246	0.94	13.024	6.720
1956	48715	1427216	1.17	12.767	2.144
1957	42979	1438905	1.66	1.748	1.817
1958	29027	1448086	0.94	−13.275	−0.424
1959	42824	1489792	1.77	−11.239	5.992
1960	49747	1508210	1.74	−19.367	2.148
1961	45449	1536569	0.81	−25.275	2.632
1962	53598	1572411	1.00	−23.833	5.776
1963	59646	1596730	1.25	−25.415	4.023
1964	67915	1661737	1.43	−11.049	5.273
1965	82141	1726134	1.58	0.884	6.036
1966	82957	1817468	1.56	8.625	5.972
1967	76248	1884607	0.87	10.772	2.701
1968	80248	1994475	1.02	15.083	4.617
1969	82918	2089362	1.47	10.213	2.788
1970	63774	2150046	1.03	8.870	−0.184
1971	67130	2246173	−0.27	13.498	3.390
1972	74196	2392514	−0.22	23.182	5.658
1973	100104	2579655	0.16	46.273	5.768
1974	75266	2761228	−1.54	17.850	−0.638
1975	48672	2753751	−1.24	4.588	−1.179
1976	57349	2868429	−1.72	7.872	5.408
1977	71904	3068650	−1.95	14.069	5.508
1978	87590	3314432	−1.26	27.160	5.030
1979	83678	3373275	−1.87	14.579	2.836
1980	52719	3332010	−2.19	−20.712	−0.297
1981	62091	3457278	1.25	−29.485	2.522
1982	22703	3595696	2.74	−42.046	−2.129
1983	24272	3739657	1.18	−29.363	3.696

Data Relevant to Table 5–3: Japan

	Real Saving	Real Wealth	Real Interest Rate	Deviation from Trend	Growth of Real Output
1957	3513	32575	7.47	1953.599	7.451
1958	3182	34402	5.07	−359.863	5.610
1959	3837	37461	4.16	−1058.062	8.890
1960	5178	42455	4.18	−936.692	13.334
1961	6401	48601	6.55	−787.287	14.474
1962	6424	52013	5.12	−1914.399	7.021
1963	6318	57456	2.13	−3011.552	10.464
1964	6459	65007	4.30	−3259.253	13.142
1965	6503	70950	2.20	−4534.212	11.252
1966	7525	77262	0.45	−3736.876	10.629
1967	9478	85751	1.48	−1844.421	10.798
1968	11315	96806	3.05	−343.661	12.714
1969	13157	110086	2.60	2019.131	12.292
1970	16316	125958	3.14	4939.825	9.862
1971	15413	142415	0.99	4024.789	12.331
1972	16823	160291	−0.49	6901.268	1.556

Data Relevant to Table 5–3: Japan

	Real Saving	Real Wealth	Real Interest Rate	Deviation from Trend	Growth of Real Output
1973	19212	178953	−4.32	10244.079	8.819
1974	16787	195063	−6.87	5007.543	−1.240
1975	13775	209408	−4.62	1172.253	2.419
1976	14592	222189	0.38	679.774	5.315
1977	14323	235455	−0.15	−744.824	5.305
1978	15466	249247	−1.13	576.562	5.118
1979	15409	265616	1.18	988.635	5.231
1980	15434	283638	6.09	−1407.026	4.775
1981	15327	295107	1.78	−3553.103	4.044
1982	14472	304742	1.99	−4755.146	3.265
1983	13915	314015	1.95	−6261.104	3.043

Notes

1. N. Sargen and R. Segal, *Japan: The World's Number One Capital Exporter* (New York: Salomon Brothers Inc., February 1985).
2. After-tax income was not available for Japan. With relatively low and stable tax rates, deviations from trend of after-tax income in Japan are likely to be highly correlated with deviations from trend of pre-tax income.
3. A time series on tax rates was kindly provided by Vito Tanzi.
4. An AR–1 model with dummy variables for oil inflation in 1973–1975 provided a very good bet.
5. Elsewhere, a time series on user cost was not significant in a U.S. investment equation that included an accelerator term and the change in U.S. debt to GNP as a proxy for prospective user cost. This work (see Makin and Sauer 1984) needs to be integrated here.

References

Bernheim, B.D. and J.B. Shoven, "Pension Funding and Saving." National Bureau of Economic Research, Cambridge, Mass., March 1985.

Blades, D., "Alternative Measures of Saving." *Occasional Studies*. Paris: OECD, June 1983.

Blades, D. and P.H. Sturm, "The Concept and Measurement of Savings: The United States and Other Industrialized Countries" in *Saving and Government Policy*. Federal Reserve Bank of Boston Conference Series no. 25.

Blinder, A.S., "Discussion of Tax Incentives to Promote Personal Saving: Recent Canadian Experience," in *Saving and Government Policy*, op. cit.

Boskin, M.J., "Taxation, Saving and the Rate of Interest." *Journal of Political Economy*, April 1978: S3–S28.

Hayashi, F., T. Ito, and J. Slemrod, "Housing Finance Imperfection: A Simulation Analysis for a Comparison of the U.S. and Japan." Mimeo, December 1984.

King, M. and D. Fullerton, *The Taxation of Income from Capital*. National Bureau of Economic Research. Chicago: University of Chicago Press, 1984.

Kotlikoff, L., "Taxation and Savings: A Neoclassical Perspective." *Journal of Economic Literature*, December 1984.

Makin, J.H. and R. Sauer, "The Effect of Debt Accumulation on Capital Formation." *AEI Studies in Fiscal Policy*, Occasional Paper no. 1. Washington, D.C.: American Enterprise Institute, November 1984.

An Outline of Japanese Taxes 1984. Tokyo: Ministry of Finance Tax Bureau, 1984.

Sargen, N. and R. Segal, *Japan: The World's Number One Capital Exporter*. New York: Salomon Brothers, Inc., 1985.

Shoven, J.B., "Saving in the U.S. Economy" in *Removing Obstacles to Economic Growth*, ed. M.L. Wachter and S.M. Wachter. Philadelphia: University of Pennsylvania Press, 1984.

Summers, L.A., "Capital Taxation and Accumulation in a Life Cycle Growth Model." *American Economic Review*, September 1981.

6

Pensions and Social Security in Household Portfolios: Evidence from the *1983 Survey of Consumer Finances*

Robert B. Avery
Gregory E. Elliehausen
Thomas A. Gustafson

P ension and social-security programs have grown rapidly since the 1940s. Pensions now cover about half the labor force, and social security covers over 90%. The claims of these programs' participants on future income has become a major asset in the household balance sheet. Munnell (1977, p. 118) estimated that the present value of social-security benefits alone accounted for nearly one-half of total household wealth in 1975. Because the value of pension and social-security benefits is so large, a number of researchers have attempted to determine the impact of these retirement programs on savings decisions and household-portfolio behavior. Unfortunately, theoretical results are ambiguous, and empirical evidence is not conclusive due to data limitations. The purpose of this chapter is to present some initial findings from the U.S. government's *1983 Survey of Consumer Finances* on the role of pensions and social security in household portfolios. The findings presented here are the first reported pension results from the survey.

This chapter is organized as follows. The first section briefly reviews previous theoretical and empirical studies of the impact of pensions and social security on the level of savings and composition of household portfolios. A second section describes the content, survey design, and data preparation for the *1983 Survey of Consumer Finances*. The third section presents results of a multivariate analysis of the effects of these retirement programs on household portfolios. The final section provides conclusions and a discussion of further work.

The views expressed in this chapter do not necessarily represent the positions of any agency of the U.S. Government. Julia Springer provided research assistance.

Previous Studies

Pensions and social security may affect household-saving behavior in two ways. First, participation in these retirement programs may affect the level of households' discretionary saving or, equivalently, the amount of nonpension wealth. Second, the composition of household savings may be affected as households substitute pension or social-security wealth for discretionary savings for retirement. Most existing studies focus on the former question, the effects of these retirement programs on saving. Recently, however, a few researchers have attempted to study the impact of pensions and social security on the composition of household portfolios.

Effects on the Level of Saving

Theoretical analysis of retirement programs' effect on saving usually begins with the traditional life-cycle savings model. This model implies that households can offset pension contributions by reducing their discretionary saving from current income, by liquidating assets, or by borrowing against future pension benefits in order to achieve preferred levels of consumption over time. As a result, pension programs would have no effect on the overall level of saving. Institutional features, however, may alter this conclusion. On the one hand, pensions may reduce saving because pension benefits are usually paid as annuities for the remainder of a worker's (and possibly his spouse's) life and because pensions often are not fully funded. On the other hand, saving may be increased because imperfect capital markets prevent households from borrowing against future pension benefits and because pensions may cause workers to retire earlier than they otherwise would. In addition, favorable tax provisions for saving through pensions have opposite income and substitution effects, while uncertainty about the receipt and value of future benefits may cause households to underestimate or to overestimate their needs for discretionary savings. Thus, theory provides no definite conclusions on the net effect of pensions on saving.[1]

Theoretical analysis of the impact of social security is similar. The simple life-cycle model suggests that social security would reduce saving because social security is financed on a pay-as-you-go basis rather than through asset-accumulation. However, if social security induces workers to retire early, discretionary saving might increase in order to finance a longer period of retirement. A further complication, introduced by Barro (1974), is that social security may simply be viewed as a substitute for intrafamily transfers. To the extent that social security induces families to reduce support for elderly parents or to increase bequests to offset children's additional payroll taxes, the overall impact of social security on saving is reduced. Thus, the effect of social security on saving is also theoretically indeterminate.[2]

Because theoretical results are ambiguous, conclusions on the impact of pensions and social security on saving must ultimately be based on empirical evidence. Early work by Cagan (1965) and Katona (1965) indicated that participation in pension programs was associated with greater discretionary saving. In a later study, Munnell (1976) found that workers covered by pensions saved more than workers who were not covered. Unfortunately, the data for this study did not include the dollar value of pension benefits; moreover, the results were based on a sample of men aged 45 to 59 for whom retirement was the primary savings objective. More recently, Diamond and Hausman (1980) and Blinder, Gordon, and Wise (1981) examined the relationship between pensions and the stock of nonpension wealth. Diamond and Hausman found an inverse relationship between nonpension assets and the dollar amount of annual pension benefits, but Blinder, Gordon, and Wise could detect no significant relationship between pension and nonpension wealth.

Evidence on the impact of social security is also inconclusive. Using aggregate time-series data, Leimer and Lesnoy (1980) found no evidence supporting the hypothesis that social security reduced savings. Cross-section studies by Feldstein and Pellechio (1979), Kotlikoff (1979), Diamond and Hausman (1980), and Blinder, Gordon, and Wise (1981), among others, have addressed this question. A few studies found an inverse relationship between the size of social-security benefits and non-pension assets, while others detected no significant relationship.

Effects on Portfolio Composition

Pension and social-security benefits have several characteristics that render them less than perfect substitutes for conventional assets. First, realization of pension benefits requires that the worker remains with the firm long enough to become vested. Social security requires a minimum period of covered employment before the worker becomes eligible to receive benefits. Realization of pension and social-security benefits also depends on the survival of the worker (or possibly his spouse) and on retirement in the sense of departure from the firm or from the labor force. In addition, social-security and most pension benefits are paid as annuities for the remainder of the worker's and spouse's lives; they are not limited to a fixed dollar amount. Furthermore, the value of these retirement benefits may depend disproportionately on the level of wages in the years immediately preceding retirement or leaving covered employment. Thus, pension and social-security benefits are highly illiquid and are subject to considerable uncertainty about realization and the eventual size of benefits.

Theoretical analysis based on portfolio-choice models provides few definite conclusions on these retirement programs' effects on the composition of household portfolios. Nevertheless, assets with similar liquidity and risk characteristics might be expected to be substitutes for pension and social-security wealth. Hubbard (1984), using data collected for the President's Commission on Pension Policy, found some evidence to support this hypothesis. He found that greater amounts of social-security wealth were associated with greater holdings of housing, stocks, and annuities and with smaller holdings of deposits and bonds. He also found that greater social-security and pension wealth were associated with greater levels of debt, suggesting that households may offset mandatory retirement saving by incurring debts. Unfortunately, the data do not include business assets of the self-employed, and the estimation technique is subject to a few reservations.[3]

The 1983 Survey of Consumer Finances

The *1983 Survey of Consumer Finances* offers new and comprehensive data for studying retirement programs' impact on households. The survey, which was jointly sponsored by the Board of Governors of the Federal Reserve System, the U.S. Department of Health and Human Services, and five other federal agencies, collected a detailed inventory of the assets and liabilities of 3,824 randomly selected American households. The survey compiled information on employment status, wages, past work history, pension-plan participation, retirement plans, and expected pension and social-security benefits. Respondents were also asked about purposes of saving, attitudes toward liquidity and financial risk, perceptions of saving in the previous year, and awareness of marginal tax rates. Interviewing was conducted by the Survey Research Center of the University of Michigan from February through July 1983.[4]

A supplementary survey collected details from pension providers on the pension formulas for respondents to the household survey. Results from the pension-provider survey are not yet available. Only data from the household survey were used for this chapter.

The unit of observation in the survey is the family, which is defined to include all persons residing in the same dwelling who are related by blood, marriage, or adoption. Families include one-person units as well as units of two or more persons.

The data used for this chapter differ somewhat from the raw-sample responses. For 3,665 observations in which the majority of dollar values were reported, a series of statistical procedures was used to impute missing values. The remaining 159 observations were discarded. A sampling weight was computed to compensate for any nonrandom exclusion of observations with missing values. This weight was used in conjunction with the survey's response weights to weight the 3,665-observation sample.

Econometric Analysis

The objective of this chapter is to investigate the relationship between the value of pension and social-security benefits and the size and composition of household portfolios. A complete analysis of this relationship requires theoretically derived structural models. Previous studies have attempted to derive such models, but their realization has been achieved at considerable cost. Previously estimated models are characterized by simple specifications with few control variables. As a consequence, their results suffer from serious concerns about robustness. This concern is especially evident when one considers the myriad of reasons for saving other than retirement.

This initial effort at studying the relationship between pensions and household portfolios using data from the *1983 Survey of Consumer Finances* employs a reduced-form model that allows for much greater control of other factors affecting household financial decisions. This control is achieved in two ways. First, separate regressions are estimated for narrowly defined subgroups of the population. While this approach limits the generality of the results, it permits much cleaner tests for the relationship between pensions and nonpension asset holdings. Second, a much greater number of family characteristics than have been considered in previous studies are included in the estimated regressions as independent variables. The proposed models regress several different measures of nonpension wealth against pension wealth, social-security wealth, and a set of control variables.

Model and Estimation

The sample selected for econometric analysis consists of families headed by persons fifty years of age or older who are in the labor force but are not self-employed. Families headed by persons in this age group are especially likely to be saving for retirement, to have accurate information about their pension benefits, and to have definite retirement plans. Moreover, fewer assumptions are required to calculate their pension wealth because their employment histories are nearly complete.

Only families in which the head is in the labor force were included because these families are the ones for whom preretirement savings choices are still relevant. Families headed by self-employed managers were excluded because their asset portfolios are dominated by their business holdings. The size of these business assets suggests that the portfolio-decisions of families headed by self-employed persons are fundamentally different from those of other families. Finally, to control further for differences among families, the sample was divided into married and unmarried groups. Separate regressions were estimated for each group. (Appendix 6A provides information on motives for retirement saving by age group and asset portfolios of the self-employed.)

Four pairs of regressions were estimated, each using a different measure of nonpension wealth as a dependent variable. They are (1) net worth, (2) total assets, (3) financial assets, and (4) liquid assets. Liquid assets include checking accounts, savings accounts, money-market deposit and money-market mutual-fund accounts, individual retirement accounts (IRAs), Keogh accounts, certificates of deposit, and savings bonds. Financial assets are liquid assets plus stocks, bonds, and trust assets. Total assets consist of financial assets, homes, other real estate, and business assets. Net worth is total assets less the amount of mortgage and consumer debt outstanding.

The independent variables of particular interest are net pension wealth, value of assets in a thrift or other savings plan (such as profit-sharing or deferred-compensation plan), and net social-security wealth. Net pension wealth was computed by subtracting the present value of the wage liability (that is, employee and employer pension contributions) from the present value of pension benefits. Pension benefits are those that the individual expects to receive upon retirement or actual benefits if the individual was already receiving benefits. Standard mortality rates, Social Security Trustees' projections for inflation (4%) and the real-wage growth rate (1%), and a discount rate equal to the long-term Treasury bond rate at the time of the survey (10.85%) were used to compute present values.[5] The value of thrift assets was reported by respondents. Net social-security wealth was computed in a manner similar to that of net pension wealth. Social-security benefits are based on social security benefit rules rather than respondent expectations.[6]

Additional variables were included in the regression models to control for other factors that may affect the size or composition of household portfolios. These variables can be grouped into several categories. The first category consists of dummy variables for age of family head. These age variables were included to account for life-cycle differences in accumulated wealth. A second category contains three family-income variables. The income variables provide an indication of the resources available to the family for asset-accumulation. These variables were constructed to allow the relationship between income and wealth to differ in the lower, middle, and upper segments of the income distribution.[7] The next two categories of variables control for differences in employment. Included in these categories are the occupation and industry in which the family head works, whether the wife works full-time, and the share of family income contributed by the wife. The fifth category contains variables for a variety of family characteristics that are related to family life cycle, human capital, and other factors. Education of family head, education of the wife, number of children, and health status are a few such variables. The last category accounts for differences in savings attitudes and characteristics, including motives for saving, attitudes toward liquidity and financial risk, and perceived marginal tax rates. A list of regression variables and their means is given in table 6–1.

Table 6–1
Regression Variables and Sample Means

	Families with Married Heads	Families with Unmarried Heads
Dependent variables		
Nonpension net worth	$193,445	$58,822
Total nonpension assets	$213,891	$67,537
Financial assets	$56,472	$14,528
Liquid assets	$24,102	$10,916
Independent variables		
Pension and social-security wealth		
Net pension wealth	$37,393	$26,182
Value of thrift assets	$6,118	$1,803
Net social-security wealth	$125,281	$28,462
Age of family head		
*Age 52–53	.136	.127
*Age 54–55	.128	.165
*Age 56–57	.138	.160
*Age 58–59	.112	.071
*Age 60–61	.117	.112
*Age 62–63	.088	.086
*Age 64–65	.050	.025
*Age 66–70	.044	.053
*Age 71 or older	.035	.034
Income		
Family income	$42,204	$18,228
Family income above $10,000 (income minus 10,000 if income greater than $10,000, zero otherwise)	$32,434	$9,393

(Table 6-1 continued)

Table 6–1 continued

	Families with Married Heads	Families with Unmarried Heads
Independent variables (continued)		
Family income above $30,000 (income minus 30,000 if income greater than $30,000, zero otherwise)	$17,188	$1,985
Occupation of family head		
*Professional or technical worker	.637	.317
*Clerical or sales	.090	.237
*Employed in agriculture, forestry, or mining	.199	.053
*Employed in wholesale or retail trade	.411	.667
*Employed by federal government	.042	.058
*Employed by state or local government	.081	.205
*Union member	.266	.237
Wife's employment		
*Wife works full-time	.475	—
Share of income contributed by wife	.190	—
*Wife self-employed	.087	—
Other family characteristics		
*Family head has high-school diploma	.431	.488
*Family head has college degree	.252	.171
*Wife has college degree	.183	—
Number of children living in household	.859	.513
Total number of children	3.356	2.565
Number of persons age 65 or older in household	.023	.065
*Family head has bad health	.293	.296
*Wife has bad health	.338	—
*Family has health insurance	.917	.810
*Nonwhite or Hispanic	.122	.251
*Family head female	—	.700
*Family head widowed	—	.394
*Family head never married	—	.141
*Rural	.400	.288
*Urban	.208	.353
*South	.303	.382
*West	.169	.208
*North-central	.271	.199
Savings attitudes		
*Saving for retirement	.513	.370
*Saving for education	.141	.078
*Willing to take high risks	.068	.074
*Not willing to take any risk	.358	.466
*Willing to tie up money for a long time	.133	.142
*Not willing to tie up money at all	.213	.285
*Most of savings from inheritance	.058	.075
*Expect to receive inheritance	.105	.074
*Aware of marginal tax rate	.634	.577
*Reported marginal tax rate	18.103%	14.348%

Source: Authors' calculations from *1983 Survey of Consumer Finances,* U.S. Government, Federal Reserve Board.

*Dummy variable.

Results

Complete results for the eight estimated regressions are presented in appendix 6B. Coefficients of the control variables are not discussed here both because they are not of specific interest to this chapter and because they are difficult to interpret due to interrelationships among the variables. The discussion focuses on the estimated coefficients for pension, thrift, and social-security variables, which are presented in table 6–2. For families with married heads, coefficients for pension wealth and thrift assets are generally significant at a 5% level. Their size indicates substantial substitution between these retirement assets and nonpension wealth. A one-dollar increase in the amount of thrift assets reduces nonpension net worth by $1.20, while a one-dollar increase in pension wealth reduces nonpension net worth by $0.66. Coefficients for social-security wealth, however, are small in size and are not significantly different from

Table 6–2
Estimated Coefficients for Pension, Thrift, and Social-Security Variables
(t-ratios in parentheses)

	Variable		
Equation	*Pension Wealth*	*Thrift Assets*	*Social-Security Wealth*
Families with married heads			
Nonpension net worth	− .664[b]	−1.200[b]	− .081
	(2.452)	(1.990)	(.675)
Total nonpension assets	− .625[b]	−1.199[b]	− .093
	(2.264)	(1.949)	(.762)
Financial assets	− .453[b]	− .562	− .031
	(2.257)	(1.256)	(.353)
Liquid assets	− .108[b]	− .087	− .010
	(3.358)	(1.213)	(.681)
Families with unmarried heads			
Nonpension net worth	− .218	− .878[b]	− .448
	(1.603)	(1.995)	(1.319)
Total nonpension assets	− .142	− .804[a]	− .322
	(.980)	(1.712)	(.888)
Financial assets	− .091[a]	− .227	− .244[b]
	(1.831)	(1.401)	(1.955)
Liquid assets	− .006	− .168	− .239[b]
	(.180)	(1.450)	(2.679)

Source: Authors' calculations from *1983 Survey of Consumer Finances*, U.S. Government, Federal Reserve Board.
[a]Significantly different from zero at the 10% level.
[b]Significantly different from zero at the 5% level.

zero, suggesting little substitution between social-security wealth and nonpension wealth.

In contrast, for families with unmarried heads, regression results indicate that all three types of retirement assets are substitutes for nonpension wealth. The size of the estimated coefficients suggests only modest substitution between pension or social-security wealth and nonpension wealth. (A one-dollar increase in pensions reduces net worth by $0.22, while a one-dollar increase in social security increases net worth by $0.45.) On the other hand, the results show substantial substitution between thrift assets and nonpension wealth. (A one-dollar increase in thrift assets reduces nonpension net worth by $0.88.) The significance levels of these thrift and pension coefficients tend to be somewhat lower than those for families with married heads, but the *t*-ratios are generally greater than one.

The impact of these retirement programs on the composition of household portfolios is shown in table 6–3. The data in this table, which are derived from the estimated regression coefficients, indicate the effects of one-dollar increases in pension wealth, thrift assets, and social-security wealth on various components of the household balance sheet after holding other family characteristics constant.[8] For example, for families with married heads, the $0.66 reduction in nonpension net worth arising from a one-dollar increase in pension wealth consists of a $0.03 increase in

Table 6–3
Effects of a One-Dollar Increase in Retirement Assets on the Composition of Nonpension Wealth
(dollars)

	Variable		
Item	*Pension Wealth*	*Thrift Assets*	*Social-Security Wealth*
Families with married heads			
Nonpension net worth	− .66	− 1.20	− .08
Total nonpension debt	.03	.00	− .01
Total assets	− .63	− 1.20	− .09
Real assets	− .18	− .64	− .06
Stocks and bonds	− .35	− .47	− .02
Liquid assets	− .11	− .09	− .01
Families with unmarried heads			
Nonpension net worth	− .22	− .88	− .45
Total nonpension debt	.08	.08	.13
Total assets	− .14	− .80	− .32
Real assets	− .05	− .57	− .08
Stocks and bonds	− .08	− .06	.00
Liquid assets	− .01	− .17	− .24

Source: Authors' calculations from *1983 Survey of Consumer Finances*, U.S. Government, Federal Reserve Board.

debts and a $0.63 reduction in assets. Of the $0.63 reduction in assets, $0.18 is in real assets, $0.34 in stocks and bonds, and $0.11 is in liquid assets.

An examination of this table suggests several conclusions. First, pension wealth, thrift assets, and social-security wealth appear to have negligible effects on the amount of debt owed by families headed by persons fifty years of age or older. Age may in part explain this result; these retirement assets might have a larger impact on families in earlier life-cycle stages whose credit use is associated with a growing need for household durables. Second, thrift assets appear to be close substitutes for nonpension assets. A dollar of thrift assets displaces about a dollar of nonpension assets. This decrease consists primarily of a decrease in real assets, although real assets decrease proportionately less than their share in household portfolios. Third, pension wealth has a substantial impact on the nonpension asset holdings of families with married heads. Over half of the assets displaced by pension wealth are stocks and bonds, and nearly three-fourths are financial assets. Fourth, social-security wealth appears to have a negligible effect on the nonpension wealth of these families. Finally, pension and social-security wealth appears to reduce nonpension wealth of families with unmarried heads by a modest amount. Financial assets contribute the largest amount to this reduction. The contribution of any single balance sheet item, however, is relatively small due to the modest size of pension and social-security effects.

Conclusions

Regressions were estimated to investigate the effects of pension and social-security wealth on the size and composition of asset portfolios of families headed by persons fifty years of age or older who are in the labor force but are not self-employed. Results provide reasonable estimates of substitution effects between pension and nonpension assets. They provide some support for the prediction of the simple life-cycle saving model that pensions and social security reduce discretionary saving.

The methods used in this chapter permit a cleaner test than those in previous studies of effects of pensions and social security on household portfolios. The results, however, cannot be generalized to the population as a whole. Additional research is required to investigate the impact of these retirement programs on families headed by persons under fifty years of age and on families headed by self-employed persons. Further work is also needed to apply the theory of portfolio choice to household behavior. The current results are only suggestive. More definitive conclusions require theoretical underpinnings which are not present in this preliminary analysis.

Appendix 6A

Descriptive Statistics

This appendix presents descriptive statistics on pension and social coverage of families, motives for saving, and the composition of uncovered and covered families' asset portfolios. The discussion focuses on families in which the family head was in the labor force. These families, which comprise 70% of the sample (table 6A–1), are the ones for whom retirement-savings choices were relevant.

Pension and Social Security Coverage

Over half of all families in which the family head worked full-time were covered by pensions in 1983, as shown in table 6A–2.[9] Family heads that were not covered by pensions tended to be younger and have lower family incomes than family heads that were covered. (See table 6A–3.) Covered families were disproportionately headed by professionals and managers, while self-employed managers were much more likely to be found among uncovered families than among covered families. However, self-employed managers were also disproportionately represented among families in which only the spouse was covered by a pension.

When social security was taken into account, coverage under a retirement program was virtually universal. Ninety-seven percent of the families in which the head worked full-time were covered by a pension or social security. It is not possible to describe accurately the characteristics of families that were not covered by a pension or social security because the number of these families was too small.

Purposes of Saving

Retirement is one of a number of motives for saving. In order to study which families were saving for retirement and for other purposes, respondents to the *1983 Survey of Consumer Finances* were asked: "People have different reasons for saving. What are your (family's) most important reasons for saving? Anything else?" Answers to this question are

Table 6A–1
Employment Status by Age of Family Head
(*percent distribution*)

Employment status	Age of Family Head (Years)						All Families
	Under 50	50–59	60–64	65–69	70–74	75 and over	
Family head unmarried							
Male, works full-time	10.7%	7.3%	3.6%	*	.5%	.7%	7.7%
Female, works full-time	14.9	15.2	7.1	2.6%	2.6	*	11.8
Temporarily laid-off or unemployed	4.5	2.2	2.0	*	*	*	3.1
Retired, works part-time	*	*	*	1.7	2.5	.9	*
Retired, not in labor force	1.0	7.4	13.7	21.0	32.8	41.8	8.9
Other	5.7	2.6	6.6	10.5	12.5	17.6	6.8
Family head married							
Works full-time, spouse not in labor force	20.6	22.0	19.7	6.4	5.3	2.6	17.6
Works full-time, spouse works full-time	29.5	28.5	17.9	4.9	2.6	*	23.3
Works full-time, spouse works part-time	3.9	2.4	3.7	.7	*	*	3.0
Temporarily laid-off or unemployed	6.0	3.6	1.4	*	2.4	*	4.3
Retired, works part-time	*	*	1.1	4.8	3.6	.6	.7
Retired, not in labor force	1.2	6.8	22.2	44.0	35.2	34.5	10.7
Other	1.9	1.5	1.1	2.9	*	1.0	1.7
Total	100	100	100	100	100	100	100

Source: Authors' calculations from *1983 Survey of Consumer Finances*, U.S. Government, Federal Reserve Board.
Note: Totals may differ from 100% due to rounding.
*Less than 0.5%.

Table 6A–2

Pension and Social-Security Coverage of Families with Head in Labor Force

(percent distribution)

	Age of Family Head (Years)		
	Under 50	50 and Over	All Families
Pension coverage			
Family head unmarried			
Not covered			
Male	6.9%	3.8%	6.1%
Female	10.4	9.6	10.2
Covered			
Male	7.1	5.1	6.6
Female	8.9	10.9	9.4
Family head married			
Neither head nor spouse			
covered	23.9	23.1	23.7
Only head covered	25.1	25.9	25.3
Both head and spouse covered	11.9	15.9	12.9
Only spouse covered	5.7	5.8	5.7
Total	100	100	100
Pension or social-security coverage			
Family head unmarried			
Not covered			
Male	.6	*	.5
Female	1.5	.8	1.3
Covered			
Male	13.4	8.6	12.2
Female	17.8	19.7	18.3
Family head married			
Neither head nor spouse			
covered	1.6	*	1.2
Only head covered	14.5	21.3	16.3
Both head and spouse covered	49.4	48.8	49.2
Only spouse covered	1.2	.5	1.0
Total	100	100	100

Source: Authors' calculations from *1983 Survey of Consumer Finances*, U.S. Government, Federal Reserve Board.

Note: Totals may differ from 100% due to rounding.

*Less than 0.5%.

presented in table 6A–4. The most frequently mentioned purpose of saving, emergencies, was named by 53.7% of all families. The next most commonly cited factor, retirement, appeared in 23.6% of all responses. Often-identified goals also included education (19.0% of families), purchasing durable goods (14.7%), and buying a home (8.8%). Among the purposes not mentioned very often were purchasing investments to earn money, investing in a business, and bequeathing money.

Table 6A–3
Pension Coverage by Various Groups
(percent distributions for families with head in labor force)

Pension coverage	Family Income (Dollars)					
	Less than 10,000	10,000– 19,999	20,000– 29,999	30,000– 49,999	50,000 or More	Total
Family head unmarried						
Not covered						
Male	35.3%	36.7%	11.7%	13.1%	3.3%	100%
Female	47.1	38.7	10.8	2.2	1.2	100
Covered						
Male	8.1	26.4	37.3	21.1	7.2	100
Female	12.0	46.8	28.8	8.8	3.8	100
Family head married						
Neither head nor spouse covered	17.3	30.7	20.0	18.5	13.5	100
Only head covered	4.0	17.2	28.7	35.3	14.8	100
Both head and spouse covered	*	7.3	16.8	50.0	25.7	100
Only spouse covered	2.0	16.3	31.9	36.4	13.5	100
All families	13.9	25.9	23.0	25.1	12.2	100

Pension coverage	Age of Family Head (Years)					
	Less than 25	25–34	35–44	45–54	55–64	65 and over	Total
Family head unmarried							
Not covered							
Male	23.8%	40.9%	16.7%	9.1%	8.2%	1.3%	100%
Female	17.3	26.2	23.1	16.8	11.6	5.0	100
Covered							
Male	10.6	39.4	21.8	18.8	9.5	*	100
Female	7.1	28.3	27.2	19.3	16.9	1.3	100

	Professional or Manager	Self-Employed Manager	Clerical or Sales Worker	Craftsman or Laborer	Miscellaneous	Total
Family head married						
Neither head nor spouse covered	11.5	30.5	22.4	17.7	13.3	4.6	100
Only head covered	2.6	26.1	31.4	24.5	14.4	1.1	100
Both head and spouse covered	2.5	27.0	28.5	22.9	16.9	2.2	100
Only spouse covered	9.1	34.6	22.4	15.2	15.4	3.3	100
All families	8.8	29.7	25.6	19.5	13.8	2.5	100

			Occupation of Family Head			
Pension coverage	*Professional or Manager*	*Self-Employed Manager*	*Clerical or Sales Worker*	*Craftsman or Laborer*	*Miscellaneous*	*Total*
Family head unmarried						
Not covered						
Male	22.7%	6.0%	10.7%	55.3%	5.4%	100%
Female	20.5	3.4	26.8	47.0	2.2	100
Covered						
Male	39.6	*	12.6	46.0	1.8	100
Female	38.2	*	35.5	25.5	.9	100
Family head married						
Neither head nor spouse covered	21.5	14.4	8.1	48.4	7.5	100
Only head covered	30.1	1.1	8.5	56.8	3.5	100
Both head and spouse covered	41.7	*	9.9	47.0	1.4	100
Only spouse covered	27.7	12.6	14.5	39.2	6.0	100
All families	29.4	5.1	13.7	47.8	4.0	100

Source: Authors' calculations from *1983 Survey of Consumer Finances*, U.S. Government, Federal Reserve Board.

Note: Totals may differ from 100% due to rounding.

*Less than 0.5%.

Table 6A–4
Purposes of Saving for Families with Head in Labor Force
(*percent of families in each group mentioning purpose*)

			Purpose				
	Emergencies	Retirement	Education	Purchase home	Purchase durables	Travel	Expenses
Family income							
Less than $10,000	49.5%	10.5%	20.7%	6.9%	18.4%	6.9%	12.7%
$10,000–19,999	53.8	18.0	16.0	10.2	15.7	10.9	7.3
$20,000–29,999	58.6	22.5	16.3	10.8	13.8	11.2	5.3
$30,000–49,999	48.8	30.9	21.7	8.8	14.3	11.4	5.1
$50,000 or more	50.9	37.8	23.4	4.3	11.1	10.8	4.9
Age of family head (years)							
Less than 25	52.5	4.9	16.2	16.1	24.2	12.0	10.2
25–34	55.6	8.8	18.6	15.3	18.5	8.9	7.2
35–44	55.4	20.7	26.4	7.6	13.9	12.6	5.4
45–54	52.4	35.9	18.2	3.1	11.5	10.0	5.2
55–64	44.5	52.0	11.1	1.9	8.2	10.9	7.3
65 and over	39.6	44.3	9.8	*	7.2	5.3	12.7
Occupation of family head							
Professional or manager	52.6	28.0	21.0	6.4	14.5	11.9	4.7
Self-employed manager	46.6	38.3	22.7	3.2	8.1	7.9	6.5
Clerical or sales worker	55.0	23.6	16.1	10.5	14.9	10.3	7.4
Craftsman and laborers	53.5	19.1	18.8	10.5	15.7	9.8	7.5
Other	44.2	27.9	12.6	6.7	13.9	13.0	11.1

Pension coverage							
Family head unmarried							
Not covered							
Male	54.0	11.7	5.5	4.1	17.0	5.0	8.7
Female	58.8	11.5	17.4	5.4	17.5	11.2	9.7
Covered							
Male	51.0	24.3	7.5	8.0	23.8	5.7	4.1
Female	60.5	24.5	12.3	7.1	18.0	14.5	7.4
Family head married							
Neither head nor spouse covered	50.4	21.1	21.4	9.3	10.6	8.3	8.8
Only head covered	50.5	28.5	21.1	10.8	14.9	12.8	4.8
Both head and spouse covered	53.0	29.2	25.7	8.1	13.5	12.6	5.2
Only spouse covered	48.2	32.0	26.8	13.9	10.9	7.9	5.0
All families	52.7	23.6	19.0	8.8	14.7	10.5	6.8

Source: Authors' calculations from *1983 Survey of Consumer Finances*, U.S. Government, Federal Reserve Board.

Note: Because each respondent could identify several purposes, totals do not need to equal 100%.

*Less than 5%.

Motives for saving varied substantially among families. The proportion of families saving for retirement rises dramatically with increasing family income and age of family head. Families headed by self-employed managers were much more likely than families in other occupation groups to save for retirement, but also a relatively high proportion of families headed by professionals and managers were saving for that end.

When families were grouped according to pension coverage, responses on savings motives appeared to support findings of earlier studies by Cagan (1965) and Katona (1965) that concluded that pensions stimulate saving. Of the families with unmarried heads, about 11% that were not covered by pensions and 24% that were covered mentioned retirement as a motive for saving. Similarly, 21% of uncovered families with married heads and about 30% of covered families with married heads were saving for retirement. At this level of analysis, however, it is not possible to separate the effects of pension coverage from those of income, age, and occupation. The higher incomes and relatively strong retirement-saving motive of families headed by professionals and managers contributed to the higher proportion of covered families saving for retirement and may have offset any negative effects of pension coverage on retirement saving. The high proportion of families headed by self-employed managers (80% of which families were not covered by pensions) mentioning retirement as a purpose of saving certainly suggests that pension coverage did influence families' motives for saving.

Pensions and Household Portfolios

The simple life-cycle savings model suggests that families covered by pensions will accumulate smaller amounts of nonpension wealth to finance retirement than uncovered families will. Statistics on average nonpension asset holdings and nonpension net worth of families with married heads appear to support this suggestion; similar statistics for families with unmarried heads, however, do not. (See table 6A–5.) The lower nonpension wealth of uncovered families with unmarried heads may in part be explained by their lower income and age.[10] Relative to their incomes, uncovered families with unmarried heads had higher average nonpension asset holdings and nonpension net worth than covered families with unmarried heads.

Regardless of marital status, families that were covered by pensions were more likely than uncovered families to own financial assets, as shown in table 6A–6. For example, covered families were about twice as likely as uncovered families to own money-market accounts and were about a third more likely to own stocks or bonds. For families with unmarried heads, nearly 20% that were covered by pensions owned IRAs

Table 6A–5
Average Family Income, Total Assets, and Net Equity of Families with Head in Labor Force, by Extent of Pension Coverage

	Family Income	Total Nonpension Assets	Nonpension Net Worth
Pension coverage			
Family head unmarried			
Not covered			
Male	$14,231	$41,146	$34,506
Female	10,272	58,537	51,192
Covered			
Male	24,068	62,212	49,015
Female	18,790	54,788	46,558
Family head married			
Neither head nor spouse covered	26,086	167,380	146,513
Only head covered	35,057	128,960	106,507
Both head and spouse covered	43,517	129,647	102,645
Only spouse covered	33,907	141,910	117,747
All families	26,170	109,681	92,468

Source: Authors' calculations from *1983 Survey of Consumer Finances,* U.S. Government, Federal Reserve Board.

or Keogh accounts, while 11% or fewer of the families that were not covered owned these accounts. For families with married heads, about 30% of covered families and 20% of uncovered families owned IRA or Keogh accounts. Homes and investment real estate were also more likely to be owned by families that were covered by pensions than by uncovered families. The lower asset-ownership figures of uncovered families may be attributed to the greater proportion of families with low incomes and young family heads among uncovered families.

In contrast to financial assets and real estate, uncovered families were more than twice as likely to own businesses than were covered families. This finding, of course, reflects the higher proportion of self-employed among uncovered families.

Asset-ownership patterns of families in which only the spouse was covered by a pension were closer to the ownership patterns of uncovered families than those of other covered families. The relatively higher proportion of self-employed managers and noticeably lower value of pension assets of families in which only the spouse was covered may explain this result. Because the groups appear to be similar, families in which only the spouse was covered will be included with uncovered families in the remaining discussion in this section.

Table 6A–7 presents average ratios of dollar amounts of holdings of

Table 6A–6
Asset and Debt Holdings of Families with Head in Labor Force, by Extent of Pension Coverage
(percent of families in each group that have asset or debt)

Pension coverage	Checking Account	Savings Account	Money-Market Account	IRA or Keogh Account	Certificate of Deposit	Savings Bonds
Family head unmarried						
Not covered						
Male	63.3	51.8	5.2	11.4	10.8	13.1
Female	60.9	53.8	8.4	5.9	12.2	11.7
Covered						
Male	75.9	66.4	16.2	19.0	11.5	16.2
Female	85.3	69.2	15.4	18.2	17.0	23.8
Family head married						
Neither head nor spouse covered	76.0	55.9	11.7	19.6	14.8	18.0
Only head covered	88.1	74.1	12.8	21.3	18.0	30.3
Both head and spouse covered	93.0	81.5	18.6	34.0	24.7	39.0
Only spouse covered	91.1	78.1	22.2	33.9	19.8	20.9
All families	80.7	66.6	13.4	20.6	16.6	23.5

	Stocks or Bonds	Business	Real Estate	House	Mortgage	Consumer Debt
Family head unmarried						
Not covered						
Male	13.4	20.0	11.2	31.9	17.1	56.1
Female	15.9	7.3	10.4	39.2	25.5	61.3
Covered						
Male	26.4	6.7	16.4	41.5	25.0	63.6
Female	25.4	2.6	14.1	45.9	29.1	73.2
Family head married						
Neither head nor spouse covered	20.8	34.6	22.0	65.3	45.2	69.9
Only head covered	27.9	15.0	21.7	78.7	61.8	81.4
Both head and spouse covered	34.7	7.8	27.2	84.1	66.6	86.2
Only spouse covered	18.5	29.4	26.3	73.1	53.8	83.8
All families	24.1	17.3	19.9	63.5	46.1	73.9

Source: Authors' calculations from *1983 Survey of Consumer Finances*, U.S. Government, Federal Reserve Board.

Table 6A-7
Average Ratios of Asset or Debt Values to Family Income for Families with Head in Labor Force, by Extent of Pension Coverage
(percent)

Pension coverage	Checking Account	Savings Account	Money-market Account	IRA or Keogh Account	Certificate of Deposit	Savings Bonds
Family head unmarried						
Not covered						
Male	6.5	11.3	16.2	25.7	52.5	3.0
Female	7.0	13.8	75.9	27.2	116.2	5.5
Covered						
Male	6.4	11.7	34.1	12.2	35.3	5.0
Female	6.0	13.7	28.2	14.0	52.7	5.4
Family head married						
Neither head nor spouse covered	7.6	12.6	40.4	29.5	50.1	3.0
Only head covered	3.9	9.6	28.3	11.5	32.7	3.1
Both head and spouse covered	2.3	8.2	22.3	12.3	29.2	3.1
Only spouse covered	5.1	7.8	41.4	20.2	51.3	3.4
All families	5.3	10.8	34.2	17.7	46.1	3.5

	Stocks or Bonds	Business	Real Estate	House	Mortgage	Consumer Debt
Family head unmarried						
Not covered						
Male	32.8	221.7	147.7	283.3	112.7	39.4
Female	166.3	515.4	305.8	639.5	380.0	37.7
Covered						
Male	48.6	161.3	190.6	204.0	112.9	22.5
Female	47.0	109.8	223.1	335.9	107.4	20.2
Family head married						
Neither head nor spouse covered	69.6	616.0	177.5	336.7	116.3	37.8
Only head covered	59.1	246.9	121.1	218.8	79.3	19.6
Both head and spouse covered	29.9	216.3	87.1	164.4	67.0	16.5
Only spouse covered	37.1	339.0	150.6	202.8	76.6	17.4
All families	59.2	434.5	153.5	272.9	106.0	25.7

Source: Authors' calculations from 1983 *Survey of Consumer Finances*, U.S. Government, Federal Reserve Board.

different asset types to family income for covered and uncovered groups of families. These ratios are computed only for families that own the assets. They indicate the size of various types of asset holdings, adjusted in a rough way for differences in incomes. Average asset-amount-to-income ratios for checking accounts, savings accounts, and savings bonds were relatively small, between 2 and 4%. Uncovered families had higher average ratios for checking accounts than did covered families, but average ratios for savings accounts and savings bonds did not appear to be related to pension coverage.

The next largest group of nonpension assets in household portfolios consisted of other financial assets. Average asset-amount-to-income ratios for money-market accounts, IRAs and Keogh accounts, certificates of deposit, and stocks and bonds generally were between 12 and 70%. Uncovered families had higher average ratios for money-market accounts (except unmarried males), IRAs and Keogh accounts, and certificates of deposit. There was no apparent relationship, however, between pension coverage and average ratios for stocks and bonds.

Real assets were the largest nonpension assets in household portfolios. Average asset-amount-to-income ratios for real assets were generally greater than 100 percent. Uncovered families had much higher average ratios than covered families for businesses, investment real estate (except unmarried males), and homes (except covered families in which only the spouse was covered).

Tables 6A–6 and 6A–7 also show the percentage of families owing mortgage and consumer debts and the average dollar amount of debt-owed-to-income ratio for covered and uncovered groups. Uncovered families were less likely than covered families to owe mortgage or consumer debt. For both types of debt, however, average dollar amount owed-to-income ratios of uncovered families were greater than those of covered families.

Appendix 6B

Table 6B–1
Regression Results: Families with Married Heads

Independent Variables	Nonpension Net Worth	Total Nonpension Assets	Financial Assets	Liquid Assets
		Dependent Variables		
Intercept	−141,009	−142,950	−12,564	−20,540
	(.823)	(.818)	(.099)	(1.013)
Net pension wealth	− .664	− .625	− .453	− .101
	(2.452)	(2.264)	(2.257)	(3.358)
Value of thrift assets	−1.200	−1.990	− .562	− .087
	(1.990)	(1.949)	(1.256)	(1.213)
Net social-security wealth	− .081	− .093	− .031	− .010
	(.675)	(.762)	(.353)	(.681)
Age 52–53	49,678	48,780	24,913	−54.699
	(.870)	(.837)	(.588)	(.008)
Age 54–55	125,155	122,000	84,579	9,353
	(2.151)	(2.055)	(1.959)	(1.358)
Age 56–57	64,895	68,361	−12,545	4,451
	(1.101)	(1.136)	(.287)	(.638)
Age 58–59	159,958	157,028	61,652	17,764
	(2.530)	(2.435)	(1.314)	(2.374)
Age 60–61	112,828	114,643	28,595	15,490
	(1.780)	(1.773)	(.608)	(2.065)
Age 62–63	134,912	131,005	45,167	3,498
	(1.967)	(1.872)	(.888)	(.431)
Age 64–65	198,441	222,071	21,041	43,297
	(2.462)	(2.701)	(.352)	(4.538)
Age 66–70	153,415	147,056	5,175	21,018
	(1.721)	(1.617)	(.078)	(1.992)
Age 71 or older	285,869	283,045	116,097	21,633
	(2.969)	(2.900)	(1.636)	(1.910)
Family income	.097	−1.412	− .043	− .199
	(.005)	(.077)	(.003)	(.093)
Family income above $10,000	6.324	8.509	1.235	.818
	(.322)	(.425)	(.085)	(.352)
Family income above $30,000	− .291	− .788	2.972	.009
	(.088)	(.233)	(1.206)	(.023)
Professional or technical worker	−28,353	−25,343	−18,767	843.885
	(.654)	(.573)	(.583)	(.164)
Clerical or sales worker	41,252	43,901	34,910	−4,995
	(.597)	(.623)	(.681)	(.611)

Table 6B–1 continued

	Dependent Variables			
Independent Variables	Nonpension Net Worth	Total Nonpension Assets	Financial Assets	Liquid Assets
Employed in agriculture, forestry, or mining	512,816 (3.172)	157,149 (3.197)	60,039 (1.680)	13,432 (2.355)
Employed in wholesale or retail trade	−30,078 (.774)	−31,259 (.788)	−19,253 (.668)	5,801 (1.261)
Employed by federal government	−14,904 (.180)	−23,550 (.278)	9,513 (.155)	−3,359 (.342)
Employed by state or local government	−13,994 (.224)	−12,161 (.191)	22,589 (.488)	676.647 (.092)
Union member	−4,137 (.102)	−12,045 (.291)	22,157 (.735)	−817.408 (.170)
Wife works full-time	−19,133 (.378)	−16,200 (.314)	−16,357 (.436)	8,202 (1.369)
Share of income contributed by wife	6,039 (.056)	4,693 (.043)	42,776 (.538)	−3,787 (.299)
Wife self-employed	47,143 (.847)	52,162 (.918)	6,406 (.155)	10,420 (1.581)
Family head has high-school diploma	92,178 (2.285)	98,738 (2.399)	20,980 (.701)	7,982 (1.672)
Family head has college degree	80,868 (1.456)	90,479 (1.596)	29,645 (.719)	7,332 (1.115)
Wife has college degree	52,589 (1.175)	52,007 (1.139)	33,405 (1.006)	−5,526 (1.043)
Number of children living in household	−19,541 (1.144)	−19,061 (.360)	−26,716 (2.019)	98.822 (.049)
Total number of children	1,971 (.236)	3,077 (.360)	1,455 (.234)	−1,031 (1.041)
Number of persons age 65 or older in household	39,150 (.410)	42,516 (.437)	16,191 (.229)	5,243 (.464)
Family head has bad health	−38,853 (1.029)	−40,407 (1.049)	26,054 (.930)	−300.263 (.067)
Wife has bad health	−35,491 (.966)	−38,939 (1.039)	52,313 (1.920)	−3,234 (.744)
Family has health insurance	−6,132 (.097)	3,194 (.049)	815.890 (.017)	3,356 (.448)
Nonwhite or Hispanic	−8,878 (.176)	16,179 (.314)	−8,230 (.220)	1,145 (.192)
Rural	139,497 (3.518)	134,458 (3.323)	44,641 (1.517)	2,871 (.612)
Urban	1,632 (.038)	−4,441 (.102)	20,236 (.639)	3,737 (.740)
South	−49,043 (1.141)	−39,392 (.898)	−57,402 (1.800)	−937.487 (.184)
West	50,781 (1.041)	72,129 (1.449)	−54,167 (1.497)	4,660 (.807)

Table 6B–1 continued

	Dependent Variables			
Independent Variables	Nonpension Net Worth	Total Nonpension Assets	Financial Assets	Liquid Assets
North-central	4,773 (.019)	17,110 (.384)	−41,448 (1.278)	8,819 (1.704)
Saving for retirement	−27,274 (.847)	−32,423 (.987)	−22,174 (.928)	2,286 (.600)
Saving for education	53,915 (1.190)	53,663 (1.161)	23,602 (.702)	5,232 (.975)
Willing to take high risks	38,122 (.592)	39,887 (.607)	−21,568 (.451)	−12,159 (1.594)
Not willing to take any risk	7,663 (.201)	6,189 (.159)	23,304 (.824)	3,877 (.859)
Willing to tie up money for a long time	−28,975 (.612)	−32,558 (.674)	8,831 (.251)	9,736 (1.737)
Not willing to tie up money at all	−54,662 (1.203)	−53,485 (1.154)	−12,053 (.358)	−9,058 (1.684)
Most of savings come from inheritance	−68,000 (1.011)	−71,621 (1.042)	−38,286 (.766)	568.127 (.071)
Expect to receive inheritance	74,172 (1.432)	71,734 (1.357)	51,181 (1.332)	1,073 (.175)
Aware of marginal tax rate	−16,924 (.369)	−20,542 (.439)	1,536 (.045)	3,875 (.714)
Reported marginal tax rate	771.545 (.618)	994.876 (.780)	139.517 (.151)	58.336 (.394)
Adjusted R^2	41.69	42.75	30.95	35.08

Note: t-ratios appear in parentheses.

Table 6B–2
Regression Results: Families with Unmarried Heads

	Dependent Variables			
Independent Variables	Nonpension Net Worth	Total Nonpension Assets	Financial Assets	Liquid Assets
Intercept	−74,701 (2.027)	−71,883 (1.829)	−16,061 (1.185)	−6,785 (.701)
Net pension wealth	−0.217 (1.603)	−0.142 (.980)	−0.091 (1.831)	−0.006 (.180)
Value of thrift assets	−0.878 (1.995)	−0.804 (1.712)	−0.227 (1.401)	−0.168 (1.450)
Net social-security wealth	−0.448 (1.319)	−0.322 (.888)	−0.244 (1.955)	−0.239 (2.679)
Age 52–53	57,708 (2.736)	61,114 (2.716)	11,801 (1.521)	9,114 (1.645)

(*Table 6B–2 continued*)

Table 6B–2 continued

Independent Variables	Nonpension Net Worth	Total Nonpension Assets	Financial Assets	Liquid Assets
		Dependent Variables		
Age 54–55	49,102 (2.587)	38,105 (1.882)	11,561 (1.656)	4,964 (.996)
Age 56–57	14,502 (.722)	6,922 (.323)	12,475 (1.689)	5,748 (1.090)
Age 58–59	10,126 (.431)	9,088 (.363)	−2,119 (.245)	−839.520 (.136)
Age 60–61	74,109 (3.288)	65,825 (2.738)	19,485 (2.350)	18,256 (3.084)
Age 62–63	66,337 (2.630)	59,835 (2.224)	18,990 (2.046)	11,165 (1.685)
Age 64–65	115,327 (3.054)	116,227 (2.886)	32,301 (2.326)	29,010 (2.925)
Age 66–70	60,795 (1.974)	46,516 (1.416)	19,869 (1.753)	17,218 (2.128)
Age 71 or older	87,243 (2.388)	74,433 (1.910)	27,179 (2.022)	25,121 (2.618)
Family income	4.081 (1.245)	3.822 (1.093)	0.641 (.532)	0.415 (.482)
Family income above $10,000	−1.717 (.454)	−1.362 (.337)	0.131 (.094)	0.139 (.140)
Family income above $30,000	−0.928 (.560)	−0.561 (.317)	−0.271 (.445)	−0.563 (1.292)
Professional or technical	43,976 (2.425)	49,144 (2.541)	3,239 (.486)	3,972 (.834)
Clerical or sales	13,024 (.798)	15,766 (.906)	−719.750 (.120)	4,181 (.976)
Employed in agriculture, forestry, or mining	120,927 (4.505)	121,326 (4.238)	4,493 (.455)	5,972 (.847)
Employed in wholesale or retail trade	19,863 (1.394)	21,405 (1.409)	5,290 (1.009)	59.488 (.016)
Employed by federal government	16,140 (.566)	10,516 (.345)	1,734 (.165)	4,688 (.625)
Employed by state or local government	2,161 (.145)	−4,443 (.280)	−360.356 (.066)	4,125 (1.057)
Union member	1,620 (.112)	−2,343 (1.52)	4,276 (.804)	−1,803 (.475)
Family head has high-school diploma	24,273 (1.745)	22,461 (1.514)	7,313 (1.429)	6,212 (1.700)
Family head has college degree	11,466 (.603)	20,574 (1.015)	6,391 (.914)	−756.935 (.152)
Number of children living in household	8,045 (1.149)	9,515 (1.275)	620.428 (.241)	2,215 (1.205)
Total number of children	−731.144 (.238)	114.903 (.035)	−773.933 (.686)	−428.646 (.532)
Number of persons age 65 or older in household	47,104 (2.446)	39,428 (1.919)	16,208 (2.287)	16,165 (3.196)

Table 6B–2 continued

Independent Variables	Dependent Variables			
	Nonpension Net Worth	Total Nonpension Assets	Financial Assets	Liquid Assets
Family head has bad health	− 19,183 (1.560)	− 16,280 (1.241)	− 3,715 (.821)	− 7,477 (2.315)
Nonwhite or Hispanic	− 21,409 (1.541)	− 22,746 (1.535)	− 8,264 (1.617)	− 5.139 (1.408)
Family head is female	17,855 (1.330)	24,325 (1.699)	3,662 (.742)	350.280 (.099)
Family head is widowed	9,473 (.720)	4,829 (.344)	6,505 (1.343)	4,133 (1.196)
Family head never married	36,799 (1.904)	35,613 (1.728)	10,507 (1.478)	7,274 (1.433)
Rural	10,960 (.755)	11,055 (.714)	866.656 (.162)	4,902 (1.286)
Urban	− 7,409 (.558)	− 10,097 (.713)	− 4,424 (.906)	1,332 (.382)
South	426.583 (.028)	1,314 (.082)	3,349 (.606)	− 1,916 (.486)
West	5,501 (.306)	5,096 (.265)	− 440.290 (.066)	948.157 (.201)
North-central	7,500 (.437)	6,612 (.361)	− 1,583 (.251)	− 3,080 (.683)
Saving for retirement	− 10,096 (.872)	− 9,183 (.743)	5,644 (1.324)	2,320 (.763)
Saving for education	− 21,728 (1.108)	− 28,192 (1.347)	2,770 (.384)	− 2,676 (.519)
Willing to take high risks	− 21,542 (1.017)	− 15,264 (.676)	− 15,325 (1.967)	− 3,888 (.699)
Not willing to take any risk	10,463 (.810)	10,092 (.732)	1,203 (.253)	1,775 (.523)
Not willing to tie up money for a long time	34,050 (2.023)	36,801 (2.050)	11,967 (1.933)	4,352 (.985)
Not willing to tie up money at all	− 23,262 (1.597)	− 26,021 (1.656)	− 7,217 (1.332)	− 8,286 (2.142)
Most of savings come from inheritance	− 6,758 (.315)	− 4,371 (.191)	9,141 (1.159)	− 283.152 (.050)
Expect to receive inheritance	4,188 (.184)	1,848 (.076)	− 3,807 (.455)	− 4,862 (.814)
Aware of marginal tax rate	7,355 (.489)	11,270 (.702)	3,575 (.646)	5,143 (1.302)
Reported marginal tax rate	− 160.709 (.324)	− 388.325 (.735)	− 96.671 (.530)	− 158.348 (1.216)
Adjusted R^2	43.22	43.25	22.22	26.92

Source: Authors' calculations from *1983 Survey of Consumer Finances*, U.S. Government, Federal Reserve Board.

Note: *t*-ratios appear in parentheses.

Notes

1. For further discussion, see Munnell (1982, 62–72).
2. See Feldstein (1974, 906–10).
3. See Auerbach (1983) for a critique of the estimation technique.
4. For further discussion of the content, design, and data-preparation of the survey and a presentation of the basic results, see Avery et al. (1984a, 1984b).
5. Specific calculations were done as follows. Any pensions currently received by household members were converted to present-value form utilizing the 1982 income-received and standard-mortality tables, assuming no survivor benefits or inflation indexing. Values for pensions of the current job (or past jobs not yet receiving benefits) were computed similarly. However, in many cases respondents gave their pension as a replacement rate of their final wage. Thus it was necessary to extrapolate wages to the date of expected retirement. This was done using estimated intraoccupation real-wage growth rates and Social Security Trustees' economywide productivity and inflation rates. The private-pension-contribution liability was also calculated applying reported contribution rates to the same wage projections.
6. Social-security benefits were calculated in one of two ways. The present value for households currently receiving benefits was computed using 1982 reported benefits, standard-mortality tables and Social Security Trustees' projections of future benefit indexing. For households not currently receiving benefits, values for both primary and spousal/widow benefits were calculated based on current and projected social-security rules. Aggregate job-history information and specific data from up to three current and past jobs reported by respondents were used to construct a year-by-year wage profile for each household. These were used with projections of future wage income and reported expectations of the starting date for benefits as inputs to current (and projected) social-security-benefit formulas. Spousal benefits were computed in a similar fashion. Assumptions about future indexing and standard-mortality tables were used to convert expected-benefit amounts into present values. The social-security-contribution liability was calculated in a similar manner to the private-pension liability using projected tax rates.
7. This specification takes into account differences in replacement rates required to maintain preretirement living standards and in social-security benefit levels at different levels of income. For example, low-income workers would need about 78% of prior earnings to maintain their preretirement standard of living. They would receive about 61% of prior earnings from social security. In contrast, workers with maximum earnings would need 56% of earnings to prevent a decline in their standard of living. Social security would replace about 28% of past income. See Munnell (1982, pp. 19–25) for further discussion.
8. Because total debt is equal to total assets less net worth, the difference in the pension-wealth coefficients in the two equations is an estimate of the effect of pensions on total debt outstanding. Estimates for real assets and for stocks and bonds were obtained in a similar fashion.
9. Coverage includes that from current job regardless of vesting and expected pensions from previous jobs.

10. See Avery et al. (1984a, 1984b) for details on asset holding and wealth by income and age groups.

References

Auerbach, Alan J. "Portfolio Composition and Pension Wealth: Comment." In *Financial Aspects of the United States Pension System,* ed. Zvi Bodie and John B. Shoven. Chicago: University of Chicago for the National Bureau of Economic Research, 1983.

Avery, Robert B., Gregory E. Elliehausen, Glenn B. Canner, and Thomas A. Gustafson. "Survey of Consumer Finances, 1983." *Federal Reserve Bulletin* 70 (September 1984a): 679–92.

———. "Survey of Consumer Finances, 1983: A Second Report." *Federal Reserve Bulletin* 70 (December 1984b): 857–68.

Barro, Robert. "Are Government Bonds Net Wealth?" *Journal of Political Economy* 82 (November–December 1974): 1095–117.

Blinder, Alan S., Roger H. Gordon, and Donald E. Wise. *An Empirical Study of the Effects of Pensions and the Saving and Labor Supply Decisions of Older Men.* Report prepared for the U.S. Department of Labor. Princeton, N.J.: Mathtech, Inc., 1981.

Cagan, Phillip. *The Effect of Pension Plans on Aggregate Saving: Evidence from a Sample Survey.* Occasional Paper no. 95. New York: Columbia University Press for the National Bureau of Economic Research, 1965.

Diamond, Peter and Jerry Hausman. "Individual Savings Behavior." Paper prepared for the National Commission on Social Security, Washington, D.C., May 1980.

Feldstein, Martin S. "Social Security, Induced Retirement, and Aggregate Capital Accumulation." *Journal of Political Economy* 82 (September–October 1974): 905–26.

Feldstein, Martin S. and Anthony J. Pellechio. "Social Security and Household Wealth Accumulation: New Microeconomic Evidence." *Review of Economics and Statistics* 61 (August 1979): 361–68.

Hubbard, R. Glenn. "Social Security and Household Portfolio Allocation." Working Paper no. 1361. National Bureau of Economic Research, Cambridge, Mass., June 1984.

Katona, George. *Private Pensions and Individual Saving.* Monograph no. 40. Ann Arbor, Mich.: Institute for Social Research, 1965.

Kotlikoff, Laurence J. "Testing the Theory of Social Security and Life Cycle Accumulation." *American Economic Review* 69 (June 1979): 396–410.

Leimer, Dean R. and Selig Lesnoy. "Social Security and Private Saving: A Reexamination of the Time Series Evidence Using Alternative Social Security Wealth Variables." Paper presented at the ninety-third annual meeting of the American Economic Association, Denver, September 1980.

Munnell, Alecia H. *The Economics of Private Pensions.* Washington, D.C.: Brookings Institution, 1982.

———. *The Future of Social Security*. Washington, D.C.: Brookings Institution, 1977.

———. "Private Pensions and Saving: New Evidence." *Journal of Political Economy* 84 (October 1976): 1013–32.

Part III
Policies toward Savings: Individual Perspectives

7
Savings and Government Deficits

Robert Ortner

Ｔhere is a widespread belief today that large government deficits and borrowing are depressing the economy by crowding out other borrowers. Another common assumption is that the inflow of foreign capital is financing and stimulating a large part of our economic expansion. These are both misconceptions. In fact, the effects of these two forces are the reverse: the large budget deficits are stimulative, while foreign capital inflows—and the trade deficits which accompany them—act as a drag on the economy. In addition, while there has been some crowding out in the U.S. economy, it is not just the traditional sectors such as housing which have been crowded out. Financial deregulation and floating exchange rates have added manufacturers to the "crowd."

One way of dealing with these popular misconceptions is to make use of the simple concept of saving and investment. For any time period, our national income accounts define saving and investment as equal. But this is purely an accounting identity. To analyze economic change, the concept of desired saving and investment is more useful. An increase in desired saving (a drop in consumption) relative to investment will tend to slow the economy, and saving and investment will equate at a lower level. Conversely, an increase in desired investment relative to saving will tend to stimulate the economy.

Government Deficits

Many people have expressed concern that government borrowing is absorbing too large a share of national resources. A typical comment about budget deficits is that "the government is consuming about 50% of the

---

The author thanks Carl E. Cox, director of the Department of Commerce Office of Economic Conditions, for his generous assistance in the preparation of the material. Responsibility for the remaining errors is mine. The opinions expressed by the author are his own and do not necessarily represent the views of the U.S. Department of Commerce.

available saving flows and there simply is not much room to finance new cars, new houses, and new factories."[1] This argument is misleading. The data on which these comments are based usually are grouped as shown in table 7–1. Using this grouping, the 1984 government deficit of $175.8 billion was 43% of net saving. Note that the government deficit is listed under investment. If one showed the federal deficit as negative saving, which would be more accurate, total net saving would be reduced from $410.4 billion to $234.6 billion. Last year's deficit then becomes 75% of net saving. Various similar calculations for 1982 show the deficit ranging upwards from 75% to over 100% of net saving. Yet after 1982, the economy managed one of its strongest recoveries in the postwar period. Obviously, something is wrong with the analysis.

The presentation in table 7–1 distorts the relationship between deficits and total saving, which only exaggerates the problem. The use of net saving vastly understates the resources available to finance real investment activity. Corporate profits shown are calculated after book (noncash) charges for depreciation are deducted; noncorporate depreciation also is not included. Total depreciation, $403 billion in 1984, is placed under investment and subtracted from gross investment.

Table 7–2 is similar to the standard presentation of saving and investment as published in the U.S. Department of Commerce's *Survey of Current Business*. Depreciation is properly included under saving as a source of funds, but net foreign investment is placed on the investment side. Despite its name, "net foreign investment" represents funds available to the financial markets and should remain under saving. The minus sign means that it was a net inflow of $93.4 billion in 1984. If shifted to the saving side, the sign would be reversed to show an additional source of funds, raising total gross saving from $544.4 billion to $637.8 billion.

The larger totals still understate financial resources available be-

Table 7–1
Net Saving and Investment, 1984
($ billions)

Investment			Saving	
Net private domestic investment		$234.6	Personal saving	$156.1
Gross investment	637.8		Undistributed corporate profits	115.4
Less capital consumption			State and local government	
allowance	403.2		surplus	52.9
Federal government deficit		175.8	Net foreign investment	93.4
			Statistical discrepancy	−7.4
Total		410.4		410.4

Source: U.S. Department of Commerce, Bureau of Economic Analysis.

Table 7–2
Gross Saving and Investment, 1984
($ billions)

Investment			Saving		
Private domestic investment		$637.8	Personal saving		$156.1
			Noncorporate capital		
Residential	153.9		consumption allowance		157.0
Business fixed investment	425.7		Corporate cash flow		361.6
			Undistributed corporate		
Change in inventories	58.2		profits	115.4	
			Capital consumption		
			allowance	246.2	
			State and local government		
Net foreign investment		−93.4	surplus		52.9
			Federal government surplus		−175.8
			Gross saving		551.8
			Statistical discrepancy		−7.4
Gross investment		544.4	Gross saving and discrepancy		544.4

Source: U.S. Department of Commerce, Bureau of Economic Analysis.

cause, in effect, borrowing and lending are netted. Tables 7–3 and 7–4 show credit market sources and uses of funds from the Federal Reserve Board's flow of funds accounts. In 1984, total credit market sources and funds raised amounted to $717 billion. Even this total understates resources. In most sectors, the term *funds raised* represents changes in loans outstanding, which are the net result of new extensions less repayments. And not all sources of credit are included. For example, trade credit, security credit, and unpaid tax liabilities are omitted.

Using this more complete picture of funds available, the federal def-

Table 7–3
Sources of Funds Supplied to Credit Markets
($ billions)

	1980	1981	1982	1983	1984
U.S. government	$20.9	$22.8	$22.5	$3.9	$20.9
U.S. government-sponsored Agencies	0.8	0.8	0.4	1.7	−2.4
Monetary authorities	4.5	9.2	9.8	10.9	8.4
Foreign	1.5	7.6	−8.6	49.2	66.5
Households	286.1	342.6	316.3	372.4	498.7
Nonfinancial corporations	15.7	20.0	30.3	46.5	15.2
Farm and nonfarm noncorporate businesses	0.6	2.8	1.9	3.8	6.1
State and local governments	15.3	12.9	31.6	36.3	42.1
Financial sector and other	26.4	−11.2	15.8	20.6	61.5
Total	371.8	407.6	419.8	545.3	717.0

Source: Federal Reserve Board, Flow of Funds Bulletin.

Table 7–4
Funds Raised in Credit Markets by Nonfinancial Sectors
($ billions)

	1980	1981	1982	1983	1984
U.S. government	$79.2	$87.4	$161.3	$186.6	$198.8
Foreign	27.2	27.2	15.7	18.9	1.7
Households	122.1	127.5	94.5	175.4	241.6
Nonfinancial corporations	78.1	102.9	70.0	59.5	163.5
Farm and nonfarm noncorporate businesses	48.1	56.5	47.1	68.2	78.5
State and local governments	17.2	6.2	31.3	36.7	33.0
Total	371.8	407.6	419.8	545.3	717.0

Source: Federal Reserve Board, Flow of Funds Bulletin.

icit (borrowing) in 1982 amounted to 38% of credit market funds raised. Among the sectors listed in table 7–4, the federal government was the largest borrower. There were dire warnings at that time that the private economy would be crowded out. Nonetheless, economic activity and private borrowing grew strongly. In 1984, despite a larger deficit, the federal government's share of borrowing had shrunk to 28%. Why did the economy grow despite the rising deficit? It didn't. It grew in part because of it.

The government deficit is a form of dissaving. In judging the impact of the deficit, one must distinguish between the effects of fiscal policy on the economy and the effects of the economy on the deficit. Measures of structural deficits attempt to remove the latter effects by holding output constant. A rising structural deficit represents declining saving which is stimulative. Yet, whether less government saving is translated into real growth depends on two other conditions: real resources available and accommodation by the Federal Reserve Board. At the end of 1982, operating rates were down to about 70%. Three years later, with the help of a strong rise in business fixed investment, capacity utilization is still a moderate 81%. The second condition—the need for monetary accommodation—requires little comment. It was recognized by classical economists and has been rediscovered in recent years through several bouts of credit- and interest-rate-crunches. Given an economy with a reasonable amount of slack and an accommodative monetary policy, one should not be surprised that the deficit contributed to growth, rather than retarded it.

Foreign Capital Inflow

The newspaper article cited at the beginning of the chapter also referred to "our dependence on foreign capital" and the dangers of a "sudden diminution of foreign savings flows." Today's conventional wisdom is that if foreign investors pull out of dollar assets, they will dampen U.S. growth and may even cause a recession.

These are misconceptions with respect to both the magnitudes involved and the direction of the effects. Foreign capital inflows do add to financial resources. Yet at the same time, the growing current account deficit is depressing the economy, because it reflects mainly the rising trade deficit. When one considers that the capital inflow equals the current account deficit (except for statistical discrepancies), it is clear that the claims that capital inflows are helping the economy and current account deficits hurting it cannot both be right.

Tables 7–1 and 7–2 show that foreign investment in the United States totaled $93.4 billion in 1984. The inflow is shown also in table 7–3 as a source of funds. The entry in table 7–3 is smaller mainly because these are funds supplied to the credit markets. Foreign direct investment in the United States (retained earnings and equity purchases) was $23 billion. While the share of funds supplied to the credit market by foreign sources has grown in recent years, it amounted to only 9% of total funds raised in 1984. This level can hardly be described as indicating a dependence. The foreign inflow could be replaced easily by domestic sources. For example, although the Federal Reserve provides a relatively small amount of funds directly, it can increase the supply indirectly by holding down interest rates and encouraging income and saving to rise.

The more important issue is the effect of this inflow on the U.S. economy. Rather than supporting and stimulating growth, as some have argued, it has been a depressant. This effect can be seen in tables 7–5 and 7–6. The data shown in table 7–5 are separate estimates made by the Commerce Department and the Federal Reserve. Net foreign investment listed in the lower portion of the table is the current account balance with some adjustments.[2]

Conceptually, the net inflow of capital is equal to the current account deficit. They differ only because of discrepancies of measurement. Since 1982, the current account movements have been dominated by the growing trade deficit. In fact, the increasing trade deficit was the means by which the net inflow of capital grew. The dollar began to rise in late 1980, reflecting a shift in preferences of both foreign and American investors. The increase in desired saving by foreigners in the United States did not result in a rise in actual saving (or in a net capital inflow) until the current account moved into deficit. Since then, foreigners have increased their income in the United States (by raising their exports to the United States), but have not increased imports from the United States. In other words, they increased their saving here. As is always the case,

Table 7–5
U.S. Capital Flows
($ billions)

	1980	1981	1982	1983	1984
Balance of Payments Basis (U.S. Department of Commerce)					
Changes in foreign assets in the U.S. (inflow)	58.1	81.3	95.2	81.7	92.8
Changes in U.S. assets abroad (outflow)	86.1	111.0	118.9	49.5	21.2
Net inflow	−28.0	−29.7	−23.7	32.2	71.6
Current account balance	1.9	6.3	−9.2	−41.6	−101.6
Allocations of SDR (Special Drawing Rights)	1.1	1.1	—	—	—
Statistical discrepancy	25.0	22.3	32.9	9.3	30.0
	28.0	29.7	23.7	−32.2	−71.6
National Income Accounts Basis (Federal Reserve)					
Changes in foreign assets in the U.S. (inflow)	29.7	34.2	0.9	63.5	87.4
Changes in U.S. assets abroad (outflow)	56.5	61.5	35.2	36.8	19.0
Net inflow	−26.8	−27.3	−34.3	26.7	68.5
Net foreign investment	5.1	4.7	−6.6	−33.9	−93.4[a]
Statistical discrepancy	21.7	22.6	40.8	7.2	24.9
	26.8	27.3	34.3	−26.7	−68.5

Source: Federal Reserve Board, Flow of Funds Bulletin and U.S. Department of Commerce.
[a]Value has been updated from published Federal Reserve data which do not include latest revisions.

increased saving tends to depress the economy, and increased saving by foreigners in the U.S. is no exception.

The result is evident in the remaining data in table 7–6. In all the major categories shown except autos (because of the auto import quotas) foreign producers have raised their U.S. market share. As a result, growth in GNP has fallen consistently behind growth in domestic purchases. It is true that the rising dollar has helped to slow inflation in this country. But the shift in capital flows toward the United States has slowed real growth, not stimulated it.

One little-noticed effect of our accumulating current account deficits is that the United States's net foreign investment position has shifted from creditor to debtor. From a peak of $149.5 billion at the end of 1982, our positive balance slipped to only $32.4 billion at the end of

Table 7–6
Effects of Net Capital Inflows

	1980	1981	1982	1983	1984
Exchange value of the dollar (December)[a]	92.0	100.3	111.3	118.0	129.5
Current account balance ($ bill.)	1.9	6.3	−9.2	−41.6	−101.6
Merchandise trade balance ($ bill.)	−25.5	−28.0	−36.5	−61.1	−107.4
Balance of receipts on income from assets ($ bill.)	30.4	34.1	27.8	23.5	18.1
Ratio of imports to final sales (1972 $ or units)					
Capital goods except autos (%)	15.6	17.4	19.5	20.2	25.9
Consumer durable goods except autos (%)	13.1	14.2	14.5	14.9	17.3
Autos (%)	26.8	27.5	27.8	26.0	23.5
Consumer nondurable goods (%)	1.3	1.5	1.6	1.8	2.3
Growth in gross domestic purchases (1972 $, 4th qtr/4th qtr, %)	−0.9	1.9	−0.4	8.0	6.7
Growth in GNP (1972 $, 4th qtr/4th qtr, %)	−0.8	1.6	−1.5	6.3	5.7

Source: Morgan Guaranty Bank and U.S. Department of Commerce.
[a]U.S. trade-weighted value of the dollar, 1980–1982 = 100.

1984. The statistical discrepancy in 1984 was almost as large. Most analysts believe that the main source of the discrepancy is an understatement of capital inflows. If so, we may have become a net debtor at the end of 1984 or, if not then, almost surely by now.

As a result of this shift, our favorable balance on asset income is also shrinking, as table 7–6 shows. In 1981, an income surplus of $34.1 billion was sufficient to cover unilateral transfers out of the country and a trade deficit of $28.0 billion, leaving a current account surplus. By 1988, our remaining surplus on asset income will also fall into deficit. That means we will have to achieve a trade surplus to bring the current account into balance.

Whatever Happened to "Crowding Out?"

Recent changes in financial markets and the strong dollar are revising our concept of crowding out. According to conventional wisdom, the large budget deficit was supposed to crowd out the interest-sensitive sectors, especially construction. Yet, the construction industry has enjoyed a strong recovery and, apart from some slippage in 1984 when interest rates rose, it has held up well. Why wasn't housing crowded out? As indicated earlier, one reason is that the impact of government borrowing was not as severe as its relationship to net saving implied. And the weakness in the economy caused by falling net exports permitted easier monetary policy than otherwise would have been the case. Two other developments have relieved homebuilding of its traditional role as financial whipping-boy: financial market deregulation and floating exchange rates.

Under the regime of Regulation Q, which set maximum interest rates that savings and commercial banks could pay on deposits, rising rates led to outflows of deposits, depriving homebuilders of their main sources of credit. Crowding out occurred primarily because of the unavailability of funds. The Federal Reserve began to remove these ceilings in the early 1970s, a process which is still continuing. During the past few years, NOW accounts and money market deposit accounts have been legalized nationwide and, in 1983, super NOW accounts were introduced. Demand for housing still falls when mortgage rates rise but the impact of high rates alone is much less than the impact of the absence of funds.

Floating exchange rates also have changed the nature of crowding out. One of the reasons for the strong dollar is high U.S. interest rates. As a result, interest rates have indirectly had a large impact on U.S. foreign trade, which is composed mainly of manufacturing and agriculture. Since mid-1984, imports have absorbed most of the growth in purchases of capital goods and consumer durables, leaving almost no net gain for domestic producers. Thus, credit restraint still results in crowding out, but part of its effect has shifted from construction to manufacturing.

Whither the Dollar and the Economy?

Since mid-1984, the economy has slowed sharply. As a result, interest rates have eased somewhat and the dollar has slipped. With the prospect of moderate growth for the U.S. economy, it is quite possible that the high reached by the dollar in February 1985 will be its peak for this cycle. If foreign and U.S. investors now begin, on balance, to try to reduce their saving in the United States and shift part of their portfolios abroad, what are the likely effects here?

First, as a group, investors probably will not succeed in reducing their saving in, or capital flow to, the United States very much if at all this year. A shift in their desired saving away from the United States will lower the dollar's value. But a lower dollar will raise U.S. exports and reduce imports only with a lag of a year or more, depending on how much and how quickly the dollar falls. By raising import prices, the nominal trade balance actually will worsen initially, until purchasers here and abroad shift the physical volume of their purchases sufficiently toward American goods. This means that the trade and current account deficits will worsen this year, and the net inflow of capital will rise. The actual net inflow of capital will not begin to shrink until the trade and current account deficits do.

A drop in the dollar would raise inflation somewhat, depending on how much the dollar falls and on other conditions in the economy. Even if the dollar falls 25 to 30%, the impact may not be very great. A large share of our imports are priced in dollars, most notably oil and automobiles. And, at this time, underlying determinants of inflation are favorable: growth has slowed, operating rates currently are a comfortable 81%, and wage settlements are moderate.

What about real growth? If investors drive down the dollar, rather than depress the economy, they will eventually stimulate it. U.S. manufacturers will be crowded in again as our trade balance improves. A critical question will be how the Fed reacts to these developments of a pickup in both inflation and real growth. If it "leans against the wind," it will add to any rise in interest rates. Thus, homebuilding may yet find itself in its familiar crowded-out role.

As a nation, we have been living beyond our means during the last few years, consuming more goods and services than we produce. This disequilibrium cannot continue indefinitely. Eventually, the pendulum will swing the other way. With a deficit in asset income, bringing the current account into balance will mean that, for a time, we will have to produce more than we consume, working harder and enjoying it less.

Notes

1. *New York Times,* February 24, 1985.
2. See footnote 10 to U.S. International Transactions Tables 1–10a, *Survey of Current Business,* June 1984.

8
Savings and Government Policy

Barry P. Bosworth

I n recent years we have witnessed a tremendous surge of emphasis on the part of economists and policymakers in the design of tax measures aimed at increasing incentives for private saving. The discussion has reached the point that the effect of such measures on saving incentives has become a major criterion for evaluating the various proposals for tax reform. From several perspectives, I believe, that focus of the discussion is misdirected.

What seems almost unnoticed in the debate on private saving incentives is that, after several decades of relative stability, the national saving rate has fallen sharply in recent years. That decline, however, does not reflect any weakening of the private saving rate. Rather it is the result of a substantial increase in government dissaving—the budget deficit. If the United States were really serious about the goal of increasing capital formation, it could achieve it by a concentrated effort to reduce the budget deficit, rather than by proposals to expand private saving incentives—particularly when we have little or no evidence on which to evaluate these proposals. In this respect, the current discussion of private saving incentives is diverting attention from the fundamental problem of government budget deficits and their link to the national rate of capital formation.

From a capital-formation perspective, the focus of our concern should be the national rate of saving, not just private saving and certainly not the personal saving rate. The distinction between personal and business saving is largely an artificial creation of the national income accounts. It matters little whether income is saved in the form of corporate retained earnings or paid out to stockholders who save in their own name. And certainly there is no reason to distinguish between the saving of corporate and unincorporated businesses, even though the latter is included within the category of personal saving. At the same time there is little benefit to any increase in private saving if it comes at the expense of increased government dissaving.

Trends in National Saving

Proposals for expanding tax incentives for private saving are often prefaced by reference to a declining trend in the private saving in the United States. As shown in table 8–1, the net private saving rate has been an extremely constant share of income over the post-World War II period, averaging 9% of net national product.[1] Although the data in table 8–1 cover only the postwar period, estimates extending back to the prior century (before the imposition of the income tax) show the same stability.

There has been a significant decline in the national saving rate since the 1960s, but it is entirely due to the rising size of the government budget deficit. In fact, the deficit has absorbed in excess of 50% of private saving since 1980. On the other hand, there has been no significant change in the private saving rate, despite a substantial decline in real rates of return on savings during the 1970s and large increases in the 1980s. Apparently, financial deregulation and the growth of investment retirement accounts (IRAs) have led to dramatic shifts in the form of saving but little or no change in its overall level.

The rate of national investment has, of course, fallen by an identical amount. Yet, the United States has been able to maintain domestic capital formation by liquidating its assets abroad. That is shown in table 8–1, where net foreign investment is reported to be a negative 2.8% of net output in 1984—a combination of lower investment (lending) abroad and increased foreign investment (borrowing) in the United States. The sharp reduction in overall investment has been overlooked in all the

Table 8–1
**U.S. Saving and Investment as Percentages of Net National Product,
1951–1984**

	1951– 1960	1961– 1970	1971– 1980	1984
Net saving[a]				
Private saving	8.4%	9.2%	8.9%	9.4%
Government saving	−0.7	−1.0	−2.0	−5.1
National saving/investment	7.7	8.1	6.9	4.4
Net foreign investment	0.3	0.6	0.0	−2.8
Private domestic investment	7.4	7.6	6.9	7.2

Source: U.S. Department of Commerce, *National Income and Product Accounts of the U.S.*
[a]Net saving and investment equals the gross flow minus capital consumption allowances (the depreciation of existing capital). Net National Product equals Gross National Product minus capital consumption allowances. Pension funds of state and local governments are allocated to the private sector.

discussion of the shift in its composition from foreign to domestic assets. How long this situation can continue, of course, is a matter of intense speculation. At current rates, the United States will become a net debtor nation sometime in 1987.

From the experience of the past several years we have also learned that we cannot take comfort in the view that government deficits raise no problem for national saving because of compensatory adjustments of the private sector. Historically, there is evidence of an inverse relationship between government and private saving. But it appears to result primarily from periods of major temporary tax changes, such as those of 1968–1969 and 1970–1975. In any case, the associated rise in private saving is far less than the change in the government budget deficit. Perhaps we could expect private saving to offset a quarter to a third of the change in the budget deficit.[2]

Saving Incentives

The responsiveness of private saving to interest rates and taxes has been a subject of much prior debate and I do not propose to review all of it here. It is, however, fair to note that it is fundamentally an empirical issue and that the question cannot really be resolved short of new data similar to the panel surveys that were developed in earlier years to examine the effects on labor supply of the negative income tax experiments. Another regression on aggregate time-series data will convince nobody on either side of the debate. The research studies of the 1970s do not predict the constancy of private saving rates in the 1980s in the face of substantial increases in the rate of return, but such studies can be defended by noting that many other things have changed in the meantime. At the same time, surveys that provide a snapshot of a single point in time contain useful information about the composition of savings, but little guidance to the response of saving to a change in taxes and interest rates. What we require is a survey that follows a group of households over a period of time, but such surveys are expensive and one for saving does not now exist.

While the theoretical analysis, which dominated the research of the past decade, cannot resolve the issue, it has highlighted many of the issues that an empirical study must address. With respect to changes in the rate of return, we need to be able to distinguish between the substitution effect (which tends to increase saving) and the income effect (which tends to reduce saving). But, at the same time, there is a third effect— the wealth effect. An unanticipated change in the rate of return creates a windfall gain or loss to existing wealth-holders and tends to alter their current consumption. Because the ratio of existing wealth to income varies by age cohort, the wealth effect can make it very difficult to infer the long-run effect on saving behavior (that of younger cohorts) from the short-run average response.

In principle, it would seem more feasible to predict the response of saving to tax changes. By appropriate redesign of the structure of the tax system, it is possible to increase marginal incentives for saving while minimizing the offsetting income effects. There are also fewer measurement problems associated with the revaluation of existing wealth that occurs with a change in market interest rates. In practice, however, the hodgepodge of existing provisions relating to the taxation of capital income greatly complicates the issue.

A recent article by Galper and Steuerle provides a summary of existing tax-preference provisions that affect saving.[3] They present three criteria for an effective incentive: (1) the benefit should be restricted to net saving and not applied to taxpayers who simply switch the composition of their assets; (2) the incentives should apply at the margin (ruling out simple exclusions of income with a low cap); and (3) the incentives should be symmetric for positive and negative saving (ruling out tax–arbitrage, or borrowing for purposes of buying tax-preferred assets). On this basis, virtually none of the existing provisions meet the criteria of an effective saving incentive. Their most common failing is in allowing individuals to borrow, claim an interest deduction, and use the loan proceeds to purchase a tax-exempt asset.

A prime example of the difficulty of relating these provisions to the overall saving rate is provided by noting that the inflow of funds to IRA accounts rose from $4.7 billion in 1981 to $32.3 billion in 1983—a change equal to 0.9% of net national product. Yet the private saving rate declined even after adjustment for cyclical effects. This seems even more surprising when we remember that we were told that the 1982–1983 personal income tax reductions would also be saved by consumers. Individuals are allowed to switch funds to IRA accounts from other forms of wealth, leading to a tax reduction with no change in saving.

Tax Policy and Capital Formation

During the 1970s the economics profession generated an enormous amount of research, both theoretical and empirical, about the taxation of capital income. But, in doing so, it failed to provide adequate guidance to policymakers about the tenuous nature of those conclusions. In practice, the research findings were applied on a very selective basis and only when they favored the position of particular interest groups seeking tax relief.

The initial research emphasized the interaction between inflation and the tax system, and reached the conclusion that inflation had led to an increased tax on capital income during the 1970s because of the failure to adjust depreciation for inflation.[4] More recently, however, several studies have concluded that inflation has little or no net effect on the tax rate applicable to new investment, and that the tax rate actually fell throughout the 1970s.[5]

The discussion of tax policy and investment has shifted to a different issue: the wide dispersion of effective tax rates across different types of capital assets and the highly differential effect that inflation has on the tax rates applicable to different investments financed in different ways. For some types of investment the effective tax rate is actually reduced by inflation; in other cases, it is sharply increased. For some types of investment tax rates are very high; for others the tax system already provides a subsidy. The new concern is not so much with the impact of taxes on the total level of investment, but with the resource distortions that result if investment decisions are based primarily on their tax advantages rather than on economic benefits.

This shift of perspective results from a fuller consideration of the tax treatment of interest payments in an inflation environment. Nominal interest payments are fully deductible as a business expense and they are included in the taxable income of recipients. Inflation increases both interest deductions and receipts. Yet the net impact on effective tax rates is negative because far more interest is claimed as an expense by borrowers than is ever reported as taxable income by recipients, while marginal tax rates of borrowers claiming that deductions are higher, on average, than those of recipients.[6]

What is most relevant for saving is that our current tax system only slightly burdens or even subsidizes users of capital (borrowers) and collects most of the revenue from suppliers (lenders). This may make little difference in a closed economy where savers and investors can be viewed simply as opposite sides of the same coin. However, in an open economy with international capital flows, the taxation of domestic investors and savers cannot be simply combined to obtain an overall tax rate on capital income. In fact, the tax system is so diverse in its treatment of different investment situations that it is virtually impossible to determine its net influence on investment or saving decisions in an overall sense.

At present the United States needs to step back from a tax system that has become so overloaded with special incentive provisions that nobody understands its net influence on capital formation. As a first step, we need an underlying conceptual framework that provides a uniform treatment of all forms of capital income, one equalizing effective tax rates across different forms of saving and investment.

The simplest means of achieving that goal is to eliminate the taxation of capital income and with it most of the complexity of the current tax system. That is the position of those who favor a consumption tax. On the other hand, a consumption tax is, in reality, a wage tax, and the notion that only wage-earners should pay for public services arouses political objections.

The alternative approach is that of the Treasury Department, which has proposed a means of measuring economic income from capital on a consistent and uniform basis and then taxing it within the income-tax framework on the same basis as wages. Both assets and liabilities would be adjusted to eliminate the distortional influences of inflation. A major feature of the Treasury plan is that it shifts the point of tax collection from the lender to the borrower's side of the market. Thus business tax collections would rise while personal taxes on capital income would decline. At the present time there are still questions about whether the simple inflation adjustments proposed by the Treasury provide a workable basis for measuring capital income.

Given the low response of total saving to tax incentives, the major goal of tax reform should be the development of a uniform treatment of capital income that eliminates the distortional effects of the tax system on capital allocation. That goal could be achieved by either a consumption tax or a uniform income tax such as that proposed by the Treasury.

The current tax system mixes features of both the consumption and the income-tax approaches. It is probably the worst of both worlds. Thus, either of these two plans would be preferable to the current system. There is, I think, no question that a consumption tax provides the strongest incentive to private saving, but we do not know the magnitude of the actual effect. The best guess would be that the effect would be small— particularly over the next decade, both because very little capital income is subject to taxation today (from that perspective we are close to a consumption tax already), and because the short-term impact on aggregate saving appears to be low. At the same time, its detrimental effect on labor supply would also have to be taken into account.

All of these issues are of great interest to economists and tax aficionados, and they are the subject of intense debate. But their consequences for long-term investment and wealth accumulation pale in magnitude when compared to the effects of basic budget policy—the balancing of revenues and expenditures.

The Economic Effects of the Budget Deficit

Skepticism about our ability to easily influence private saving leads me to conclude that the United States must deal with the budget deficit if it hopes to find the means of restoring national rates of saving and investment to prior levels. But, again, efforts to do so are highly controversial for both political and economic reasons. On the political side, the existence of a budget deficit is seen by conservatives as a highly effective tool for cutting government social programs. Deficits may be bad, but a tax increase would be even worse because it relieves pressure for further expenditure cuts. Neither they nor the supporters of these programs yet seem prepared to compromise.

Deficits have both good and bad effects on the economy. Thus far in the public mind, the short-term economic benefits have outweighed the longer-term cost. A major reason for this is that the costs of deficits, as reflected in a lower rate of national wealth accumulation, are not immediate. They build up gradually over time.

The growth in the deficit provided a major stimulus in lifting the United States out of the 1980–1982 recession. And the combination of fiscal stimulus (to maintain output growth) and monetary restraint (to reduce inflation) has yielded substantial short-term benefits. The rise in the value of the dollar lowered import prices by an amount that is estimated to be contributing about three percentage points to the decline in inflation in the United States. That is, about half of the six percentage points of decline in the U.S. inflation rate since 1980 can be attributed to the exchange rate. The result was a major reduction in the unemployment cost required to get to a lower rate of inflation. Of course, the inflation gains may be purely transitory, if our exchange rate declines in future years, but that is a qualification with little public impact. Nor are we particularly impressed with the argument of other countries that it was a beggar-thy-neighbor policy of exporting the burden of adjustment onto them.

Several years ago, the standard forecast of economists was that the decline in national saving, pictured in table 8–1, would initiate a heightened competition for credit within the United States, raising interest rates and reducing domestic investment. The investment forecast was wrong because it failed to anticipate the ease with which the United States could borrow abroad, increasing domestic capital by reducing our net foreign holdings. Ever since then, we have said that the situation could not last— the dollar would fall and the trade deficit would decline. That forecast also has proved to be wrong. A decline in the U.S. saving rate has been far more in the best interest of the world economy than we envisioned.

It is true that the United States is short of saving, but the rest of the world has been plagued by an excess of private saving relative to domestic investment, and the export of that surplus to the United States has provided an important means of propping up economic activity in the rest of the world. The shift in U.S. policy imposes substantial cost on other countries, particularly the indebted countries of Latin America. But the basic problem of stagnating growth abroad predated that shift.

The foreign counterpart to the imbalance between U.S. domestic saving and investment is illustrated in table 8–2 which shows saving and investment rates for Japan. There has been some decline in the net private saving rate since 1979 from 18 to 25% as of 1984, but it appears to be largely a cyclical phenomenon related to higher capital consumption allowances per dollar of output. At the same time, the government budget deficit has shrunk, so that the overall national saving rate has fallen only slightly, from 13 to 12% of net output. Meanwhile, there has been a precipitous decline in the rate of domestic investment of five percentage points. The offset has been a sharp rise in foreign investment—the trade surplus. The Japanese share of output devoted to wealth accumulation is still about three times that of the United States.

In several respects, the current situation is not very different from that following the mid-1970s rise in oil prices. The accumulation of large trade surpluses (increased saving) by the OPEC countries focused concern on the need to recycle those funds. The recycling occurred when the OPEC countries deposited the surplus in U.S. banks who in turn loaned the funds for investment in Latin America. A similar process was at work with the increased lending to the eastern European countries. Today the United States is playing the role of a large, less-developed country. The only problem is that we have used the loans to support our own consumption—both public and private—rather than increasing

Table 8–2
Japanese Saving and Investment as a Share of National Product, Fiscal Years 1979–1984

	FY1979	FY1983	FY1984
Net saving			
Private saving	17.8	14.8	15.2
Government saving	−5.1	−3.6	−3.2
National saving/investment	12.7	11.2	12.1
Foreign investment	−1.7	2.4	3.0
Private domestic investment	14.4	8.5	9.9
Statistical discrepancy	0.0	−0.3	0.8

Source: Constructed by the author from data published in Japan Research Center, *Quarterly Forecast of Japan's Economy* 58 (December 1984).

capital formation. But, at least we hear no more Reagan administration lectures to the LDCs about their need to live within their means.

Some of the potential adjustment problems for the world economy are illustrated by considering the response to a reversal of U.S. economic policy. A substantial reduction in the U.S. budget deficit would remove much of the rationale for the current large trade deficit. Some offset would occur as lower interest rates promoted additional investment in the United States and abroad. However, it is difficult to believe that lower interest rates in Europe and Japan would add to domestic investment more than those countries would lose in exports to the United States. Even with lower interest rates, Latin American and other LDCs could not be expected to revert to the status of capital-importing countries in the near future.

Here in the United States there is a general belief that an easing of monetary policy could offset the depressive effects of a shift in fiscal policy toward restraint. Much of the presumed adjustment, however, relies upon a fall in the value of the dollar and thereby a smaller trade deficit. If other countries resist such a loss of exports, the adjustment could be more difficult than generally believed.

The conclusion should not be that the United States is not paying a cost for the fall in its national saving rate. Future generations will inherit a much smaller net wealth as a result of the current consumption binge. But a consideration of the role of the U.S. deficit in the world economy does suggest that the current situation is more sustainable than the frequent forecast of a near-term economic crisis has implied.

The most immediate costs of the budget deficit are reflected in the foreign trade deficit and the loss of competitiveness for U.S. industries engaged in international trade. But here too, what seems to be missing from the policy discussion is a recognition that, given its domestic fiscal-monetary policies, the United States *needs* a large trade deficit. Without it, the United States could not simultaneously maintain both a high level of consumption and current rates of domestic investment. Without the trade deficit, interest rates in the United States would be far higher as the budget deficit crowds out private domestic spending. Instead, the public's attention is directed to the unfair trade practices of other countries. In most cases, the problem of a large trade imbalance generates pressure for additional government expenditures (to aid agriculture, for example) or trade restraints (to benefit industries competing with imports), but not reductions in the budget deficit.

At present, there is little public pressure to force the painful adjustments of policy that would be required to restore the U.S. rate of capital accumulation to prior levels. It is more comfortable to blame foreigners for the most evident cost, the trade deficit, rather than to admit that we shot ourselves in the foot by the particular choice of policy. The costs of a lower rate of capital accumulation are only dimly perceived by the current generation and are unlikely to have immediate consequences for as long as the rest of the world remains so willing to lend its resources. We might also ask where else are they going to go with their funds. The United States does offer a rate of return in excess of that available in most other regions of the world.

Why Is the Deficit So Hard to Reduce?

Table 8–3 provides one perspective on how the United States got into its current budget quandry. It compares the budget projections under the tax laws and programs in effect in 1981 with the service budget projections made in early 1985. The table highlights several aspects of the current budget debate.

First, the recession of 1980–1982 would have created a large budget deficit even under the budget policies in place in 1981. But with continued economic recovery the deficit would have declined, as it did in prior expansions, and move into a modest surplus by the end of the decade.

Second, the changed priorities of the Reagan administration are clearly evident in the rise in defense spending (adding $95 billion annually by 1990), and the cutbacks in nondefense spending. The debate over budget priorities, however, has resulted only in a reallocation of outlays between defense and nondefense. There has been no net reduction in government expenditures.

Third, despite the failure to reduce total program expenditures, the Tax Reduction Act of 1981 lowered revenues by an amount that will reach an annual rate of $335 billion in 1990. Every year since 1981 the Congress has acted to raise taxes, but the net reduction still totals about $225 billion annually. That fact alone creates a large budget deficit.

Finally, the major growth in government outlays is coming from the cost of financing the public debt. The added annual interest payments required to finance the legislated additions to the deficit during this decade alone will add $123 billion to annual outlays by 1990. That does not include the interest cost that would have resulted from financing the debt generated in prior decades and under the 1981 budget program. It is also, in all likelihood, an underestimate because the Congressional Budget Office assumes that interest rates will decline in future years, despite the magnitude of the deficit.

An alternative perspective is provided in table 8–4, where major program costs are shown as a percent of the Gross National Product. The period from 1960 to 1980 shows a shift in budget priorities which

Table 8–3
Effect on Deficits of Policy Changes since 1981, Constant 1984 Economic Assumptions
($ billions)

	FY1982	FY1983	FY1984	FY1986	FY1988	FY1990
Deficit under policies in effect in 1981	-$106	-$151	-$95	-$64	-$17	$68
Effect of legislative changes						
Defense increases	-3	-16	-23	-41	-65	-95
Nondefense spending cuts	40	48	50	63	73	88
Tax actions						
1981 program	-42	-93	-141	-208	-270	-335
1982 program	*	18	38	53	61	58
1983 program		1	7	12	26	24
1984 program			1	16	24	30
Effect of legislative actions on interest costs	*	-3	-10	-35	-69	-123
Total changes	-5	-45	-81	-143	-223	-359
Deficit under policies in effect in 1985	-111	-195	-175	-206	-240	-290

Source: Compiled from published material of Congressional Budget Office.

Table 8–4
Sources and Disposition of Government Revenues, United States

	Actual					Projected	
	1960	1970	1980	1984	1986	1988	1990
Billions of dollars							
Revenues	$ 92.5	$192.8	$517.1	$666.5	$788	$934	$1,088
Outlays	92.2	195.7	576.7	841.8	995	1,174	1,378
Deficit	0.3	–2.8	–59.6	–175.3	–206	–240	–290
Public debt	237.2	284.9	715.1	1,312.6	1,740	2,220	2,786
Percentage of GNP							
Expenditures							
National defense	9.7%	8.4%	5.2%	6.4%	6.8%	7.2%	7.6%
Social security and medicare	2.3	3.7	5.8	6.6	6.5	6.6	6.6
Other nondefense	5.2	6.6	9.4	7.4	7.1	6.6	6.3
Net interest	1.4	1.5	2.0	3.1	3.5	3.9	4.1
Total	18.5	20.2	22.4	23.5	23.9	24.3	24.6
Revenues							
Social insurance taxes	2.9%	4.6%	6.1%	6.7%	6.8%	6.9%	6.9%
Individual income taxes	8.2	9.3	9.5	8.3	8.7	8.9	9.2
Corporate taxes	4.3	3.4	2.5	1.6	1.7	2.0	1.9
Excise taxes	2.3	1.6	0.9	1.0	0.8	0.7	0.6
Other	0.8	1.1	1.0	1.0	0.8	0.8	0.8
Total	18.6	19.9	20.1	18.6	19.0	19.3	19.4
Deficit	0.1	–0.3	–2.9	–5.2	–5.2	–5.1	–5.3
Public debt	47.6	29.4	27.8	36.7	41.8	46.0	49.7

is precisely the reverse of the 1980s—the share of GNP spent on defense declined by 4.5 percentage points while nondefense programs, other than social security, grew by 4.2 percentage points. During that period, the major growth in the budget was in providing for the retired—a 3.5 percentage point increase in the share of GNP devoted to Social Security and Medicare. However, there was one crucial difference between the past and current situations. Regardless of whether it was a good idea to expand these programs, at least taxes were raised to pay for them. In fact, the only significant increase in tax rates was the tax on labor income. Corporate and excise taxes have declined sharply and personal income taxes are roughly unchanged.

In future years, government expenditures will continue to grow as a share of GNP, but none of that growth comes from the expansion of programs—it is all increases in interest costs on the public debt, which will rise from $715 billion in 1980 to $2.8 trillion in 1990. As a share of GNP the debt will rise from 28% in 1980 to 50% in 1990 and continue to grow every year thereafter. While that share is not much greater than in 1960 and earlier postwar years, the burden will be much greater because of higher interest rates charged on today's debt. Indeed, interest payments as a share of GNP should rise from 1.4% in 1960 to 4.1% in 1990.

Long-term budget projections are notoriously unreliable because future economic conditions are never as assumed and the government is always modifying the budget. But we should also point out that those projections have been wrong in the past because government was too optimistic. Reality is even worse than we anticipate. These projections are no different from previous ones in assuming eight years of economic growth without a recession.

The magnitude of the deficit has proved difficult for the public to grasp, and most discussions still imply that minor adjustments in a few programs will solve the problem. Yet, each year's deficit of $200 billion adds $20 billion of interest payments every year into the future. By 1990, if nothing is done, nearly half of personal income taxes will go each year to pay interest on the debt. By failing to address the problem today, taxes will have to be raised even higher in future years. Furthermore, the deficit cannot be eliminated by focusing on nondefense programs alone. With the cuts that have already been put in place, spending on those programs will be, as a share of GNP, below the levels that preceded the Johnson administration. That is, in many respects we have achieved President Reagan's goal of eliminating the Great Society programs, yet the deficit remains at $200 billion.

In one important respect, this chapter understates the magnitude of the budget imbalance. Social Security and Medicare costs are not projected to rise as a share of GNP in the near future because there is no projected growth in the share of the population that is retired until early in the next century. Then the number of retired individuals per worker will rise sharply, increasing the burden on future generations. In recognition of this problem in 1983 Congress substantially reduced future Social Security benefits by 8 to 16%, while increasing social insurance taxes on the current generation. The object was to build up a reserve of about $18 trillion by the year 2045. It will rapidly decumulate after that date, but the surplus eliminates the need to raise Social Security taxes in the next century.

However, in order to actually reduce the real burden on future generations, it is crucial that this surplus be invested in real capital that raises national income in future decades. If, as is currently planned, the surplus is simply used to finance current consumption—borrowing from the social insurance fund to finance the general fund deficit—no net reduction in the burden on future generations will occur. This problem exists quite independently of the issue of whether the Social Security system should be fully funded or operated on an actuarial pay-as-you-go basis.

The demographic trend toward a rising retired population implies that the United States should have a rising and not a falling rate of national saving and investment in order to moderate the burden on future workers. The current focus on the unified budget deficit (inclusive of Social Security and Medicare) camouflages the distinction between the trust funds and the general fund. If these programs were separated out, we would observe that general-fund revenues are only sufficient to pay for less than two-thirds of current expenditures. Alternatively, the appropriate long-run policy would be to aim for a substantial surplus in the unified budget.

Economists are accustomed to analyzing the effects of budget policy on the economy. Curiously, the current situation seems to rely on the opposite flow-of-causation. The costs of the budget deficit are simply too indirect to arouse the public's concern. Until a deteriorating economic situation makes those costs more immediate, it is unlikely that the public will support any of the painful actions that would be required. There is currently no support for a tax increase. Moreover, while the public generally favors cuts in expenditures, there is majority support for a reduction in only one specific category—welfare. Yet, at the same time, a majority is opposed to cuts in either Aid to Families with Dependent Children (AFDC) or food stamps.

This situation is likely to continue until foreign reluctance to invest in the United States leads to greater domestic competition for resources plus either inflation or rising interest rates. Earlier I expressed skepticism about the effect of tax reform on private saving. Similarly, a consideration of the political and economic forces impacting on the budget indicates little immediate progress toward reducing the budget deficit. From a long-run perspective the fall-off in national saving and investment is a serious mistake, but there is little reason to expect a dramatic correction in the near future. Instead, the United States may muddle through for several more years with some modest rise in private saving, a stabilizing of the budget deficit at the current level, continued large trade deficits, and a moderation of domestic investment as more firms consider moving their production facilities overseas. That should be a sufficiently murky outcome to enable us to continue the current vigorous but inconclusive debate.

Notes

1. The only change I have made to the data published in the National Income Accounts is to shift pension funds of state and local governments to the private sector so that they are treated in a fashion identical to those of private firms. The adjustment adds about half of a percentage point to the private saving rate. It is also possible to define private saving to include investment in consumer durables. Such a change raises the rate of saving by 1 to 2% of NNP, but leaves the trend unaffected. The net saving rate does have a substantial cyclical component, falling in recessions and depressions, because of the fixed nature of depreciation of existing capital. No such cycle is evident in the gross saving rate.

2. This statement is supported by noting that a simple regression of the net private saving rate on a time-trend, the utilization of the potential GNP (a cyclical adjustment) and the government deficit yields a coefficient of 0.3 on the deficit for the 1951–1984 period with marginal statistical significance. Furthermore, the actual saving rate in 1984 is within 0.5 percentage points of the predicted level.

3. Harvey Galper and Eugene Steuerle, "Tax Incentives for Saving," *The Brookings Review*, Winter 1983: 16–23.

4. For a recent example, see Martin Feldstein and Lawrence Summers, "Inflation and the Taxation of Capital Income in the Corporate Sector," *National Tax Journal* 32 (December 1979): 445–70.

5. Mervyn A. King and Don Fullerton (eds.), *The Taxation of Income from Capital: A Comparative Study of the United States, the United Kingdom, Sweden, and West Germany* (Chicago: The University of Chicago Press, 1984); and Don Fullerton and Yolanda K. Henderson, "Incentive Effects of Taxes on Income from Capital: Alternative Policies in the 1980s" in *The Legacy of Reaganomics: Prospects for Long-Term Growth*, ed. Charles R. Hulten and Isabel V. Sawhill (Washington, D.C.: The Urban Institute, 1984), pp. 45–90.

6. Fullerton and Henderson, op. cit., p. 54.

9
In Defense of Savings

Paul Craig Roberts

I am encouraged to see that there now is a Savings Forum and that it has academic economists on its executive council. This is a big change. Only a few years ago economists and public policymakers looked upon saving with suspicion. For example, in December 1977 the Congressional Budget Office published a Technical Analysis Paper titled *Closing the Fiscal Policy Loop: A Long-Run Analysis* in which CBO argued that healthy economic growth required strong spending, which meant not saving. The study reported that in order for the U.S. to achieve an average annual growth in real GNP of 5.16% over a five-year period and balance the budget by 1982, Americans must spend a lot. Spending a lot meant a personal savings rate of less than 6% of disposable income. CBO calculated that if the savings rate exceeded 6%, "an increasing federal deficit would be necessary" to achieve the growth goal.

In other words, the Keynesian point of view was that saving is not spending, and if savings amount to anything much, the government must sop them up with deficits if the economy is to grow. This is the kind of advice that economists fed Congresses and administrations throughout the postwar era. As we all know, Nobel economist Paul Samuelson warned about the paradox of thrift through many editions of *Principles of Economics*. Sophisticated and unsophisticated students alike easily reached the conclusion that the less we save the faster we grow. In the minds of many, private saving became an antisocial act.

The economists' suspicion of saving affected economic policy in many ways. For example, the GNP multipliers showed that an increase in government spending was a more effective way to stimulate the economy than a reduction in taxation. As recently as April 1978 CBO warned the Congress that "a permanent income tax cut is a relatively expensive way of reducing unemployment in terms of budget dollars (net or gross costs) per additional job."[1] Since in Keynesian analysis personal income taxation only affects disposable income and the level of demand, the balanced-budget multiplier taught that government could increase GNP by raising taxes and spending the money. The reasoning was that people would partly pay the higher taxes by reducing their savings. Consequently, government spending would rise by more than private spending would fall, and aggregate demand would increase. The Keynesian point of view that taxes have no adverse impact on the economy turned out to be good for the growth of government, but not for capital formation and growth in labor productivity, which collapsed in the 1970s.

The neglect of the behavioral effects of taxation led to the proposition that progressive income and wealth taxes can be used to redistribute income at no cost to investment or aggregate economic activity. In other words, the argument is that private property rights can be infringed upon with impunity. These faulty conclusions played a major role in the transformation of the U.S. from a free society toward a welfare state. The sharp drop in the growth of U.S. labor productivity from a 3.1% annual rate of increase over the 1948–1968 period to 0.6% from 1973 to 1980 brought to a halt the growth in real labor income and increased the demand for government programs that further infringed upon property rights. Now the threat to free trade posed by poor U.S. productivity performance threatens the future of the western alliance, which depends on European and Japanese access to U.S. markets. A defense of saving is not only a defense of a higher real GNP growth path and better productivity performance, but also a defense of the western alliance.

There can be no doubt whatsoever that it was supply-side economists who rescued saving. Supply-siders stressed that taxation affects relative prices and not just disposable income.[2] Marginal tax rates affect the price of current consumption in terms of foregone future income, and thereby affect the saving rate. The price of additional current consumption is the amount of future income foregone by not saving and investing. The higher the tax rate, the smaller the value of the income stream foregone by enjoying additional current consumption. In other words, the higher the tax rate, the lower the price of current consumption.

Supply-siders reinterpreted the so-called Kennedy tax cuts of the 1960s and demonstrated empirically that it was not a consumption-led expansion.[3] Real consumer spending actually declined as a percentage of income. Saving, investment, and tax revenues rose sharply. A burst of saving and investment activity spurred the economy to faster growth of the ability to produce.

Ironically, saving owes much of its new support from economists to the fact that enactment of President Reagan's supply-side tax program in 1981 coincided with the Federal Reserve's engineering the worst recession in the postwar period. The large and unexpected budget deficits resulted primarily from the collapses in the inflation rate and nominal GNP growth path, which were both sharp and unexpected, even by the Fed itself. This gave the president's opponents the opportunity to attack his supply-side policy on supply-side terms. They could not resist, and economists, who had always denied any crowding-out effects from budget deficits caused by government spending, were suddenly and unabashedly warning of severe crowding-out effects from budget deficits that they hoped to pin on tax-cutting. Economists with a long tradition of refuting the crowding-out hypothesis, urging instead the need for budget deficits to soak up leakages known as private saving, were born again and preached the old Republican doctrine against Ronald Reagan and supply-side economics. The economic establishment discovered a new principle of fiscal policy: only tax cuts result in budget deficits that crowd out private investment.

In 1982, a year of recession, the budget projected a deficit of 3.8% of GNP (including "off-budget" items), with a forecasted decline to 3.1% in 1983. Normally, these deficits would have been viewed as automatic stabilizers. Instead, there was the hue and cry that the deficits would keep interest rates high, crowd out private investment, and prevent an economic recovery. The administration itself fell victim to this belief, and the chairman of the President's Council of Economic Advisers failed to predict the economic recovery that was visible the week that the 1983 *Economic Report of the President* was published. Indeed, the CEA chairman and the budget director were running around advocating a "contingency" tax increase to help pull the economy out of recession.

It is interesting to compare the response to the 1981–1982 recession with the response to the previous recession of 1974–1975. 1976 was the first year of recovery, with a real growth rate of 5.4% in spite of (Keynesians claimed because of) a deficit that measured 4.5% of GNP, while 1977, the second year of economic recovery, showed real economic growth steaming along at 5.5%. Yet the argument then was that the recovery would stall without higher deficit spending. I remember very well since I was directly involved as chief economist of the minority staff of the House Budget Committee.

After winning the 1976 presidential election, the Democrats reopened the 1977 fiscal year budget. An unprecedented third budget resolution was introduced to provide an additional stimulus package, including a $50 rebate, with the goal of increasing the 1977 deficit from $50 billion to $70 billion (3.7% of GNP). Testifying before the Senate Budget Committee in support of more stimulus, Walter Heller, chairman of the Council of Economic Advisers under President Kennedy, was asked if he thought the larger deficit posed a problem for the economy. He replied that a deficit measuring 3.7% of GNP was minor and did not raise "even a remote specter" of inflation.[4]

The argument that the deficit would mean high interest rates, less investment, and an aborted recovery was also dismissed. In the same hearings Senator Cranston asked Heller and Alice Rivlin, director of the Congressional Budget Office, if the deficit would crowd out business investment, raise interest rates, and destroy business confidence. Heller dismissed the possibility with a shake of the head. Rivlin said it was not a serious concern. She reminded the senator that some people (Republicans) had worried about the same thing a couple of years ago but that it did not happen. She had the same answer for the House Budget Committee two weeks later on January 24. Indeed, it was the standard answer. The previous year she had assured the Senate Budget Committee that " 'crowding out' of private spending by the federal sector does not appear to have occurred. In spite of the large federal deficit and modest rates of money supply growth over the year, interest rates generally did not increase."[5]

When Reagan cut tax rates and a recession appeared instead of the excess demand inflation that many economists had predicted, the conventional wisdom changed overnight. The minute a conservative president was vulnerable, large numbers of economists instantly changed their lifelong positions and began preaching the old Republican doctrine of crowding-out against Ronald Reagan. No new discovery or empirical study coincided with this doffing and donning of policy positions. Confronted with the new development, I assigned the economic policy staff of the U.S. Treasury Department to an exhaustive study (including a review of all academic studies) titled *The Effect of Deficits on Prices of Financial Assets: Theory and Evidence*. The burden of managing the study fell upon my deputy and successor, Manuel Johnson. When it was published in the spring of 1984, born-again budget-balancers dismissed it as an argument that deficits don't matter. So much for the role that facts and objective analysis play in what is essentially an ideological attack on private-property rights disguised as a concern that insufficient taxation has dangerously reduced the societal saving rate.

Previously, deficits were justified when economic policy was being used to create new entitlements and to redistribute income. Today, essentially the same people are attacking deficits and advocating higher taxes in the name of increased saving. The selective use of the crowding-out argument has no economic content. Neither does the selective argument that Treasury borrowing, but not taxation, crowds out private investment.

We do not yet know whether the 1981 tax cut will duplicate the effect of the 1964 tax cut in raising the real personal savings rate. The effects of severe recession, robust recovery, and large increases in the values of stocks and bonds will swamp in the short run the relative price effect of changes in marginal tax rates on the personal savings rate. We do know, however, that gross private saving has risen substantially. Indeed, it is impossible to allow businesses faster write-offs without raising business saving. The facts also reveal no increase over the 1982–1984 period in the rate of foreign-owned capital inflows. Instead, U.S. capital outflows have collapsed. In other words, the money is staying at home, and we have been financing our own deficit.

We must carefully examine the argument that higher taxes will increase total saving by reducing government dissaving. Just as it is difficult to find governments that don't spend additional revenues, it is difficult to find taxes that do not raise the cost of capital. Colleagues and I presented the results of our studies at an international conference in Milan in November 1984. We found that the effect of taxation on the cost of capital can easily swamp the effect of interest rates.[6]

There has been a revolution in macroeconomics. It came out of the policy process in Washington. Academics are just beginning to catch up with it. Previously they could neglect the relative price effects of taxation on the basis of the argument that the elasticities of response were zero (or even negative). This argument has been proven to be theoretically and empirically wrong. Moreover, the concept of public saving has lost its credibility. Researchers are finding that the communist and third world governments that achieved relatively high ratios of investment to GNP misused the capital and achieved what some call "industrialization without prosperity" and "investment without growth."[7] Today disillusionment with government seems strongest where there is the most government. The Chinese communists are talking about opening a stock market so that they will have some notion of the value of capital in different uses, and on March 25, 1985, the *New York Times* reported that the prime minister of socialist India "in a notable break with past policies, has proposed a sweeping program to cut taxes for businesses and wealthy individuals and reduce government regulation of key parts of the economy." If this keeps up, disillusionment with government might one day even spread to academic economists in Cambridge, Massachusetts and Cambridge, England. If not, they will end up in the dustbin of history.

Notes

1. *Understanding Fiscal Policy* (Washington, D.C.: Congressional Budget Office, 1978), p. 38.

2. Paul Craig Roberts, "The Breakdown of the Keynesian Model." *The Public Interest*, Summer 1978.

3. Paul Craig Roberts, *The Supply-Side Revolution*. (Cambridge, Mass.: Harvard University Press, 1984).

4. *The Economy and the Federal Budget,* hearings before the Senate Budget Committee, 95th Congress, January 11, 1977, p. 34.

5. *Review of the President's Budget,* hearings before the Senate Budget Committee, 94th Congress, 1976, p. 88.

6. Aldona Robbins, Gary Robbins, and Paul Craig Roberts, "The Relative Impact of Taxation and Interest Rates on the Cost of Capital," in Ralph Landau and Dale W. Jorgenson, eds., *Technology and Economic Policy* (forthcoming, 1986) (Cambridge, Mass.: Ballinger Press).

7. See, for example, Nick Eberstadt, "Famine, Development, and Foreign Aid," *Commentary,* March 1985, and Peter T. Bauer, *Reality and Rhetoric: Studies in the Economics of Development* (Cambridge, Mass.: Harvard University Press, 1984).

10
International Aspects of Saving

Lawrence R. Klein

The Significance of Saving: Conceptual Issues

The advice given by Polonius to his son was obviously virtuous:

> Neither a borrower nor a lender be; For loan oft loses both itself and friend, and borrowing dulls the edge of husbandry (*Hamlet,* act I, scene III).

After Shakespeare, Benjamin Franklin passed on many sayings about the virtues of thrift. Some of his wisdom was set aside or possibly even ridiculed during the Great Depression when we aimed at building pyramids or leaf-raking just to put people to work, but, in a fundamental sense, saving retained its inherent importance, as I shall try to make clear. As a starting point, I would like to try to explain what an economist means by saving.

From an accounting point of view, for either the micro or macro economy, saving can be approached from two sides:

$$\text{Saving as a residual: saving} = \text{income minus expenditures} \quad (10.1)$$
$$S = - C$$

$$\text{Saving as a } \textit{direct} \text{ concept: saving} = \text{change in net worth}$$
$$= \text{change in assets minus}$$
$$\text{change in liabilities} \quad (10.2)$$
$$S = \Delta NW$$
$$= \Delta A - \Delta L$$

The importance of saving tends to be understated if we treat it as a mere residual. Also, it is error prone, combining the errors in income measurement and expenditure measurement. In spite of the presence of residual errors, many statisticians favor the income-expenditure definition because income and spending data are generally considered to be far more reliable than are data on specific assets and liabilities. In particular, the problem of capital revaluation plagues the capital-accounting approach. Also, the residual calculation tends to be uninformative about the source of savings. By building up the total from changes in specific assets and liabilities, it is possible to construct components of saving such as *contractual,* as distinguished from *discretionary,* saving; *financial,* as distinguished from *real,* saving; *direct,* as distinguished from *imputed,* saving; or *liquid,* as distinguished from *illiquid,* saving. These are only some of the main categories and among them, *contractual* vs. *discretionary* savings appears to be the most significant among the various distinctions that have been drawn.

People make genuine decisions about most asset and liability changes; therefore, savings are not really a residual process. That is a strong reason for preferring the direct concept viewing savings as a change in net worth.

The residual concept was popularized as a typical representation of personal saving. During the Great Depression saving could be portrayed as an economic inhibitor because it appears to be the withholding of funds from the spending stream. This promotes the idea that spending is good (expansionary) and saving is bad (restrictive). In a depressed state, short-run expansions of spending in place of saving can be interpreted as desirable, but in the longer run—even in the intermediate term—savings form the resource base from which growth can take place. According to this view, the virtue of thrift comes into its own and facilitates economic growth and expansion. It is, indeed, one of our great hopes for the future.

But the concept of saving extends far beyond the purely personal decision to spend or not to spend. An important aggregate is national saving, which is the sum of all components of saving: national savings = personal saving + business saving + government saving + foreign saving. These different types of saving have some independent characteristics and need not always move in unison. At the present time in the United States, personal saving is somewhat disappointing in strength; business saving is quite strong; and government saving is a peril for the stability of the economy, as is foreign saving. In other countries, the situation may be structured entirely differently. Personal saving has traditionally been strong in Japan, while business saving is not so strong, but foreign saving is large in absolute value but opposite in sign to the corresponding U.S. component. The structure of national saving changes over time and varies from country to country.

A tabular picture of national savings is provided by the national accounting statement of sources and uses of funds. A statement for the U.S. is provided in table 10–1.

Personal saving and undistributed profits have had wide cyclical swings, as have the price adjustments for changing valuations (inventory valuations and capital-consumption allowance, or CCA, adjustment). Sometimes the personal component is strong; sometimes the business component is strong. In the recent period when there has been an enormous drain from the federal budget deficit, corporate savings have improved significantly, to compensate for a drop in personal savings in 1983, but the real strength in business saving has come from the source of capital consumption allowances. Favorable tax treatment of depreciation enabled companies to source a great part of their financial capital internally. This is a significant reason why federal deficit finance has not brought about extreme crowding out. Capital-consumption allowances have been steady, large, and growing. That is an American savings phenomenon and provides an institutional structural difference in comparison with a number of other countries. Sources and uses statements always balance; it is mainly a question of whether they balance easily, without the strain that would generate undue fluctuations and high levels of interest rates. That is how we use this accounting statement in savings analysis at Wharton Econometrics.

Having tried to establish an understanding of the meaning of savings, let us look at some analytical issues involving the concept. Elementary students are generally introduced to the "paradox of thrift." By striving to save more, a society may end up saving less. This happens, in the short run, because a surge in saving withholds funds from the spending stream, and declining demand (or a demand shortfall) induces a decline in aggregate economic activity, bringing down national income levels. From a reduced income base, the populace can save less, not more. In the textbook analytics, we find a savings function shifting upwards along a more gently rising investment function and finding a new intersection point at a lower income level.

This is a valid short-run effect and accounts for the fact that our present administration cheered the expenditure surge that accompanied the large tax cuts of 1981–1983. These cuts were put forward as promoters of saving, but they actually promoted spending according to the tenets of mainstream macroeconomics and generated an expanding volume of aggregate economic activity.

But the expansion is not necessarily sustainable unless all the components of aggregate activity continue along a healthy path. In particular, investment spending can be restrained or even obstructed by a perverse movement of interest rates. This is the point at which a sources-and-uses

Table 10–1
Sources and Uses of U.S. Gross Savings
($ billion)

	1973	1974	1975	1976	1977	1978
Gross saving	235.5	227.3	218.9	257.9	309.1	375.0
Private	227.7	232.0	282.7	294.4	326.9	374.2
Personal	79.0	85.1	94.3	82.5	78.0	89.4
Corporate saving	49.6	55.2	50.7	65.1	81.2	98.9
Corporate IVA	−20.0	−40.0	−11.6	−14.7	−16.2	−24.0
CCA adjustment	2.7	−1.8	−10.1	−13.5	−11.3	−12.7
CCA	116.5	136.0	159.3	175.0	195.2	225.5
Wage accrual less adjustment	−0.1	−0.5	0	0	0	0.2
Government	7.8	−4.7	−63.8	−36.5	−17.8	0.8
Federal	−5.6	−11.5	−69.3	−53.1	−45.9	−29.5
State/local	13.4	6.8	5.5	16.6	28.0	30.3
Capital grants	0	−2.0	0	0	0	0
Gross investment	236.3	231.5	224.4	263.0	310.4	372.3
Private domestic	229.8	228.7	206.1	257.9	324.1	386.6
Net foreign	6.5	2.9	18.3	5.1	−13.6	−14.3
Statistical discrepancy	0.8	3.7	5.5	5.1	1.4	−2.6

Source: Wharten Econometrics Forecasting Associates.

IVA = inventory valuation adjustment

CCA = capital consumption allowances

balance at favorable interest rates, without crowding out, becomes relevant. If savings are not sufficiently plentiful, there may be crowding out, and a resulting fall in investment spending could precipitate a decline in activity. This is why saving, in the medium term, beyond the immediate shifts displayed in the paradox of thrift, becomes important. In the short run spending (not saving) is immediately strategic for promoting economic activity; in the longer run, saving (not consumer spending) is strategic for maintaining economic expansion. As in many economic processes, there is a double-edged effect. It could also be viewed as a distinction between cyclical and secular needs for saving in a healthy, growing economy.

It should be noted in the sources-and-uses statement that foreign saving (called *net foreign investment* and listed negatively as a use of funds or positively as a source of funds) provides an international component in the total balance. In recent years this entry has changed sign and grown, as a deficit figure, to the amazing level of about $100 billion. In a very real sense, we can conclude that we are depending on a source of international funding to supply our financial capital needs caused by a large domestic budget deficit. The foreign inflow does not fully offset

					Wharton Forecast			
1979	1980	1981	1982	1983	1984	1985	1986	1987
422.5	405.8	484.4	408.8	436.8	552.4	568.4	601.3	673.4
408.2	436.5	511.1	524.0	571.3	675.2	698.4	742.7	820.4
96.7	110.2	137.4	136.0	118.1	156.1	137.1	146.3	167.0
112.4	91.2	73.5	35.6	54.5	65.6	61.7	59.8	72.2
−43.1	−42.9	−23.6	−9.5	−11.2	−5.6	−8.8	−15.5	−22.2
−14.8	−16.3	−7.6	3.1	33.2	55.7	76.6	86.6	94.6
256.0	293.2	330.3	358.8	377.1	403.3	431.8	465.5	508.9
−0.2	0	0.1	0	−0.4	0.1	0	0	0
14.3	−30.7	−26.7	−115.3	−134.5	−122.8	−130.0	−141.4	−147.0
−16.1	−61.2	−64.3	−148.2	−178.6	−175.7	−190.6	−197.9	−210.0
30.4	30.6	37.6	32.9	44.1	52.9	60.6	56.6	63.0
1.1	1.2	1.1	0	0	0	0	0	0
421.2	408.2	490.0	408.3	437.7	544.4	566.2	610.4	678.9
423.0	401.9	484.2	414.9	471.6	637.8	678.2	742.5	821.1
−1.8	6.3	5.8	−6.6	−33.9	−93.4	−112.0	−132.2	−142.2
−1.5	2.3	5.6	−0.5	0.5	−7.9	−2.3	9.0	5.4

the domestic budget drain, but it is getting uncomfortably close to doing so. Foreign flows tend to be volatile; that is why many economists view with alarm the fact that we are not funding our domestic capital needs from our own saving, but are depending heavily on foreigners to supply funds to our capital market. This obviously has serious implications for the strength of the dollar in foreign exchange markets and generates an entirely fresh train of other international problems. This international dimension of our sources-and-uses picture is unusual; as shown in figure 10–1, the normal pattern of the dynamics of our current account is for the net balance to fluctuate in a fairly narrow range (in the low double-digits at the extreme) about a zero balance.

The Distribution of Saving over the World

There are uniform systems of accounts and other statistical tabulations for many countries maintained at well-known international organizations such as OECD, the Common Market, the World Bank, International Monetary Fund, and United Nations. The fact that many diverse

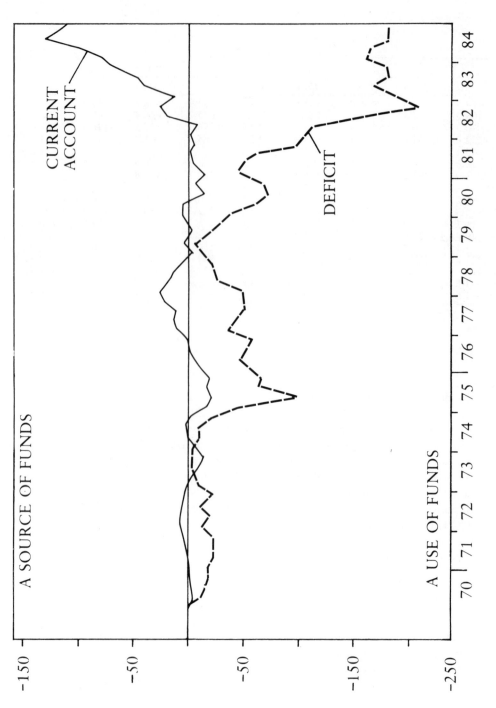

Figure 10–1. The Current Account and Federal Budget Deficit

countries fit into a common mold does not mean that they are necessarily very much alike as far as behavior is concerned. Some countries grow quickly; some grow slowly. Some are export-led and some are import-led. Some are big savers, and others are big spenders. Economic behavior is wide ranging. The variability of savings propensities is quite revealing about the economic situation of different countries.

First, let us look at the distribution of savings behavior, worldwide. Gross domestic saving as a percent of gross domestic product has been tabulated for more than 100 countries by the World Bank. Figures for individual countries (all the OECD countries, individually, and groups of developing countries) are given in table 10–2.

These figures refer to total national savings. The table includes both public and private saving, and covers the saving of foreigners through net exports. Both business and personal saving are included since it is a macro figure. There is no general time-drift discernible here. On the whole, the developing world had a higher propensity to save in 1982 than in 1960, while many of the developed countries had a slightly reduced saving propensity between the two years. The high saving pro-

Table 10–2
The Average Propensity to Save, 1960 and 1982: Gross Domestic Saving as a Percent of Gross Domestic Product

	1960	*1982*
Low-income countries	18%	21%
Middle-income countries	19	21
Upper-middle-income countries	21	23
High-income oil-exporters	NA	53
OECD nations	22	20
Australia	25	20
Austria	28	24
Belgium	18	13
Canada	21	23
Denmark	25	17
Finland	28	25
France	25	17
Ireland	11	22
Italy	24	20
Japan	33	31
Netherlands	28	21
New Zealand	21	21
Norway	28	32
Spain	21	18
Sweden	24	17
Switzerland	29	25
United Kingdom	17	20
United States	19	15
West Germany	30	24

pensity of rich oil-exporting countries in 1982 is probably associated with their sudden increment in wealth, after oil prices went up so markedly in 1974.

Among low-income countries, the rate of saving would not be so high were it not for the figures for China (24 and 30%) and India (14 and 22%). Many of the low-income countries and a few of the middle-income countries, too, had negative saving rates, a bit more in 1982 than in 1960.

There are many interesting savings statistics for individual developing countries, but the most significant contrast in table 10–2 is the high rate for Japan and the low rate for the United States. There are some other high savers and low savers, but these approach the extremes. Japan's high saving rate is associated with a high investment rate and fairly low interest rates. The United States has a lower investment rate and relatively high interest rates. There are institutional differences in financial systems that account for the disparity in interest rates, and investment appears to be growing fast in the United States, even if its level is not a high fraction of GDP. Japan's edge in export competitiveness and in productivity growth is partly explained by its high saving rate. This is a primary reason for our interest in savings patterns.

The figures in table 10–2 show Japan's two-to-one margin of superiority over the United States in the area of average propensity to save at the gross national level. The margin of superiority is even greater when we look at personal saving alone. The ratios of household saving to household disposable income are: 17.1 percent for Japan, FY 1982, and 6.2 percent for the U.S., calendar year 1982 (personal saving/personal disposable income). These figures for 1982 are fairly typical of other periods and indicate a margin that is almost three-to-one. Behavior may not be so dissimilar for other kinds of domestic saving or investment, but there are real differences in saving–spending behavior among households.

Japan's high savings rate allows it to tolerate fiscal deficits better than the U.S. can because in a total sources-and-uses analysis, private saving can offset public dissaving. America is a relatively high-consumption economy and runs a danger of carrying large public deficits. There may be a crowding out. This is less likely to happen in Japan.

Why is Japan a high saver and the U.S. a low saver? For that matter, why are Germany and Switzerland fairly high savers and why are the United Kingdom and Belgium on the low side like the United States? These are not easy questions to answer, and they undoubtedly have no single-factor explanations. It is a matter of early training in values, business and financial practices, retirement systems, and defense needs, among other causes.

It is unusual for the United States to have such a large foreign deficit. It is unusual for the U.S. to have to pay so much attention to external factors, but the nation is now fully involved in the world economy and cannot ignore developments in merchandise trade, international financing, and the interest-exchange rate drain on the national economy. The U.S. is now a net debtor country and were it not for the willingness of people everywhere to elect to hold dollars without significantly questioning their value, the nation would be facing some serious adjustment problems, like those in front of many heavily indebted developing countries who are forced by IMF conditionality to adopt austere policies.

The fact that the U.S. has become a net debtor country means that it has significant interest payments to make to the rest of the world. Payments on foreign assets (mainly interest) amount, in 1985, to more than $60 billion per year. Of this, the federal government is paying about $18 to $20 billion per year. When interest rates go up, the U.S. servicing burden abroad becomes more onerous, as does the need to pay on the domestically held debt. As long as the saving–investment balance (or total sources–uses balance) is robust, the U.S. can hold interest rates in check and manage the debt service burden at home and abroad without serious problems.

However, under a crowding-out scenario generated by unpleasant developments at home, it will be difficult to hold foreign capital in the U.S. and the burdens will become even more oppressive. This is why the sources-and-uses statement deserves close scrutiny and continued monitoring to ensure the abundance of funding sources from savings. This is a key development for a worsening debt servicing burden. The most volatile and uncertain component in the whole sources-and-uses statement is the net capital inflow from abroad. It is in the economic and general national interests of the U.S. to be able to stimulate saving, bringing forth a greater flow than is now being realized, at prevailing interest rates. If this were to happen, interest rates would not be under pressure and the U.S. could continue to meet debt-servicing charges without undue financial distress. This is why saving is so important for the economy today. It is a new situation, however, for the U.S. to have to treat this problem in the open international economy. I choose to look at the total saving pattern, and that involves a great deal of international economic analysis.

The Federal Reserve authorities hold a wild card in this savings picture. By supplying or withholding reserves from the banking system they can influence the course of interest rates beyond the effects of the flows laid out in table 10–1. Their role is important in analyzing the two principal scenarios confronting the future of the U.S. economy:

1. Hard- or crash-landing scenario: Adverse events trigger a loss of confidence in the U.S. economy or its financial system. Funds flow out of the United States causing a sharp drop in exchange value of the dollar. This induces price rises. If the Federal Reserve authorities restrict reserves to fight the inflationary pressures or hold capital, as much as possible, in the United States, there will be crowding out, and interest rates will rise. There will be a recessionary adjustment to hold down imports and put the current account in better balance. This is the hard-landing scenario that was imposed on Mexico and Brazil. They devalued, had high interest rates, monetary restraint, recession, and a turnabout on current account.

2. Soft-landing scenario: Adding to the source of funds for the U.S. capital market, the Federal Reserve authorities supply more reserves to the banking system, bringing down interest rates. The lower rates cause foreign capital to flow out of the United States and the dollar falls. Exports are stimulated, imports are restrained, and the adjustment to the current account is made without a significant recession. Capital-formation and other interest-sensitive spending is encouraged by the more favorable rates, thus bringing about a cyclical revival.

Naturally, we hope that the present foreign imbalance in our national savings total will be taken care of by the second scenario.

11
Toward a National Consensus on Saving

F. Gerard Adams
Susan M. Wachter

Presented as papers at the 1985 Savings Forum conference, the chapters in this book illustrate how close and yet how far we are from a consensus on saving. We recognize that saving is important. We understand that it is *national* saving, not just *personal* or *public* saving that counts. We are aware that saving in the United States is at a low extreme compared to other countries, rich and poor. We know that the tax system and our public sector have important negative impacts on saving. But we do not know for sure what determines saving. We do not know the magnitude of the impacts of public policies on saving. And we cannot agree on what is important to do about saving, except for reducing the deficit. Hence, savings policy is intertwined with the central political economic debate of our time.

A number of important questions can be asked on the basis of the evidence presented at the conference. Fewer can be easily and conclusively answered.

First, do we have a national consensus on savings? Savings and, of course, capital investment relate deeply to the nation's growth and productivity potential. And growth represents an important dimension of the nation's economic performance. The broad feeling that the savings rate of the United States is too low derives from the facts that we would like to see higher rates of capital investment and that we anticipate that more investment would result in more rapid growth of productivity and income. It is not surprising, consequently, that savings and investment are seen as targets of economic performance in their own right, and that most economists and even most citizens will applaud an increase in savings and investment. It would appear from this perspective that there is a national consensus on saving.

But the consensus that low saving and investment are responsible for a low rate of growth is in conflict with the reality of public deficits. Almost every day the still floundering attempts to resolve the controversy on the federal budget remind us of the drain of the public sector on the economy's saving. The crowding-out issue has been termed the "dog that does not bark." But as is pointed out repeatedly in the chapters of this book, were it not for the inflow of foreign capital—an international dimension which poses new challenges—and for the willingness of the Federal Reserve to feed dollars into the system, public expenditures would be crowding out private investment ever more strongly. The dog would "bark." A consensus on savings involves making some fundamental decisions, many of which have been elusive in recent years.

Another paradox is, as Roberts and others point out, that taxes have incentive effects and that taxes imposed to balance the budget risk further reducing incentives to save and to invest. There is some agreement on the advantages of reducing marginal tax rates on capital and on creating a "level playing field" among investments, as well as on the advantages of reducing marginal tax rates on labor, if these reductions were possible without increasing the deficit or choosing among cuts in public expenditures. Clearly, the structure and level of taxation (the taxes which are already in effect and those which might be imposed) are an important element of savings and investment policy on which we lack consensus.

A second question is do we need consensus on saving? One approach in this regard might be to argue that we rely on market forces to determine other aspects of our economy and we can rely on market forces to achieve an optimal savings objective. It is interesting to note that many proponents of the free market would not agree with this statement. Perhaps this reflects the fact that savings is seen to have some merit in itself, in a Benjamin Franklin sense, or that market-determined growth is not sufficiently rapid when compared to aspirations or to the growth record being achieved by our competitors, such as Japan. But putting the philosophical question aside, we surely need a consensus on saving because of the interventions of the public sector. Our discussion above has focused on the resources going into public consumption (though public investment is all too often forgotten) and the need to raise taxes to finance public expenditure. These have impacts on saving. In the absence of a completely neutral public sector (an unachievable target), we require a consensus on saving. Policy impacts on saving, which means we must have some notion of what that policy should be.

A third question is what should the consensus on savings policy include? Beginning with the macro dimensions, the savings consensus should focus on the share of our nation's product which should go for saving and investment. As we will note further, this is not an easy call. Aside from the fact that most people would argue that the savings rate should be higher, we do not know how much higher—surely that depends on the yield from the investments toward which this added saving should be directed. Two critical dimensions in this regard are where that saving should be effected—at the level of consumers, business, or government?—and how it should be used—for equipment, business structures, residential construction, or infrastructure? Again, there is no easy answer.

An important source of disagreement with respect to saving is the failure on the part of many to see saving and investment in the context of the total economy. Partial analysis generally produces only partial results. Thus, the emphasis on spending to stimulate economic activity in a demand-deficient economy (which has sometimes been termed the Keynesian argument) misses the point that saving and investment are the source of capital accumulation and productivity growth. Few economists would deny this supply-side approach even as most will accept the demand-side stimulus. Which one applies and which one is appropriate depends on the situation of the economy, its need for stimulus, and the possibility of productively employing additional capital.

A similar paradox occurs with respect to saving and taxation. It is frequently argued that saving and investment are impeded by taxes, and with respect to most types of taxes that view has some justice. On the other hand, there is also general agreement that, in principle, taxes should be sufficient to finance government spending to avoid deficits. The two views require reconciliation. It is not enough to be opposed to taxes, nor for that matter to be opposed to deficits. The picture must be examined in a dynamic macro framework to determine what is the optimal level of government spending and taxation, and to recognize impacts on savings and investment behavior.

The chapters of this book reveal how much additional knowledge is required before we can hope for a consensus on saving. The Savings Forum is dedicated to the development and dissemination of that knowledge. We propose here an agenda for research. As in most topics the research potentials are almost without end as our understanding of the basic facts is deepened and confirmed and as more detailed questions can be examined. Thus, the best one can do is to outline a set of priorities. In view of what we need to know and now do know, what are the central themes which require additional research? These themes can be ordered in two dimensions, from the macro to the micro and from the theoretical to the applied.

From the macro to the micro perspective, we begin with the dominant issues of economic growth and their relationship to saving and investment. From a theoretical perspective, growth theorists have obtained important results linking the growth path to the savings rate under varied assumptions. But the linkage between savings and growth on a macro empirical level are much more tenuous, reflecting the difficulties of measuring and evaluating real-world conditions. At any point in time, different countries are at very different stages of their economic development process, use diverse technologies, have different industrial structures and economic institutions, calling for the analytical tools of both the empirical economist and the economic historian.

The national accountant makes an important contribution in establishing quantitative dimensions for savings flows—sources and uses of funds, gross and net investment, for example—which can serve as the basis for improved understanding. On the micro level, the determination of saving in households and businesses poses similar challenges. The theoretical constructs are far developed, if not always realistic in the eyes of some observers, but the empirical information—the surveys and household records of saving and asset holdings—leave much to be desired. More challenging still is the need to reconcile what can be observed at the macro level with the micro behavior of the individual savers and investors.

From a macro perspective, we can identify five principal concerns which offer opportunities for productive study. (Of necessity, these topics are broad and we suggest some more detailed objectives.)

The role of savings and investment in economic growth—optimal savings rates, investment and productivity, tradeoffs between alternative economic targets, reconciliation between short term and long term objectives, and intergenerational transfers

Allocation of savings and investment in economic development—priorities between various types of investment, and sources of savings

International savings flows—long-term relationships between high-saver and low-saver countries, the role of international capital flows and the adjustment process, savings flows and alternative exchange rate regimes, savings flows and development of the poor countries and the international debt and macro instability

Macroeconomic relationships—historical and intercountry perspectives on savings, macro empirical determinants of saving, interrelationships between public-sector and private-sector savings, and impact of taxation and investment incentives

Measurement—measurement of aggregate savings concepts, statistics on sources and uses of funds, reconciliation between national accounts, flows of funds, and international statistics.

Macro relationships, theoretical and observed, require microeconomic underpinnings. That has been the challenge in many aspects of modern economics. Some of the critical micro questions are:

Theory of savings and investment—determinants of consumer and household savings behavior, savings and investment behavior in business, optimal micro savings behavior, and theory of the public sector

Public sector interventions and savings behavior on the micro level—effect of tax structure on savings and investment

Measurement—savings and asset holdings by consumers, micro data on business savings and financing, micro data on public assets and savings, and pension statistics

Micro empirical studies—determinants of consumer saving and asset holding, the role of pensions, the role of demographic characteristics and household structure, business savings and investments, internal and external business financing, and influence of taxation on micro savings behavior.

Clearly there is still much to be learned about saving, its role in the economy and policy trade-offs. We hope that, on the basis of such additional knowledge, a consensus can be built which will lead to a more optimal national policy.

Index

About the Contributors

Robert B. Avery, an economist at Financial Studies Section, Division of Research and Statistics, Board of Governors of the Federal Reserve System. Author or coauthor of two books and numerous articles including "Application of Classification Techniques in Business, Banking and Finances," 1981.

Marshall E. Blume, Howard Butcher Professor of Finance and chairman of the finance department at the Wharton School, University of Pennsylvania, has written numerous books, monographs, and articles on investments and finance. He has served as managing editor of *Journal of Finance* and associate editor of *Journal of Financial Economics* and *Journal of Financial Quantitative Analysis.*

Michael J. Boskin is professor of economics, chairman of the Center for Economic Policy Research at Stanford University and research associate at the National Bureau of Economic Research. Author of many papers and editor of six volumes of essays on taxation, fiscal policy, capital formation, labor markets, social security, and related subjects, he was keynote speaker at the White House Conference on Aging in 1981.

Barry P. Bosworth is senior fellow in the economic studies program at Brookings Institution. Director of the U.S. Council on Wage and Price Stability from 1977 to 1979, he is author or coauthor of *Tax Incentives and Economic Growth* (1984), *Lowering the Deficit and Interest Rates* (1984), *Primary Commodities and the New Inflation* (1975), and numerous articles.

Gregory E. Elliehausen serves as economist in the Financial Structure Section of the Division of Research and Statistics, Board of Governors of the Federal Reserve System. He is author or coauthor of *1977 Consumer Credit Survey, The Impact of Federal Interest Rates on the Small Saver,* and *1983 Survey of Consumer Finances.*

Irwin Friend, Hopkinson Professor of Finance and Economics at the Wharton School, University of Pennsylvania, is director of the University's Rodney White Center for Financial Research, and a fellow of the

American Statistical Association and Econometric Society. He has also served on the editorial boards of *Journal of Banking and Finance, The American Economic Review, The Journal of Finance,* and *The Journal of the American Statistical Association.* Author and coauthor of numerous books, monographs and articles on capital markets, saving and investment, corporate finance and investments, economic forecasting, and tax policy, he was president of the American Finance Association in 1972.

Thomas A. Gustafson, economist and chief of Medicaid Branch of the Division of Policy Analysis, Health Care Financing, Administration, U.S. Department of Health and Human Services. He is author or coauthor of several articles relating to retirement and household wealth.

Lawrence R. Klein was a Nobel laureate in economic sciences in 1980. Founder of Wharton Econometric Forecasting Associates, he served as its chairman from 1969 to 1980, and since then has chaired its professional board. Professor of economics at University of Pennsylvania, he was president of the American Economic Association in 1977 and has authored *The Keynesian Revolution* (1966, 1974), *A Textbook of Econometrics* (1953, 1974), and many other books and articles.

John H. Makin is director of fiscal policy studies at the American Enterprise Institute. Former professor of economics and director of the Institute for Economic Research at University of Washington, he is the author of *Elements of Money,* (1971), *Theory of Economic Policy* (1972), *Macroeconomics* (1984), and *The Global Debt Crisis* (1984).

Robert Ortner, chief economist at the U.S. Department of Commerce, directs the Office of Economic Conditions and Office of Economic Policy, which provide analysis and policy options for the Secretary of Commerce. Formerly senior vice president and chief economist at the Bank of New York, he has also taught statistics, economics, and finance at the Wharton School, University of Pennsylvania.

Paul Craig Roberts, William E. Simon Professor of Political Economy at Georgetown University, was assistant secretary of the U.S. Treasury for Economic Policy from 1981 to 1982. Author of *The Supply Side Revolution* (1984), and *Alienation and the Soviet Economy* (1971), he currently writes the column "Economic Watch" in *Business Week.*

Lawrence H. Summers is professor of economics at Harvard University, research associate of the National Bureau of Economic Research, and domestic policy economist on the President's Council of Economic Advisers. He is author of more than forty articles on macroeconomic topics and a forthcoming book, *The Asset Price Approach to Capital Income Taxation.*

About the Editors

F. Gerard Adams is professor of economics and finance, director of the Economics Research Unit and codirector of the Center for Analysis of Developing Economies (CADE), at the University of Pennsylvania and senior consultant for Wharton Econometric Forecasting Associates, Inc. He is also coauthor and editor of *Stabilizing World Commodity Markets* (1978), *Industrial Policies for Growth and Competitiveness* (1983), *Industrial Policies for Growth and Competitiveness: Empirical Studies,* vol. II (1985), *Commodity Exports and Economic Growth* (1982), *The Business Forecasting Revolution* (1986) and other books and articles.

Susan M. Wachter, associate professor of finance at the Wharton School, University of Pennsylvania, serves on the editorial board of the *American Real Estate and Urban Economics Journal,* is associate editor of *Housing Finance Review,* and is a member of the board of directors of the American Real Estate and Urban Economics Association. She is author and coeditor of *Latin American Inflation* (1976), *Towards a New U.S. Industrial Policy?* (1981), *Removing Obstacles to Economic Growth* (1984), and the forthcoming *Inflation's Impact on Pensions.*